THE
GARDENER'S
LABYRINTH

THE GARDENER'S LABYRINTH

Thomas Hill

Edited with an introduction
by Richard Mabey

Oxford New York

OXFORD UNIVERSITY PRESS

1987

Oxford University Press, Walton Street, Oxford OX2 6DP

Oxford New York Toronto
Delhi Bombay Calcutta Madras Karachi
Petaling Jaya Singapore Hong Kong Tokyo
Nairobi Dar es Salaam Cape Town
Melbourne Auckland

and associated companies in
Beirut Berlin Ibadan Nicosia

Oxford is a trade mark of Oxford University Press

British Library Cataloguing in Publication Data

Hill, Thomas, fl. 1590
The gardeners labyrinth.
1. Gardening — England
I. Title   II. Mabey, Richard
635'.0942   SB453.3.G7

ISBN 0-19-217763-X

Library of Congress Cataloging-in-Publication Data

Hill, Thomas, b. ca. 1528
The gardener's labyrinth.
Includes index.
1. Gardening — England — Early works to 1800.
2. Gardening — Early works to 1800.
3. Vegetable gardening — England — Early works to 1800.
4. Vegetable gardening — Early works to 1800.
I. Mabey, Richard, 1941—   .   II. Title.
SB453.3.G7H48   1987   635   87-11174

ISBN 0-19-217763-X

Produced for Oxford University Press by
Curtis Garratt Limited, The Old Vicarage, Horton cum Studley, Oxford OX9 1BT

Picture Research by Suzanne Williams
Index by Barbara James

Filmset by SX Composing Ltd
Printed in Hong Kong

CONTENTS

INTRODUCTION

The Gardener's Labyrinth was the first popular gardening manual to be published in the English language. It is not a great book, nor – at least in terms of the information it contains – a particularly original one. As a study of plants it is overshadowed by the massive herbals of the Elizabethan botanists Turner and Gerard. Even as a garden encyclopaedia it can't compete with John Parkinson's *Paradisi in Sole*, published fifty years later in 1629. But from its very first pages, *The Labyrinth*'s descriptions of how to test soil between the fingers, build a rose arch, mulch a vegetable bed, leave you in no doubt that this is a pioneering work, a new way of addressing what was fast becoming, so to speak, a common or garden pastime. Here is Thomas Hill's typically engaging account of the rituals of watering:

> The common watering pot for the Garden beds with us, hath a narrow neck, big belly, somewhat large bottom, and full of little holes, with a proper hole formed on the head to take in the water, which filled full, and the thumb laid on the hole to keep in the aire, may on such wise be carried in a handsome manner ... the beds at one instant shal not fully be watered, but as the earth and plants drink in, so gently sprinkle forth the water, in feeding the plants with moisture, as by a brest or nourishing Pap, which like handled, shall greatly prosper the tender plants comming up, where they otherwise by the hasty drowning with water, are much annoyed, and put in hazard of perishing.

Hill's tips are unusual not just for their practicality, but for their informality and directness. These were novel qualities in the sixteenth century, but today Hill's tone seems unmistakable. It is the enthusiastic, coaxing, down-to-earth voice of the incipient garden columnist.

It is no surprise that this now familiar form of garden writing should have first emerged during the Elizabethan era. England was enjoying a rare spell of peace and prosperity. Discovery and innovation flourished in the prevailing mood of self-confidence, and the first stirrings of an open-minded and observational science were beginning to challenge at least some of the old superstitions And from the far corners of the globe Queen Elizabeth's adventurous explorers were sending back a steady stream of new plants for the glory of her gardens and the curiosity of her scientists.

Flowers were the symbols and *motifs* of the age. They were celebrated in poetry and painting. They adorned plasterwork and tapestry. And though their domestic and often bizarre medical uses were still the chief preoccupation of those who studied them seriously, the illustrated herbals that began to be published from the middle of the sixteenth century gave increasing attention to plants as pure objects of pleasure.

The major landmark in Elizabethan botanical literature was the publication in 1551 of William Turner's *Herball*, the first major book on plants to be originally written in English. It was followed in 1597 by a far more enduring work, John Gerard's *The Herbal or General History of Plants*. Gerard was a notorious plagiarizer, and much of his celebrated work is an unacknowledged – and by no means always accurate – adaptation of the Belgian Rembert Dodoens *New Herbal* (translated by Henry Lyte in 1578). But he was a skilled gardener and blessed with an infectiously lively writing style, and his book proved as popular and stimulating to his contemporaries as it has done to four centuries of readers since.

Gerard did include some notes on the cultivation of the one-and-a-half-thousand plants described in his book, but works devoted to gardening were either in private manuscripts, or biased towards small-scale agriculture – as, for example, John Fitzherbert's *Boke of Husbandry*, 1523. What finally ensured the appearance of gardening books with a more obviously popular appeal was the rapid extension of the middle class during the latter half of the sixteenth century. An increasing number of families had the money and leisure to indulge in 'pleasure grounds', and to some extent gardens became status symbols, fashionable insignia of wealth and taste. Yet there is no doubt that they were also sincerely viewed as perfect expressions of the era's devotion to art, romance, and learning.

Thomas Hill, or Hyll as he occasionally spelt his name, was the first writer to attempt to meet the needs of this new readership. Sadly, not a great deal is known about him. He was born in 1529, and practised both as an astrologer and a jobbing writer. He did compilation and translation work, and brought out a string of books and pamphlets on a range of subjects that seem to have been of perennial fascination in popular publishing. As well as gardening, he covered astrology, cooking, popular medicine, and psychology. In 1571 he published 'A Prognostication for the Year 1572'; in 1576 'The moste pleasaunte Arte of the Interpretacion of Dreames'; and fourteen years later, 'A Contemplation of Mysteries: contayning the rare effectes and significations of certayne Comets'. His scope was vast, and he coped by sticking to the time-honoured journalistic principle of quoting reputable – or at least distinguished – sources, and recycling and exploiting his works for all that could be squeezed out of them.

That Hill was adept at digesting specialist writings and composing a good story from them is apparent from his gardening writings. His first book on the subject – 'A most briefe and pleasaunte Treatyse, teachynge howe to Dress, Sowe, and set a Garden' – appeared in 1563. A rejigged and expanded version entitled *The Profitable Arte of Gardening*, including short appendices on bees and on the planting and grafting of fruit trees, appeared five years later. Both were practical guides which leaned heavily on the recommendations of classical writers.

The Profitable Arte sold well, and went into three more editions before the close of the century. Hill and his publishers, obviously recognizing a winning streak, put together a much more extensive edition entitled *The Gardener's Labyrinth*, and launched it in 1577. Mindful, perhaps, of the dangers of over exposure, Hill this time wrote under the pseudonym of Didymus Mountaine.

The Gardener's Labyrinth reworked a good deal of material from its predecessors and, like them, borrowed much of its contents from Greek and Roman sources. A score of different classical writers are quoted, notably Pliny, Palladius, Varro, Columella, and Cato. But the structure and preoccupations of the book faithfully reflect the current English style of gardening. It begins with a section of good gardening practice, on the qualities of soils, the making of hedges, how to gather herbs and deter pests. The second part is a detailed account of the cultivation, qualities, and uses of more than fifty different herbs, vegetables, and flowers. These included extensive derivative notes on their supposed medicinal properties, as established according to various astrological and magical systems (these have been omitted from this edition).

The Labyrinth seems to have been an instant success, and a new edition was put in hand the following year. There were four more editions during the next seventy-five years, and the publishers were increasingly extravagant with their blandishments on the title pages. 'A New Art of Gardning, Wherein is laid down New and Rare inventions and secrets of Gardening not heretofore known' announced the 1652 edition, 'Collected from the best approved Authors, besides forty years experience in the Art of Gardning; by D.M.'

Many passages in the book betray its hybrid origins. It can be repetitive, disjointed, and gullible. The writing is occasionally crabbed, and the whole text looks as if it has been rushed a little too speedily through its proofing stages. Yet in the end it is those 'forty years of experience in the Art of Gardning' that shine through. Hill was a man who clearly enjoyed getting his hands dirty, and who relished the practical business of gardening every bit as much as Gerard did the plants. He enjoyed its sociability, its rewards, and the ingenuity it demanded. Describing how his book was put together, Hill can't disguise the fact that he found the practice of garden-craft just as much a part of the fun as its finished products. The knowledge he was passing on, he explains, was 'parte purchased by friendshippe and earnest suite, of the skillful observers and wittie searchers in our tyme of laudable secrets in garden matters, serving as well for the use and singular comforts of mannes life, as to a proper gayne and delight of the mind'.

Hill's text is full of the kind of knacks and wrinkles that nurture green-fingeredness. He has sensitive ideas about how to hand weed so as not to disturb young seedlings, and why it should *never* be attempted in over-dry weather. He gives clear instructions about how to ensure a regular supply of fresh herbs in the winter by cutting the plants right back regularly. His delightful method of establishing a quickset hedge – 'mix and steepe for a time, all the Berries and seeds in the bending meale of Tares, into the thickness of Honey: the same mixture lay diligently into old and untwisted Ship or Wel-ropes' – was still being recommended in farming manuals 300 years later.

Some of his advice is remarkably precocious. He warns against using the same kind of dung repeatedly on the same piece of ground, because of the dangers of disease and 'noisome wormes'. He knew how to blanch vegetables by forcing them in the dark, and how to cook them conservatively. His 'salad ball', made by *growing* half-a-dozen different salad vegetables closely intertwined from a mixture of their seeds in a pellet of dung, would be a sensation today in any *cuisine naturelle* restaurant. At one point Hill describes the garden as a 'ground plot for the mind', and it is clear that for all his astrological whimsy, it was the power of plants over the senses and emotions that he admired most.

The life of man in this world is but thraldom, when the Sences are not pleased [he wrote] and what rarer object can there be on earth . . . than a beautifull and Odoriferous Garden plot Artificially composed, where he may read and contemplate on the wonderfull works of the great Creator, in Plants and Flowers; for if he observeth with a judicial eye, and serious judgement their variety of Colours, Sents, Beauty, Shapes, Interlacing, Enamilling, Mixture, Turnings, Windings, Embossments, Operations and Vertues, it is most admirable to behold, and meditate upon the same.

There would be no better site for such meditation than one of Hill's bowers or 'herbars', bosky retreats built of ash or willow poles and draped with sweet-smelling plants like rosemary, jasmine, privet, and climbing roses. Hill adored scented plants. His favourites – roses, pinks, stocks, sweet violets, lavender – would still head most plant lists today. And he recommended that they should be used to edge and overhang the 'Walks and Allies' by which the formal Elizabethan garden was divided up into geometrically regular beds.

Most of Hill's indulgences have this kind of practical edge to them. The planting of orange trees in wheeled tubs, so that they could 'be rolled hither and thither' was in the eighteenth century to become a delightful conceit by which dwarf fruit trees could be brought straight to the dessert table; but it began as a device for ensuring that they could be removed rapidly from unexpected spells of bad weather.

Yet running through the book is a stranger and, to most modern minds, patently impractical line of advice which springs from the old tradition of natural magic. Some of this results from Hill's own interest in astrology, and he suggests abstruse zodiacal schemes for planting and harvesting that I suspect will only be comprehensible to the initiated (though it would be as well for the rest of us to remember that many peasant societies still plant and harvest according to the phases of the moon, and that science has discovered frequent calendrical rhythms in plant growth). There are also some extraordinary suggestions for pest control, whose origins are hard to guess at. Eagle or kite's dung, buried in the garden, would drive away all 'venomous worms'. Ants could be banished by stuffing an owl's heart in their nest holes.

But chiefly the suggestions came from the most ancient and widespread of pre-scientific systems: the doctrine of sympathetic magic. Even weather control was thought possible by adherence to the principle of like repelling like. Firing a gun or ringing bells would disperse thunderstorms. The ominous pelt of a seal or crocodile, hung at the entrance of a garden, would keep dark clouds away; failing that, the clouds' own image could be reflected back at them with 'a mighty glass'. More farcically, Hill recommends the sowing of the infamously flatulent seeds of lentil to keep seedling beds free from wind damage.

Many of what might be regarded as the old wives' tales of this book result from a fascinatingly vulgarized version of sympathetic magic translated into day-to-day garden practicalities. In this version, antagonisms, resemblances, sympathies, all carry much the same weight. So Hill frequently recommends watering plants with the juice of their own leaves – or, in the case of parsley, with Aquavit! And sowing conglomerations of seeds together, in the same hole, is a way of guaranteeing large specimens of vegetables.

It is these passages that I personally find most fascinating in Hill. They give an insight into this crucial moment in history, when the old beliefs were colliding with the burgeoning mood of reason and practicality. Hill juggles these disparate elements with endearing journalistic bluster, dashing from fact to ancient fantasy without the slightest concern for consistency or continuity. For the true flavour of this first garden gossip, read him on onions; on how to grow monsters by sowing them *inside* gourd seeds, how to string them up in winter, pickle them, and turn them into invisible ink. Or his masterly essay on cucumbers, in which he slips effortlessly from hints on how to 'stretch' the plants by a system of tantalizing watering (and the fruits by growing them inside hollow canes) to gleefully exact instructions on how to etch 'strange figures' on their skin. These tips are four centuries old, but they could be coming fresh over the garden wall.

Note on the text

This edition is based on the 1652 edition. Hill's astrologically based notes on the medicinal uses of specific plants have been omitted but the extended table, which was published as a guide and index to these notes, has been retained as a precis of their contents. The somewhat erratic spelling is reproduced as in the original, except where it obviously results from a printer's error.

All plant names, and their variations, plus unfamiliar gardening terms, are explained in the glossary.

GLOSSARY

Note to glossary

The purpose of this glossary is to catalogue all the plants mentioned by Hill, and to translate unfamiliar, vernacular, or obsolete namings.

The information is ordered as follows:
1   the name or names used by Hill, and their variations. Some of these may be misspellings or misprints but, given the natural flexibility of sixteenth-century spelling, no attempt has been made to correct or regularize them;
2   the modern English and scientific names;
3   the status and uses of the plant are given, together with its country of origin, concluding, where appropriate, with a few notes on the extent and advancement of its cultivation. All these notes refer to sixteenth-century status and practice.

The main primary sources for this information are: the contemporary works of John Gerard, *The Herball* (1597; enlarged and amended by Thomas Johnson, 1633); *A New Herball*, William Turner 1551; *Paradisi in sole Paradisus terrestris*, John Parkinson, 1629.

Glosses on a few unfamiliar or obsolete gardening terms have also been added, and are listed alphabetically. References to other entries in the glossary are printed in small capital letters.

adamant, adamantstone in this context probably a magnetic or lodestone, though the term was also used for diamond and for mythically hard substances.

agaricke bracket fungi of the group *Polypores*, especially those growing on larch.

alexanders *Smyrnium olustratum*. Medicinal herb and vegetable. Mediterranean. Introduced by the Romans and naturalized in coastal areas.

angelica *Angelica archangelica*. Medicinal and culinary. Eastern Europe.

arach, arage *see* ORAGE.

aristolochia birthwort, *Aristolochia clematitis*. Medicinal herb. Southern Europe. Introduced by monks in the twelfth century.

artichoke globe artichoke, *Cynara scolymus*. Vegetable. Mediterranean. Probably reached Britain in the late medieval period. (The Jerusalem artichoke, *Helianthus tuberosus*, was not introduced from North America until 1616.)

ash-tree *Fraxinus excelsior*. Native tree.

balme sweet or lemon balm, *Melissa officinalis*. Medicinal and culinary herb and bee plant. Southern Europe. Anciently introduced and occasionally naturalized.

barberry *Berberis vulgaris*. Native shrub. Fruit used as pickle or candied decoration for meat.

basill basil, *Ocimum basilicum*. Medicinal and culinary. Asia.

batchelors-buttons: a vernacular name applied to a large number of small and usually double flowers, including buttercups, campions, feverfew, and tansy.

battle (of soils) fertile, rich.

bay-tree, bay *Laurus nobilis*. Aromatic shrub. Mediterranean. Probably introduced to English gardens during the climatically warm period between the twelfth and fourteenth centuries.

beanes, beans leguminous vegetables from Europe and Asia. Some dozen different varieties were in cultivation in England in the sixteenth century, including broad and tick beans, and an increasing number of kidney and 'runner' beans from the New World. The young pods of these were cooked and eaten whole, exactly as today, but the showier varieties were also grown as ornamental climbers.

beets root vegetables, cultivated varieties of the native *Beta vulgaris*. White beets were being eaten in Anglo-Saxon times; the red beetroot was just arriving from Italy at the time Hill was writing. Gerard mentions growing one as a curiosity in 1596.

bittony betony, *Betonica officinalis*. Medicinal herb. Native.

blessed thistle *Carduus benedictus*. Medicinal herb and vegetable. Mediterranean. Probably a monastic introduction to England during the Middle Ages.

blete blite, a generic name for leaf vegetables of the goosefoot family (*Chenopodium*), sometimes also applied to docks, ORAGES etc. The word derives from a Latin term for 'insipid'.

bloodwort probably red-veined dock, *Rumex sanguineus*, though the term was also a local name for a number of other species, including herb-robert, centaury, and yarrow, used to staunch bleeding.

borage, burrage *Borago officinalis*. Medicinal. Southern Europe. Introduced by the Romans.

bramble *Rubus fruticosus*. Fruiting rambler. Native.

brionie, briony probably the native white bryony, *Bryonia dioica*, whose roots were used as a medicinal herb.

buckshorne *see* HARTSHORNE.

buglass, buglosse alkanet, *Anchusa officinalis*. Medicinal. Europe.

bulles bullace, *Prunus insititia*. Wild plum tree, possibly native.

bytonie BITTONY.

cabbage *Brassica* varieties. Vegetable. Europe. Loose-leaved varieties, mostly derived from the wild European sea cabbage, *Brassica oleracea*, were traditionally known as coleworts; the tighter-headed, paler-leaved modern cabbages, known as Savoys, were introduced to Britain from Holland in the 1570s.

camomile, camomel various species and cultivated varieties of the chamomile family (*Anthemis, Chamaemelum*). Medicinal and ornamental. Native.

Carduus benedictus BLESSED THISTLE.

carnation *Dianthus* varieties. Ornamental and medicinal. Europe. Already very popular and diverse in the late sixteenth and early seventeenth centuries. John Parkinson alone grew almost thirty different varieties.

carret carrot, *Daucus carota*. Root vegetable. The white roots of the native wild carrot were eaten in prehistoric times. The sweeter, orange-coloured strains came from the Middle East during the fifteenth and sixteenth centuries.

celondine greater celandine, *Chelidonium majus*. Medicinal. Southern Europe. Anciently introduced and widely naturalized.

centory centaury, *Centaurium erythraea*. Medicinal. Native.

chervil *Anthriscus cerefolium*. Culinary and medicinal. Eastern Europe. The name was sometimes also applied to the related sweet cicely, *Myrrhis odorata*.

chibuls, chibouls spring or Welsh onions, *Allium fistolosum*. *See* ONION.

citrone, cytrone citron, *Citrus medica*. Fruit tree. The first of the citrus fruits to be brought out of Asia to Europe about 300 BC. It has a long, pear-shaped fruit with a thick, rough, yellow rind; today it is used as the basis for 'candied peel'.

cives chives, *Allium schoenoprasum*. Culinary and medicinal. Native.

clary various native and European sages, *Salvis* species. Medicinal and ornamental.

colewort CABBAGE.

coliander coriander, *Coriandrum sativum*. Culinary and medicinal. Probably introduced by the Romans.

colocynthis a wild GOURD.

columbine *Aquilegia vulgaris*. Ornamental and medicinal. Native. Double, variegated, and split-petalled varieties were already grown.

corne name covering the various kinds of wheat. Turkey-corne was the common English term for maize which had been brought back to Britain from the New World early in the sixteenth century. '

costmary *Balsamita major*. Medicinal and culinary. Asia.

couslip cowslip, *Primula veris*. Ornamental and medicinal. Native. Several different varieties were in cultivation, including doubles and 'hose-in-hose'.

cowcumber, cucumber *Cucumis sativus*. Vegetable. Probably not grown in England until the fifteenth century.

crab crab apple, *Malus sylvestris*. Fruit tree. Native.

cress a generic term applied to a wide range of green vegetables, all with sharp-tasting leaves, including garden cress, *Lepidium sativum*, and nasturtiums, *Tropaeolum* species, introduced from the New World in the late sixteenth century.

crevices crayfish, probably the native freshwater species, *Astacus pallipes*.

crocuss *Crocus* species and varieties. Ornamental bulbs. Native and European. At least a dozen – including doubles – were in cultivation in England in the late sixteenth century.

cucumber, wild squirting cucumber, *Cucumis agininus*. Medicinal. A climber from central Europe.

currans 1 currants, *Ribes* species and varieties. Fruiting shrubs. Red, white and black currants are all British natives. They were just beginning to be improved by cultivation in the sixteenth century. **2** small raisins.

cynocrambe dog's mercury, *Mercurialis perennis*. Medicinal. Native. A wild, woodland flower, rarely cultivated.

cypresse *Cupressus sempervirens*. Evergreen tree. Mediterranean. Introduced in the early sixteenth century.

daffadown dillie daffodil, *Narcissus pseudonarcissus*. Bulb. This name was chiefly used for the native wild daffodil, though at least fifty varieties of *Narcissus* were in cultivation by the end of the sixteenth century.

dandelyon dandelion, *Taraxacum officinale*. Medicinal. Native.

date date palm, *Phoenix dactylifera*. Fruiting tree. Asia, Africa. Dates could not be grown in Britain, and were chiefly imported from Syria and Palestine.

dazie, dasey daisy, *Bellis* and *Leucanthemum* species and varieties. Ornamental and medicinal. Native. Doubles were popular in cultivation.

dil, dill, dyl *Anethum graveolens*. Culinary and medicinal. Southern Europe.

dittany 1 dittander, *Lepidium latifolium*. Medicinal and culinary. Native. Its hot, spicy root was used as a precursor of horseradish in the kitchen. **2** dittany, or 'burning bush', *Dictamnus albus*. Aromatic flowering shrub. Southern Europe. Introduced to Britain in the sixteenth century.

dutch-rose cabbage or Provence rose, *Rosa centifolia*. *See* ROSE.

earth-apple 1 CUCUMBER. **2** SOWESBREAD. Later, the potato.

eglantine SWEET BRYER.

elder *Sambucus nigra*. Fruiting shrub. Native. Used as a hedging plant, and valued medicinally for its flowers and berries.

elicampane elecampane, *Inula helenium*. Medicinal. Near East. Anciently introduced to Britain, and locally naturalized.

ellebore HELLEBORES.

endive *Cichorium endivia*. Salad vegetable. Asia. First cultivated in England in the sixteenth century. Curly leaved varieties, comparable to modern endives, were known by the end of the century.

erum, ervum generic name applied to various VETCHES including the chickling vetch, *Lathyrus sativus*.

fenel, fenell fennel, *Foeniculum vulgare*. Culinary and medicinal. Mediterranean. Introduced to Britain by the Romans, and widely naturalized.

fenny-greek fenugreek, *Trigonella foenumgraecum*. Culinary and medicinal. Mediterranean.

fetherfew feverfew, *Tanacetum parthenium*. Medicinal. Europe. Introduced by the Romans.

figge fig, *Ficus carica*. Fruit tree. Originally domesticated in Asia Minor, and probably first grown in Britain by the Romans.

filipendula dropwort, *Filipendula vulgaris*. Medicinal. Native.

fitch VETCH.

flebane common fleabane, *Pulicaria dysenterica*. Medicinal. Native. Burnt on fires as a fumigant.

flower armoure *Amaranthus* species, including love-lies-bleeding, etc. Ornamental and medicinal. Europe, New World.

flower de luce *Iris* species and varieties. Ornamental and medicinal. Native and European.

flowers of the sun sunflower, *Helianthus* species. Ornamental flowers. Introduced from the New World, sixteenth century.

fluelline, hearb fluellin members of the speed-well family, *Veronica* species. Medicinal. Native.

french balme *see* BALME.

french-mallow an annual or biennial mallow (probably a *Lavatera*) with pale green leaves 'plaited or curled about the brims like a ruff'.

galbanum a gum derived from giant fennel, *Ferula galbanifera*. Large aromatic perennial from the Eastern Mediterranean, introduced to British gardens at an unknown date.

garlike, garlick garlic, *Allium sativum*. Culinary and medicinal. Asia. Anciently introduced to Britain.

gellyflower, gillyflower pinks, etc, *Dianthus* varieties. *See* CARNATION.

gentiane, gentian various *Gentiana* species. Medicinal and ornamental. Europe. The great yellow gentian, *G. lutea*, from southern Europe, was the kind most often grown for medicinal use.

gooseberry *Ribes uva-crispa*. Fruiting shrub. Native. Gooseberries were used in cooking as well as in medicine, and about six varieties were in cultivation in the sixteenth century. But the fruit had not been improved much from the small, slightly sharp wild form.

gourd various members of the Cucurbitaceae family, especially snake and bottle gourds. Ornamental, Asia. The fruits were occasionally eaten, baked, but they did not always ripen properly in the English climate, and were grown largely as curiosities.

great mallows probably HOLY OKES.

hartichock *see* ARTICHOKE.

hartshorne 1 buck's-horn plantain, *Plantago coronopus*. **2** swine-cress, *Coronopus squamatum*. Both native medicinal herbs. **3** deer antlers, used as a source of gelatine.

hartstongue hart's-tongue, *Phyllitis scolopendrium*. Medicinal fern. Native.

hastings local, vernacular term for an early cropping field pea.

haythorne hawthorn, *Crataegus monogyna*. Shrub. Native.

hearb-grace, herb of grace RUE.

hearb heliotropium various *Heliotropium* species. Medicinal and ornamental. Mediter-ranean. Known as tornesole in Britain.

hearb perforata probably perforate St John's-wort, *Hypericum perforatum*. Medicinal. Native.

hearb sticas *see* STICAS.

hearts ease, hartsease wild pansy, *Viola tricolor*. Ornamental and medicinal. Native. Larger varieties were raised in cultivation, but modern pansies were not developed until the nineteenth century.

hellebores *Helleborus* species. Ornamental and medicinal. Native and European. The native black or stinking hellebore, *H. foetidus*, was the species most commonly brought into gardens.

henbane *Hyoscyamus niger*. Strongly narcotic herb. Native. Anciently cultivated for medicinal purposes.

hisop hyssop, *Hyssopus officinalis*. Medicinal and culinary. Mediterranean.

holy okes hollyhocks, *Althaea rosea*. Ornamental. Reputedly first brought to Britain from the Near East by the Crusaders. A number of double varieties was in cultivation by the end of the sixteenth century.

honeysuckle *Lonicera periclymenum*. Climbing shrub. Native. Grown in gardens for decoration. The berries were occasionally used in medicine.

housleek houseleek, *Sempervivum tectorum*. Medicinal and ornamental. Central Europe. Anciently introduced to Britain and planted on roofs as a protection against lightning.

isop hyssop, *see* HISOP.

jacemine summer or white jasmine, *Jasminum officinale*. Scented climber. Middle East.

july-flowers CARNATIONS.

lavender *Lavandula officinalis*. Ornamental and medicinal shrub. Mediterranean. Anciently introduced.

leek *Allium ampeloprasum* var. *porrum*. Vegetable. Eastern Mediterranean. Probably a Roman introduction. As well as being cultivated for their stems, leeks were cropped for their green tops, as if they were a giant chive.

lemmon lemon, *Citrus limon*. Fruit tree. Mediterranean. Not commonly cultivated as far north as Britain.

lettice, littice lettuce, *Lactuca sativa*. Vegetable. Originally cultivated in the Near East. Cabbage, cos, and curly leaved were all in cultivation in English gardens. The leaves were used medicinally as well as in salads.

lilly lily, *Lilium* species and varieties. Ornamental flowers. At least fifteen European and Near Eastern species were in cultivation.

lionsfoot probably edelweiss, *Leontopodium alpinum*. European alpine, occasionally cultivated in sixteenth-century gardens.

liver-wort 1 liverworts, members of the Hepaticae group. **2** hepatica, *Hepatica nobilis*. Medicinal and ornamental. Europe.

lovage *Levisticum officinale*. Medicinal and culinary herb. Mediterranean.

lung-wort *Pulmonaria officinalis*. Medicinal herb. Europe. Anciently introduced and widely naturalized.

lupines *Lupin* species. Ornamental flowers. Mediterranean. American species were not brought over until the early seventeenth century.

marigold *Calendula officinalis*. Ornamental and medicinal flower. Mediterranean. Introduced about 1580. Several varieties were in cultivation.

marjoram *Origanum* species. Medicinal and culinary herbs. Native and Mediterranean.

melon *Melo cucumis*. Fruit. Originally from Africa, probably first introduced to Britain in the late Middle Ages. A number of varieties were in cultivation on primitive hot-beds (not always very successfully), including musk and Spanish melons. The water-melon was brought over from the New World in the mid-sixteenth century.

mercury good King Henry, *Chenopodium bonus-henricus*. Green vegetable. Europe. Anciently introduced to and naturalized in Britain.

mints *Mentha* species and varieties. Culinary and medicinal herbs. Native. A dozen or so species and hybrids were known and used.

mirtle, myrtle *Myrtus communis*. Aromatic shrub. Mediterranean. Popular in arbours, and occasionally used in medicine.

monks-hood *Aconitum napellus*. Highly toxic flower. Native. Occasionally cultivated for its poisonous properties (and only much later as a decorative species).

mugwort *Artemisia vulgaris*. Medicinal herb. Native.

musk mellions musk, galia, and netted varieties of MELON.

mustard black mustard, *Brassica nigra*. Medicinal and culinary. Native. Anciently cultivated for leaves and seeds. White mustard, *Sinapis alba*, also native, was not cultivated until the sixteenth century, then chiefly for medicinal purposes.

navew, navewe a kind of RAPE.

neeswort, nosewort probably sneezewort, *Achillea ptarmica*. Medicinal. Native.

nigella romana love-in-a-mist, *Nigella damascena*, and other *Nigella* and *Delphinium* species. Ornamental and medicinal annual flowers. Europe.

oculus christi CLARY.

oke oak, *Quercus* species. Deciduous tree. Native.

olive *Olea europaea*. Mediterranean tree, not cultivated in Britain.

onion *Allium cepa* (and related species). Vegetable. Central Asia, probably introduced by the Romans. Varieties grown included the scallion or shallot, and the winter, spring, or Welsh onion, *A. fistulosum*.

ophioscoridon wild garlic. *See* RAMSRES.

orage orache, *Atriplex hortensis*. Green vegetable. Europe. The name was also applied to other *Atriplex* and *Chenopodium* species, including fat hen, *C. album*.

orenge orange, *Citrus* species. Fruit tree. South-east Asia, first brought to Britain by the Normans.

organy wild MARJORAM.

orpiment arsenic trisulphide, used as a pigment and a poison.

osier, ozier *Salix viminalis*. Native species of willow, used for basket weaving.

palma christi castor-oil plant, *Ricinus communis*. Medicinal shrub. Middle East.

pansie HEARTSEASE.

parcely, parsley *Petroselinum crispum*. Culinary and medicinal. Mediterranean, introduced to Britain in the fifteenth or sixteenth century.

parsnep parsnip, *Pastinaca sativa*. Root vegetable. Native. Began to be improved as a vegetable during the Middle Ages.

patience patience dock, *Rumex patientia*. Green vegetable and medicinal herb. Europe.

peason, pease peas, *Pisum* varieties. Vegetable. Introduced from the Near East by the Romans. A food staple principally used in the dried state. Half-a-dozen varieties were in cultivation.

pellitory pellitory-of-the-wall, *Parietaria judaica*. Medicinal herb. Native.

peny-royal pennyroyal, *Mentha pulegium*. Medicinal herb. Native.

pepperwort dittander, *see* DITTANY.

peucedanum hog's fennel, *Peucedanum officinale*. Medicinal herb. Native.

pinck pinks, *see* CARNATION.

piony, pyonie wild peony, *Paeonia mascula*. Medicinal and ornamental. Mediterranean, probably introduced to Britain as a medicinal herb by medieval monks. A number of other varieties – including doubles – were being grown in sixteenth-century gardens.

pomecitron CITRONE.

pomegranet, pomegranate *Pumica granatum*. Fruit tree. Originally from Asia, anciently naturalized in the Mediterranean region. Grown in England since at least the sixteenth century.

pompons, pompions, pumpion MELON.

poppy *Papaver* species. Medicinal, culinary, and ornamental. Native and European. The introduced opium poppy, *Papaver somniferum*, was occasionally grown for its seeds, which were used to season bread and as a source of oil.

primrose *Primula vulgaris*. Medicinal and ornamental. Native. Several different varieties – including some doubles and compacted flowers – were in cultivation, and were probably first found as wild 'sports'.

privet *Ligustrum vulgare*. Shrub, used medicinally and for hedging. Native.

purselane purslane, *Portulaca oleracea*. Salad vegetable. Introduced from the Middle East in

about the fifteenth century.

quince *Cydonia vulgaris*. Medicinal and culinary fruit. Native of the Near East, probably introduced to Britain by the Romans.

radish *Raphanus sativus*. Root vegetable and medicinal herb. Uncertain origins, but probably a Roman introduction.

ramsres ramsons, wild garlic, *Allium ursinum*. Culinary and medicinal herb. Native. Also applied to field garlic, *Allium oleraceum*.

rape turnip, *see* TURNEP.

raponticke rhapontic – obsolete name applied to a number of different astringent herbs, notably rhubarb (*see* RUBERB) and centaury (*see* CENTORY).

rhodophanes, rhododaphne oleander, *Nerium oleander*. Poisonous shrub. Mediterranean.

rocket *Eruca sativa*. Salad vegetable and medicinal herb. Mediterranean.

roman worme-wood *Artemisia pontica, see* WORMWOOD.

rose *Rosa* species and cultivars. At least forty different varieties were in cultivation in Britain, including the multi-petalled Dutch or cabbage rose, and the first musks and damasks, recently introduced from Asia.

rose campion *Lychnis coronaria*. Ornamental. Mediterranean, introduced in the late Middle Ages.

rosemarie, rosemary *Rosmarinus officinalis*. Medicinal, culinary, and ornamental shrub. Mediterranean.

ruberb rhubarb, *Rheum rhaponticum*. Medicinal herb. Asia. Rhubarb did not begin to be used as a food until the eighteenth century.

ruddel ruddle, a red ochre used as a dye, and for marking sheep.

rue *Ruta graveolens*. Aromatic shrub. Mediterranean, introduced by the Romans and used chiefly medicinally.

saffron *Crocus sativus*. Stigmas from flowers used as spice, cosmetic, and dye. Bulbs occasionally used medicinally. Native to Asia Minor, introduced by the Romans, and once grown commercially in Britain.

sage *Salvia officinalis*. Culinary and medicinal herb. Mediterranean.

saudaracha sandaracha, the gum of the juniper.

savery summer savory, *Satureja hortensis*, and winter savory, *S. montana*. Culinary and medicinal herbs. Mediterranean, probably introduced by the Romans.

savin-tree savin or sabine, *Juniperus sabina*. Evergreen shrub. Near East. The poisonous berries were used medicinally.

scalions most commonly shallots, but also used for various kinds of small, clustering onions. *See* ONION.

scamonie, scammonie various species of Mediterranean and Near-Eastern bindweed, *Convolvulus* species, valued as medicinal herbs.

self-heale selfheal, *Prunella vulgaris*. Medicinal herb. Native.

senae bladder-senna, *Colutea arborescens*. Medicinal herb. Mediterranean, introduced in the early sixteenth century.

sesamium sesame, *Sesamum indicum*. Oil-bearing pulse. Originally from Africa, anciently introduced to India and the Mediterranean. Not grown in Britain, though the oil was used medicinally.

siler possibly a variety of willow, though Gerard glosses it as a pseudonym for the Italian black alder, *Alnus nigra*.

singreen HOUSLEEK.

skerrot skirret, *Sium sisarum*. Root vegetable. East Asian, introduced to Britain in about the fifteenth century; fell out of fashion in the late seventeenth century.

skiff in this context, presumably a shallow, boat-shaped wooden container for strewing water.

slow sloe or blackthorn, *Prunus spinosa*. Fruiting shrub. Native. Fruits used in cooking, medicine and for making dye.

smallage wild celery, *Apium graveolens*. Medicinal and culinary herb. Native.

smyrnium ANGELICA.

sorrel, sorrell *Rumex acetosa*. Medicinal and culinary herb. Native.

sotherenwood, sothernwood southernwood, *Artemisia abrotanum*. Medicinal and ornamental. Southern Europe.

sowesbreade sowbread, *Cyclamen* species. Ornamental and medicinal bulbs. Europe.

speradge, sperage asparagus, *Asparagus officinalis*. Vegetable. Native, but cultivated forms did not begin to appear in Britain until the sixteenth century.

spiknard spikenard, various plants of the Valerian family with scented roots. Celtic spikenard, *Valeriana celtica*, from the Alps, was the form occasionally grown in gardens. The roots were used medicinally and in perfumery.

spinedge spinach, *Spinacea oleracea*. Vegetable, originally from Persia. Introduced to Britain in the mid-sixteenth century.

spingled possibly sprung, already shooting (Italian, *spingere*).

squill onyon squill, *Scilla* species. Bulbs, used as a vegetable and medicinally. Southern Europe. The practice of eating squill bulbs appears to have died out by the end of the seventeenth century.

stecados French lavender, *Lavandula stoechas*. Ornamental and medicinal 'sub-shrub'. Southern Europe.

sticas Uncertain. Possibly 'stoechas', French lavender (*see* STECADOS); or one of the horehounds, *Stachys* species.

stock july-flowers stocks, *Matthiola* species and cultivars. Ornamental and medicinal. Europe. Doubles were already in cultivation. (Yellow stock july-flowers were WALLFLOWERS.)

storax gum from trees of the *Styrax* family.

strawberry wild strawberry, *Fragaria vesca*. Culinary and medicinal fruit. Native. In the sixteenth century, cultivation of strawberries consisted of transplanting and manuring the wild varieties. The alpine or hautbois strawberry, *F. moschata*, was grown in some gardens, but the larger American species were not introduced until the early eighteenth century.

succory chicory, *Cichorium intybus* and cultivars. Salad vegetable and medicinal herb. Native. Larger, softer-leaved varieties were in cultivation, and the practice of over-wintering roots in the dark to produce blanched leaves was well known in the sixteenth century.

sweet-bryer sweet briar, *Rosa rubiginosa*. Flowering shrub. Native. Popular in arbours for its apple-scented leaves.

sweet johns *Dianthus* varieties closely related to sweet william, *D. barbatus*. Ornamental flowers. Southern Europe.

sweet-sisley sweet cicely, *Myrrhis odorata*. Medicinal and culinary herb. Introduced from Europe but widely naturalized.

tansie tansy, *Tanacetum vulgare*. Medicinal and culinary herb. Native.

taragone tarragon, *Artemisia dracunculus*. Medicinal and culinary herb. Southern Europe.

tares VETCHES.

time, tyme thyme, *Thymus* species. Medicinal and culinary herbs. Native and Mediterranean. A number of varieties and species were grown, including the lemon-scented type.

tulips *Tulipa* species and cultivars. Ornamental bulbs. Southern Europe and Near East. Gerard lists thirty different species and varieties.

turbith probably an extract of the root of the giant fennel, *Ferula communis*.

turks-cap martagon lilies, *Lilium* species. Ornamental. Europe.

turnep, turnup, turen turnip, *Brassica rapa*. Root vegetable. Anciently cultivated in Britain as a staple.

valeriane valerian, *Valeriana officinalis*. Medicinal herb. Native. (Some other species were grouped under this name. Greek valerian, for example, was jacob's ladder, *Polemonium caeruleum*.)

vetches *Vicia* species. Medicinal and fodder plants. Native.

vine grape vine, *Vitis vinifera*. Fruiting climber. Originating in Asia, introduced to Britain by the Romans, and cultivated sporadically since.

violet *Viola* species. Ornamental and medicinal. Native and European.

wall-july-flowers, wallflowers *Cheiranthus* species. Ornamental and medicinal flowers. European, possibly introduced by the Normans.

walworte 1 WALLFLOWERS. **2** biting stonecrop, *Sedum acre*. Medicinal herb. Native. **3** danewort, dwarf elder, *Sambucus ebulus*. Medicinal herb. Europe.

wardens variety of large pear for baking, developed at Warden Abbey in Bedfordshire in the Middle Ages.

white-thorne hawthorn, *see* HAYTHORNE.

willow *Salix* species. Trees and shrubs. Native.

woodbine HONEYSUCKLE.

wormwood *Artemisia* species. Medicinal herbs. Mediterranean.

Jacob Grimmer (c. 1626-89), The Spring. *The seventeenth-century garden was a hive of activity in spring with levelling of beds, planting, sowing, and raking of the raised beds, as well as pruning of young trees.*

Tree planting and digging in a well-ordered Swiss garden in 1637.

A TABLE EXPRESSING
THE CONTENTS OF EVERY CHAPTER
CONTAINED IN THIS LABYRINTH.

The
Gardeners-Labyrinth.
**Wherein is laid down New and Rare inventions
and secrets of Gardening not heretofore known.**

CHAP. I

he worthy *Pliny* (in his XIX. Book) reporteth, that a Garden plot in the ancient time at *Rome*, was none other, then a smal & simple inclosure of ground, which through the labour & diligence of the Husbandman, yielded a commodity and yearly revenue unto him. But after years (that man more esteemed of himself, and sought an easier life) devised and framed this ground plot for the mind, as for pleasure and delight: as may well appear by that Epicure, of whom *Cicero* maketh mention, in his book, intituled, *De natura Dearum*, who living at ease, and conceiving a felicity in the Garden, endeavoured first to place and frame the same within the wals of *Athens*, which before (as it should seem) lay open, and undefended in the wild field, and the culture of it not had in so much estimation, as to place them nigh to their townes and houses: For which cause, doth *Plinie* (by good reason) rightly attribute the invention of the delectable Garden to him. The Garden plots, which the ancient *Romans* possessed (as *Plinie* reporteth) were only set about with trees, having a dead enclosure made onely of bushes that needed repairing every year: in which especially were sown the red Onions, Coleworts, great Leeks, Cresses, great Mallows or holy Olies, Endive, Rocket, and sundry sallet herbs: In these they found such a commodity, as marvellously pleased them, feeling they by injoying the herbs, spared the charge of flesh, besides a daily profit that they got, by the herbs brought to the City to be sold. The meaner sort of that time so little cared and

The invention of Garden plots, by whom first devised, and what commoditie found by them in time past.

OPPOSITE *A view painted in the style of Paul Brill shows that the Roman garden of the seventeenth century seems to have suffered from exactly the ramshackle method of enclosure that Hill censures in his opening chapter.*

BELOW *Enjoying the fragrance and spectacle of a well-laid-out seventeenth-century garden. From the Hortus Floridus.*

esteemed the eating of flesh (who in generall accounted it a kind of reproach, to be known to have eaten flesh) that they refusing this taunt, did (as to a shambles or fresh market) haunt daily to the Garden.

Columella reporteth, *lib.* 10. that the ancient husbandman so slenderly looked unto (or rather forced of) Gardens, that they in furthering the grouth and yield of their fruits and herbs, bestowed small travel and diligence. And as they appeared negligent in their labours of the Garden, so were they well pleased with a mean living, insomuch that the common sort fed and lived willingly on grosse and simple herbs. But after the age and people were reformed, and brought by the instruction of the Epicure, to a more delight of themselves in coveting to feed on dainty herbs and sallets, with meats delectable, and taking an earnester care for the pleasing of their mouths, they laboured then to become skilful, and to use a greater care about the ordering and apt dressing of Garden plots, by wel fencing and comely furnishing of their ground, with sundry needful & delectable trees, plants, and herbs: in which travels and diligence of the husbandmen, so good successe and commodity ensuing, procured not onley the willing carriage of herbs, fruits, and other commodities far off to be exercised unto Cities and Market townes, by which these through the sale obtained a daily gaine and yearly revenue, for the aid of their houshold charges, but allured them also to place and frame Gardens, as well within Cities and Towns as fast by, that a cost

Mid-seventeenth century English embroidery showing Abraham and the Angels. This displays in artly fashion *the pleasures of eating out of doors in a well-stocked garden.*

bestowed, might after possesse the procreation and delight of minds, besides the proper gaine made by the fruits, flowers, and herbs, gathered in them. The Garden plots at length grew so common among the meaner sort, that the charge and the chiefest care of the same, was committed unto the wife, insomuch that these accounted not the wife of the house to be a huswife indeed, if she bestowed not paines and deligence, as *Cato* reporteth, in the weeding, trimming, and dressing of the Garden: but to be brief, and leaving further to report of antiquity, I thinke it high time to declare the effects and commoditie of this worke taken in hand; and first to treat of the care, helps, and secrets to be learned and followed in the Garden ground: All which in a pleasant manner, shall after be uttered in distinct Chapters, to the furtherance and commodity of many Gardeners, and all such having pleasure therein.

CHAP. II

he husbandman or Gardener shall enjoy a most commodious and delectable Garden, which both knoweth, can, and will orderly dresse the same: yet not sufficient is it to a Gardener, that he knoweth, or would the furtherance of the Garden, without any cost bestowed, which the works and labours of the same require; nor the will againe of the workman, in doing and bestowing of charges, shall smally availe without he have both art and skill in the same. For that cause, it is the chiefest point in every faculty and businesse to understand and know what to begin and follow; as the learned *Columella* out of *Varronianus Tremellius* aptly uttereth. The person which shall enjoy or have in readinesse these three, and will purposely or with diligence frame to him a well dressed Garden, shall after obtaine these two commodities, as utility and delight; the utility yieldeth the plenty of herbs, flowers, and fruits right delectable, but the pleasure of the same procureth a delight, and (as *Varro* writeth) a jucundity of mind. For that cause a Garden shall workmanly be handled, and dressed unto the necessary use and commodity of mans life, next for health, and the recovery of strength by sicknesse feebled, as the singular *Paladius Rutilius* both learnedly uttered, and the skilful *Florentius*, that wrote enchantingly of husbandry in the *Greeke* tongue, certain years before him: Lastly, by sight, unto delectation through the fragrancy of smell; but most of all, that the same may furnish the owners and husbandmans table, with sundry seemely and dainty dishes to him of small cost. The Garden ground (if the same may be) ought rather to be placed near hand, whereby the owner or Gardener may with more ease be partaker of such commodities growing in the Garden, and both oftner resort, and use diligence in the same. So that this is the whole care and duty required

What care and diligence is required of every Gardener: to these, what increase and commoditie a well laboured earth yieldeth.

of every owner and Gardener in their plot of ground. Yet may I not be unmindful, that the Garden doth require a dunging at the apt times, of which in the proper place we shall after treat.

CHAP. III

What consideration and choosing is to be used in any Garden-plot, with the goodnesse and worthinesse of every earth.

s to the nature and goodness of a Garden ground, that especially that ought to be eschewed, is bitter & salt earth of tast, if so be we meane to make a fertil, commodious and well yeilding ground: for these two natures of earth, were very much disliked in ancient time, as may appear by the skilfull Poet *Virgil*, who sayeth that every earth is not allowed or commended, for the yeeld of Garden hearbs. For which cause, the mind of the ancient Husbandman is, that the

While the clothes and the exact form of the spade may have changed from medieval times to the present day, it has always required effort and determination for the gardener to produce a well-turned bed. This illustration dates from c. 1480.

Gardener by taking up a clod of earth, should esely trie the goodness of it after this manner: in considering whether the earth be neither hot and bare, not leane by sand, lacking a mixture of perfect earth: nor the same found to be wholly chalk, nor naughty sand: nor barren gravel, nor of the glistering pouder or dust of a leane stony ground, nor the earth continual moist; for all these be the special defaults of a good and perfect earth. The best ground for a Garden, is the same judged to be, which in the Summer time is neither very drie, nor clayie, nor sandy and rough, nor endamaged with gapings, procured by heat of the Summer, as the worthy *Didimus* in his Greek instructions of Husbandry writeth. Wherefore the earth which in summer time is wont to be drie, either perisheth or loseth all the seeds sowne, and plants set in it, or yeildeth those thin, and weak proving on the ground. For the clayie ground of itselfe, over-bindeth: but the sandy and rough, in a contrary manner: so that neither is wont to nourish plants, nor retaine water. Therefore an apt earth for a Garden, shall you readily trie and find out, if the same thorow wet and dissolved with water, you shall see to have a much clamminess and fastness. In which ground, if a watriness shall exceed, then shall you judge the same disagreeable and unfruitful: if dissolving the earth with water, you shall find the same very clammie, or much cleaving to the hand and fingers as if it were wax, this earth man you account as wholly unprofitable. *Pliny* willeth that a Garden plot before all other matters done to it, be very well clensed of stone, and to these, that the earth prove not full of chaps, or but few to be seene, lest the Sun beames entring between, may so scorch and burne the roots of the plants. For which cause, the best and gentle or worthiest earth shall be chosen, in which you mind to commit your seeds: or for the same, that the nurse as a Mother, may often agree to the fruit, or yeild to be an aider and furtherer to it.

Follower of Joos de Momper II, detail from A Music Part before a Village *(1633). A rather sophisticated moated garden with arbour walks and corner shelters from which to look out on to the beauties of the garden and the surrounding countryside. Hill advised against the use of moated gardens on the grounds that water evaporating from the moat may make seeds and plants 'wax old' and that the earth may become 'overmoist'.*

CHAP. IV

Certaine plainer
instructions, much
furthering the Gardener,
in the knowledge and
choice of a good and battle
ground, with other
matters necessarie.

he Gardener minding to trie and know a fat earth, for the use of a Garden, shall worke after this manner: in taking a little clod of the earth, and the same to sprinckle with fair water, kneading it well in the hand: which after appearing clammie, and cleaving or sticking to the fingers, doth undoubtedly witnesse that earth to have have a fatness in it. And other trial of a battle earth may be thus purchased, if you dig up a rotten clod, in a manner black, and the same able enough to cover it selfe with the growth of its own grass, and appearing also of mixt colour, which earth, if it be found thin and close, may well be fastened and made clammy, through the adjoyning and mixing of a fat earth to it. The Garden ground doth also require a sweetness to consist in it, which the Gardener shall easily find and know by tast of it: if so be he take up a clod of the earth in any part of the ground which most misliketh him, and moistning the clod with faire water in an earthen potsheard, doth after the dipping of the finger in this moist earth and water, let a drop softly fall on the tongue, he shall incontinent feele and perceive (by reason of the taste) of what condition the same is. Further, every fat earth being reasonably loose, is evermore commended and chosen, which of it selfe requireth smal labour, and yeeldeth the most increase. But worst of all others is that ground, which shall be both drie and grosse, lean and cold. In the kinds of ground, the chalk is to be refused: which properly the ancients name the clayish, the reddish earth. The worthy *Varro* commended the same ground, which of it selfe being drie and pliable, yeildeth properly walworts. The same earth doth *Columella* greatly allow, which of its owne accord yeildeth or bringeth forth Wilding or Crab-trees, young springs, the Slow or Bulles trees, Elme trees, and such like. So that a battle ground, is on such wise found and known: the rather of the crescent things, seene in it of its own accord: yet of necessity may every ground well agree, to be mixed and turned in with dung. *Florentius* uttereth an other trial of a fruitfull ground: if so be the Gardener diggeth up a furrow, of a foot and a halfe deep, and filleth the same againe with its owne earth, which in short time after gapeth or choppeth, this no doubt is a weake and leane earth; but if the earth thus ordered, swelleth or retcheth out, then is it a sure note, that the same is a battle and fat ground. And this is noted to be a meane earth, which after the digging and raking even, gapeth but a little. This I thought not good to be covered, nor willingly over passed: that a Garden plot situated or standing near to a mote, or compassed by a mote, is not alwaies laudable, in that the seeds bestowed in the same, and divers plants set in it, doe lightly and soon through the water vapourating forth, wax old: yea the fruits (whether those shall be of the hearbs) are trees or for the more part caused unpleasant, and overmoist. Further conceive, that a Garden ground, ought to be of a moderate increase, and easie dressing, which neither is very moist, nor over drie of it selfe. To these such a earth is greatly commended as being digged. Birds covet to it: and that Crows especially follow the new casting of the digger. If the earth shall be found naughty or unfruitfull, as the clayie, sandy, and chalkie, then ought the same to be amended, after the mind of the skilfull, with marle and dung laid three foot deepe, and well turned in with the earth: if this be perceived over thin, and leane, then to be mixed and holpen by a fat earth: or to a barren and over drie ground, may be mixed a moist and very fat earth. A watery ground is made the better, if the same be mixed with a sandy or smal gravelly earth, and deep Allies made, for the conveying and shifting of the water falling in the night. But to use such tedious paines in these, *Pliny* accounteth it a madness, for what fruit or gaine may be hoped after, in bestowing such a travel and diligence in the like ground plot? To conclude, every reasonable earth may very much be holpen, through the wel dunging and labouring of the Gardener: of which matter (in the proper place) we meane fully to treat.

CHAP. V

t is right necessary (saith *Varro*) to place Gardens near to the City, as wel for the benefit of Pot-hearbs and roots, as all manner of sweet smelling flowers, that the City greatly needeth. Were these placed in a soile far off, that they cannot so conveniently and in due time be brought to the Market to be sold, in such places they are altogether disallowed, & thought frivolous for the turne. *Cato* doth very much commend the Garden plot placed near to the City, in which both young trees to beare up Vines, and Willow or Ozier trees be planted nigh to water sides, and in all places watery: and that through the Garden ground, water or springs be seene running. To these the seeds of most hearbs committed into a wel dunged, dressed, and faire or large open plot, in which besides all kindes of fruits, for the use of man, workmanly planted and set in apt times of the yeare. Flowers, and all manner of round and delectable roots, with the sweet and pleasant smelling trees; as all the kindes of the Roses, the sweet Iacemine, the Eglantine brier, the Mirtle tree, and all others of like fort, be sowed and planted in due seasons of the yeare. But a Garden plot, onely serving for the use of Pot-hearbs and the Kitchin, ought especially to be a battleground, sufficient moist of it selfe, and well turned in or workmanly laboured with dung. Garden plots ought to be placed far from Barnes, Hay-lofts and Stables, if the same possibly may be refused, or otherwise chosen for the turne; that in the chaffe or dust of the straws (as enemy to them) the plants hardly brook and suffer, insomuch that the very straws blowne abroad with the winde,

Of the placing and standing of a Garden plot, with the necessary benefit of a water to a Garden, and other matters profitable.

Detail from a sixteenth-century painting of a market where growers and traders are busily exchanging their wares. Hill recommended that the garden should be close to the town or city so that produce could be brought freshly to market.

and falling on herbs, do greatly annoy and harm them, as the singular *Florentius* in his Greek instructions of Husbandry skilfully uttereth. For these, saith he, by cleaving to the plants in the falling, pierce the leaves, which once pierced, are incontinent burned with them. All Gardens as wel prosper by the dunging with with roots, as with the proper dung allowable: yet dunging the Garden earth, with the branches and leaves of trees, is of the skilfull Gardeners very much disallowed, as unprofitable and noyous to herbs.

A splendid wall affording the ultimate protection to a garden. From a late fifteenth-century manuscript illustration of the Roman de la Rose.

As to the wel standing of a Garden behooveth; the aptest and most laudable placing of a Garden plot shall be, if the plain ground lying somewhat aslope, that have a course of spring water running thorow by several parts. But this course of water running thorow the Garden plot, may in no wise be big. And the smallnesse of the labouring and dressing of a Garden ground, is more likely to yield, fruit then the largeness of it, not laboured in a manner at all.

It behooveth to have a Well or Pump in a Garden, unless some

A thorn hedge was another method of enclosure. This example is from the Bradford Table Carpet. *Sixteenth-century English embroidery.*

This kitchen garden shows that the principles of Hill's ideas continued to be employed into the eighteenth century. The enclosed beds of the sloping garden are well disposed and irrigated, and situated far enough from the barns and haylofts to prevent the plants being 'annoyed' by windblown straws.

running water, as either ditch or small River be near adjoyning; for that a sweet water sprinkled on young plants and herbs, giveth a special nourishment. If a Well be lacking in the Garden, then dig a deep pit in some convenient place of the Garden, to draw water out of the same. For a Garden ground needeth often to be watered, through which all seeds committed to the earth, as *Pliny* reporteth, both sooner break forth, and speedier spread abroad. That a pit with water of long continuance may be purchased, the same at that time *Columella* willeth to be digged when the Sun shall obtain or occupy the last degrees of *Virgo*; which is in the moneth of *September*, before the equinoctial harvest. For the vertue then of wel-springs are throughly tried and found out: at which time through the long drought of Summer, the earth lacketh the due moisture of raine. If a well or pit to purpose cannot be made in the Garden, then frame up a square pit or Cestern levelled in the bottom with Brick and Lime to receive the Raine-water falling, with which in the hottest Summer daies, you may water the beds of the Garden. But if all these manner of helps and wayes shall faile the Gardener, or cannot wel be compassed in the Garden ground, then shall he dig the ground after the mind of *Palladius Rutilius*, three or four foot the deeper or lower. For the beds on such wise ordered, being workmanly laboured and sowen, may the better endure through the low standing, the whole drought of the Summer dayes. In the Garden ground besides, this shall you observe, that when the Allies or pathes of the beds be over cloyed with water, to dig deep gutters here and there after your discretion, in such order, that the water falling and running along, may be guided into a convenient pit, made at the lower side or end of the Garden, for that onely purpose. Here further learn, that what Garden plot the nature of the moisture helpeth not, the same may you aptly divide into parts, in converting the spaces, digged and dressed for the Winter time to lie open to the South, and those prepared for the Summer time, like unto the North quarter.

CHAP. VI

What aire commended for the benefit of a Garden, and which be noyous as well to Man as the Plants; and the reason why Garden plots ought to be placed nigh to the owners house.

 very ground-plot lying near to the City, as well the Garden as Orchard, ought to be placed near to the house, for the oftner recourse and diligence to be bestowed of the owner; and the Garden especially to be laboured and wel turned up with dung: through whose juyce and fatning, the earth may yield herbs of her own accord. As touching the aire commended for a Garden, the same being clear and temperate is best allowed, in that this not only cherisheth and prospereth the herbs growing in it, but procureth a delight and comfort to the walkers therein. An evil aire in the contrary manner, troubled with the vapours of standing pits, ditches, and such like mixed to it, doth not only annoy and corrupt the plants and herbs growing in that Garden fast by, but choke and dul the spirits of men, by walking in the same. Besides, the winds biting, and frosts mortifying, do both harm and destroy Plants. *Avicen* writing of the aire, doth in a skilful manner utter, that the same aire, which after the Sun setting is soon cold, and after the Sun rising speedily hot, is both subtile and healthful to man. So that a contrary aire to this, worketh the contrary to man and Plants. Yet that aire is accounted worser,

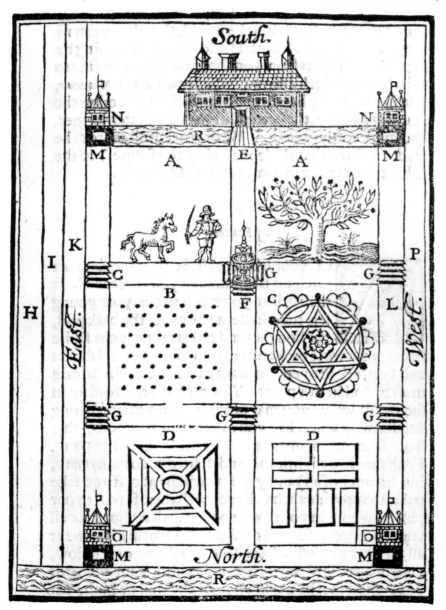

A plan for a garden from Gervaise Markham, A New Orchard and Garden, *1638. A. All these squares must be set with Trees, the Garden and other Ornaments must stand in spaces betwixt the Trees, and in the borders and fences. B. Trees twenty yards asunder. C. Garden Knots. D. Kitching Garden. E. Bridge. F. Conduit. G. Staires. H. Walks set with great wood thick. I. Walks set with great wood round about your orchard. K. The outfence set with stone fruit. M. Mount. To force Earth for a Mount or such like, set it round with quick, and lay boughes of Trees strangely intermingled, the tops inward, with the Earth in the middle. N. Still house. O. Good standing for Bees, if you have an house. P. If the River run by your door, and under your Mount, it will be pleasant.*

which seemeth as it were to wring or bind hard together the heart; yea, making strait or letting the attraction of aire. The learned Neapolitane *Rutilius,* besides these reporteth, that the subtileness or healthiness of the aire, do declare those places free from low vallies, and stinking mists or fogs in the night, that might annoy both men and the plants. Here it doth not much disagree from the matter, to write in general of the qualities of the winds, and of these in the briefest manner. First, the Easternly and Westernly winds be in a manner temperate of quality, as between a hotness and coldnesse, yet of the two, the Easternly winds be known drier. Further, the Easternly winds are for the more part hotter then the Westernly, and the Westernly by report of the ancient, somewhat more moist then the Easternly. Of all the winds for the benefit of the Garden, is the South-west wind especially commended; as the worthy *Florentius* in his *Greeke* rules, and others experience affirme.

Besides these, as unto the clemency or temperateness of aire, and healthfulness of the place belongeth, a Garden plot in cold Countries ought in a contrary manner to be placed, either to the East or South quarter, if the same be such a plot of ground, which both containeth trees and plants, or herbs coming up in it, left the Garden plot excluded from these two parts, by the object or standing against of some most great and high hill, be so nipped, frozen, and withered, with the extream cold long continuing, or the Garden plot otherwise far distant from the comfort of the Sun on the North part, or else the Sun only shining low and weake, at the West quarter of the same: The singular *Cato* willeth, that the Garden, if a man can, be placed at the foot of an hil; and the same beholding or lying open to the South, especially in a healthful place. For a Garden plot thus defended by an

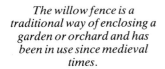

The willow fence is a traditional way of enclosing a garden or orchard and has been in use since medieval times.

high hil, on the North part, and all the day comforted by the open face of the South quarter, is procured to yield the sweeter and timelier fruits, in the seasons of the year. But in hot Regions or Countries, the open place of a Garden ground must be rather scituated towards the North quarter, which may through the like standing, availe as well to health of body and quickning of the spirits, as to profit and pleasure.

This besides conceive, that the placing of a Garden ground, near to a Fen or Marsh, is every where to be misliked and refused; if the same lie open towards the South or West, and yearly in the Summer time is accustomed to be dry; for on such wise happening, the aire thereabout gathered up, doth in the falling again, engender either the pestilence, or wicked vermin, much harming the Garden plot lying nigh to it. There is also a great regard to be had to the water, mote, or ditch, standing nigh or round about the Garden ground; whether this for the most part be want to vaporate or breath forth any noysome aire, that may both to men & the plants be harmful. For peculiar and proper is the same (or rather such is the propertie) of very many still waters and Motes. So that it is the counsel of the skilful (if any like be known) to refrain from placing any Garden plot or Orchard, if the owner may chuse, near to the same.

CHAP. VII

ORASMUCH as the same may be thought a meere madness, to have chosen out a fit plot of ground, and to cast, digge, and dresse it seemly in all points; yet lying open day and night, as wel to the incursions and common haunt, as the injuries to be wrought and done by Robbers or Thieves, fowls and beasts; for that cause I here mind to treat of sundry manners of fencing, and compassing in of the Garden grounds in ancient times. First, the skilful and wary Husbandmen in time past, being those of good ability, built them wals about of Free-stone artly laid, and mortered together, and some did, with baked bricke like handled. Others of lesser ability, and of meaner sort, framed them inclosures, with stones handsomely laid one upon another with morter or clay; and some of them couched the broad salt Stones, with other bigge and large stones (in like order about) where such dwel by quarries of stone. But very many of the baser and poorer sort, made them fences and wals about, with mudde of the ditch, dung, chaffe, and straws cut short, and wel mixed together. Others there were, which with bigge Canes set upright, by smal poles bound together, so fenced their Garden plot, in handsome manner round about. Some also with young Willow trees, set by certaine distances, and the drie black thorne (purchased from the wood) being bound in (between the spaces) so framed their inclosure: but this manner of inclosing wrought or built by Art, the skilfuller named a dead and

The forme of the Inclosures, which Husbandmen and *Romans* in time past invented.

rough inclosure, made especially for the keeping and defending of Cattel out of the Garden ground. Yet the hedge or inclusure erected after this manner, requireth every yeare to be new repaired and bound up in the places needful, to the tediousnesse and great paines of the Husbandman.

The learned *Columella* in his Husbandrie reporteth, that the *Romanes* in time past, fenced and inclosed their Garden grounds, with big quarters set upright, and poles with lathes, very thicke fastened to them by smal rods of the Ozier tree, walling them in. Some bored large holes thorow big bodies or stocks of trees, that quarters or great poles made for the purpose might passe thorow them, either by two or three together, in reasonable distance, with paile bord raised and fastened along to them. Some also through the Timber of trees, (set into the earth) fastned pig poles or long quarters round about, much like to the usual Cattel pounds in our age. But some attaining to more skil, erected as *Varro* reporteth, a natural inclosure, set about with black or white thorne trees, and young Willows; which had besides the roots of a quick set hedge, that in time growing up, withstood tempests, windes, land-floods, yea fire the consumer of all things put to it. The ancient Husbandmen did besides these, invent the casting up of banks and countermures of earth, round about the Garden plot, much like to the trenches in time of war about Bulwarks and Tents: and these they specially made neare to high waies or by Rivers, or Marshes, or Fens lying open, or other fields, that the Garden plot might on such wise be defended, from the damages and harmes both of Theeves, Cattel, and Land-floods.

For a plainer conceiving of the abovesaid, learn these following; that the ancient Husbandmen did cast up, and made a deepe ditch about their Garden ground (standing in the open field) which might receive all the raine water falling: and this they so digged with a slope passage, whereby the water might runne the easier and freelier from the bottom. The earth and clay cast up on the inside (fast by the brinke) they so wrought up together, that hardly any person (after the drying of the countermure) could clime over the same. Some also made high Banks or countermurs, without a ditch digged about, and the same so served in the open fields in stead of a wal.

To be brief, the inclosure which longest endured, surest, and of least cost, was the same that the *Romanes* in ancient time made with brambles, and the white thorne laid orderly in bankes, for the better growing up. For this inclosure or hedge (after years sprung up) endured by report of the learned *Cato* an infinite time; yea experience in our age, doth likewise confirme the same. For which cause, this inclosure was very much commended of the ancient *Romanes*, who wel conceived and knew, that the bramble decayed and dyed not at any season, except it were digged and plucked quite up by the roots. Yea they learned by practise, that the bramble singed or scorched with straw flaming, recovered and grew every yeare after, both stiffer, rougher, and thicker together.

How to erect a pole fence to protect the whitethorn quickset hedge around the garden while it is growing. It must be high enough to prevent poultry from flying over it. From Gervaise Markham, Cheap and Good Husbandry, *1616.*

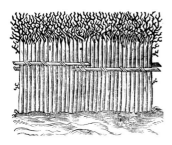

CHAP. VIII

he most commendable inclosure for every Garden plot, is a quick-set hedge, made with brambles and white thorne: but the stronger and more defensive hedge is the same, which the singular *Democritus* in his Greek instructions of Husbandrie (that wrote long before *Columella*, and *Palladius Rutilius*) cunningly uttereth, and the same with ease and smal cost after this manner: Gather saith he, in a due season of the yeare, the seeds found in the red berries of the biggest and highest Briers (which by a more common name with us, are called the wild Eglantine Briers) the thorow ripe seeds of the brambles (running low by the ground) the ripe seeds of the white Thorne, and to these both the ripe Berries of the Goose-berry and Barberry trees: this done, mix and steepe for a time, all the Berries and seeds in the bending meale of Tares, unto the thickness of Honey: the same mixture lay diligently into old and untwisted Ship or Wel-ropes, or other long worne ropes, and fittered or broken into short pieces, being in a manner starke rotten, in such order, that the seeds bestowed or couched within the soft haires of them, may be preserved and defended from the cold, unto the beginning of the spring. At which time where you be minded that the inclosure or hedge shall runne and spring up, there digge in handsome manner, two smal furrows, and these either two or three foot asunder, and a mans foot and a halfe deep: into which lay your ropes with the seeds, covering them workmanly with light earth, and (if need shal require) water by sprinkling, or moisten the seeds, in the same wise again.

The latter inventions of erecting a natural and strong hedge, which in time growing, may prove a most sure defence and safeguard of the Garden.

Conversation and gentle music in the seclusion of a garden with its humble quick-set hedge and vine arbour. From an engraving of 1626.

The worthy *Columella* (in his Husbandrie) and the Neapolitane *Palladius Rutilius* writing the like instruction, in a manner will, that the ground plot in which a hedge shall be erected, be compassed with two narrow furrows, digged three foot distant one from the other, and a mans foot and a halfe deep: but these to be made in the equinoctial Harvest, at what time the ground shal be wel moistened with showers. The furrows thus prepared, they appointed to lye open all the winter thorow; after in the moneth of *February*, the ropes with the seeds, laid into each furrows to be covered not thick over with light earth, for hindering the growth of the seeds, especially of the white Thorne: and that this action be rather wrought, when as the winde bloweth from the South or South-west. The seeds thus covered with diligence, shall appeare within a moneth either more or lesse, and the tender young Thornes sprung up to some height, must be holpen and stayed with Willow twigs, or rather smal props, set betweene the empty spaces, until the Thornes by their further growth, joyned together, may stay one the other, which within few yeares, wil grow to a most strong defence of the Garden or field, and a sure safeguard against outward injuries. *Columella* besides willeth, that a willow or Osier hedge, be set on either side, and in the middle roome or space between the two furrows, covered and even raked, that these might so stay the tender thornes, springing up in either furrow, unto the time they joyned, and were grown above this willow hedge, or at least unto such strength, that they wel staied one of the other. Others there are as the famous *Diophanes* (among the *Greek* writers of Husbandry) and with him many the like, which wil a quick-set hedge to be erected, and made after this manner. The bigger arms or rods of the bramble, they willed to be cut into short portions or parts, and these laid a slope into open furrows of a span deep, to be diligently covered with earth: after to use about the plants, a daily digging or rearing up of the earth, and watering of them if need so requireth, until the plants bud forth, and the leaves of the stems open, which by this manner of comforting and cherishing, shall grow in a few years to a strong, sure and continual hedge.

The Neapolitane *Palladus Rutilius*, instructeth the way and manner of erecting another quick-set hedg on this wise: plant saith he, young Elder trees near three foot asunder, then the seeds of the brambles, lapped diligently in long lumps of softned and moist clay or tough earth, lay the same orderly in a shallow furrow, between the Elder trees, which aptly covered with light earth, and watering the places if need so requireth, wil within three years following, grow to such a strength and surenesse, that the same will be able enough to defend the injuries both of the thief and beast. *Palladius Rutilius* reporteth, that this hedge of brambles after three years growth, ought to be singed with flaming straw; for on such wise handled, it prospereth afterward the better: In that the bramble as he saith, through the very yeares singing or burning with straw, joyeth and increaseth the better: yea through the yearely burning, as the skilful

Husbandmen affirm, they shoot out harder rougher and pricks.

And this manner, to be brief, is a general way of inclosing Garden grounds, with smal cost, and easily performed. Although the comlier inclosure or hedge of a Garden be the same, which is made of the white thorne artely laid: that in few yeares with diligence cut, waxeth so thick and strong, that hardly any person can enter into the ground, saving by the Garden doore: yet in sundry Garden grounds be hedges framed with the Privet tree, although far weaker in resistance; which at this day are made the stronger, through the yearly cutting, both above, and by the sides: yea the same also causeth through the like doing to grow the evener and thicker, to the beautifying of the Garden ground, and for other necessary purposes. To conclude, I have uttered here the making of certain natural inclosures for a Garden, which may with the meanest cost be erected in any ground.

CHAP. IX

here were in ancient time, as *Pliny* recordeth, certaine wittie Husbandmen, that wholly refused and forbad the dunging of Gardens placed nigh to the dwelling houses: in that this dunging might not onely infect the aire thereabout, but cause also the crescent things to prove both unsavourier and more corrupt. And in this matter the worthy writers of Husbandry commended highly the Greek Poet *Hesiodus*, which writing very cunningly of Husbandry, omitted the dunging of the fields, and Gardens plots, contented rather to counsell unto healthfulnesse, then willed the same to fertility. Insomuch as it was supposed enough at that time, to have fatned the fields and Garden plots, with the leaves and empty cods of the Beanes, Peason, Tares, and such like, turned work-manly in with the earth in due season of the yeare, and not to have employed or dunged the ground with a rotten and pestilent matter, incommodious to man and the Plants. Which wise men have wel found out, in that the sowen plants sprung up in such an earth, yeeld for the most part a harmful quality to the daily feeders on them, hardly to be amended.

Yet for that neither the ancient, nor latter Husbandmen, seeme to follow the instruction of this precept, nor approve or allow any proper dunging, prescribing and commending the same in general: for that cause, I here purpose to treat in a brief manner, of the nature and use of the same. But first of all to warne you that a good and battle ground needeth smal dunging, where a dry and thin or lean earth in contrary maner requireth plenty of dung. A earth onely drie (as *Maro* reporteth) well joyeth to be often fed, and diligently laboured with fat dung: But the ground that hath a meane substance in it, requireth in like manner a meane dunging to be used. Further conceive, that good dung doth (for the more part) procure a good and battle earth

The cause why certaine skilful Husbandmen in ancient time misliked the dunging of Gardens near to the house: and what dung best allowed for the Kitchin or pot-hearbs.

A team of gardeners turning in the dung. From a garden manual of 1706.

the better, yea this helpeth and amendeth the evil and naughty earth: But the evil dung in a contrary manner, doth evermore cause all earths the worser: And this behoveth the Gardener and Husbandman to know, that as the earth not dunged, is both cold and stiffe: even so the ground by the over much dunging may be burned altogether. For which cause (*Columella* reporteth) that more available and better it is, often to dung the earth, then overmuch at one time to bestow in the ground. The earth digged up to serve for the spring, ought to be dunged in the wane or decrease of the Moone about St. *Martins* day: that the same lying all the Winter thorow, may so be dissolved against the time of committing seeds to the earth: and in moneth of *March* to be dunged again, that the earth well moistened with showres (in the moneth of *April* may be procured the apter, for the bestowing of your finer and dainty seeds in the same. Herein consider the leanness or fatness of your earth in the often dunging of it, and the worthinesse of your seeds, which may require a like paines to be bestowed on the ground. The plot of earth prepared for the Winter seeds, ought to be wel turned in with dung about the end of *September*, and the seeds committed to the earth, after the ground be wel moistened with showers. The dung in a Garden plot, for the planting of young sets ought not to be couched or laid next to the roots of the plants: but in such order the dung must be used, that a thin bed of earth be first made, for the setting of the young herbs, next laid to this a handsome bed of dung, as neither too thicke or thin spread on that earth: above that let another course of earth be raked over of a reasonable thicknesse: workmanly handled and done, see that your plants be set handsomely into the ground, and in a chosen time. For the earth and beds (on such wise prepared) helpe that the plants bestowed shal not at all be burned: neither the heat of the dung, hastily breath forth to them.

CHAP. X

s touching the worthinesse and exellency of dung, the Greek writers of Husbandry (to whom many of the Latin Authors consent) affirm that the Doves dung is the best, because the same possesseth a mighty hotnesse, for which they willed this dung to be strawed the thinner, and in a manner (as thin to be scattered abroad) as seeds on the earth, whereby the same may so season the earth measurably, and not on a heap or thick bestowed (as Mr. *Varro* reporteth) much like to the dung of Cattel thrown abroad on the ground. The dung also of the Hen and other fowls greatly commanded for the sourenes, except the dung of Geese, Ducks, and other water fowls, for their much and thin dunging. And although this dung at last, be weaker than the others, yet may the same be profitable, as the selfe same *Varro* witnesseth out of the Greek instructions of Husbandry. A commendation next is attributed to the Asses dung, in that the same beast for his leisurely eating digesteth easier, and causeth the better dung, which bestowed in the earth, for that the same is most fertil by nature, bringeth or yeeldeth forth least store of weeds, and procureth very much all plants and hearbs: yes, this causeth the most sweet and pleasantest hearbs and roots. The third in place is the Goats dung, being most sower, which insueth the sheeps dung yet fatter. After this, both the Oxe and Cow dung, next the swines dung, worthier then the Oxen or Kine, but greatly disallowed of *Columella*, for the mighty hotnesse in that the same burneth the seeds immediately bestowed in the earth. The vilest and worst of all dungs, after the opinion of the Greek writers of Husbandry, is the Horses and Mules, if either of these be bestowed alone in the earth; yet with the sower dungs mixed, either will profitably be abated or qualified. But the same especially is to be learned and observed of every Gardener and Husbandman, that they fatten not the earth, if it be possible, with dung of one yeare for the

Of the kindes of dung, and which well commended for the dunging of Gardens.

same, besides that it is of no utility, it engendreth also many noisome wormes and kinds of vermine. But of the contrary mind is *Columella*, who willeth the earth to be fatned with dung which hath lyen a yeare, and not above; in that the same, as he reporteth, bringeth forth least weeds, and possesseth as yet a sufficient strength for the turn. But how older the same be, so much the lesse profitable, in that is lesser availeth: yet the newest dung (saith he) wil wel agree for Meadows or the fields, in that the same procureth the more yeild of grasse, being bestowed in the moneth of *February* and *March*, in colder Countries, and the Moone increasing of light. The mud also of a running water, as the ditch or river, may be imployed in the stead of dung. The dung besides of three yeares is esteemed very good, for that in the longer time lying, whatsoever this shall have of the evil quality, and stinking savour, the same by that time vapoured forth: and if any hard matter consisted in the same, the age thorowly resolved it. Howsoever it shall happen, that the earth be the worthiest dung of all, for flowers and kitchin hearbs in the very thin ashes reported to be, which in nature is hot. For the kinde of dung either killeth or driveth away the Garden Fleas, the Wormes, the canker Wormes, found commonly on Coleworts, Snailes and all other creeping things, wasting the stems of Plants and Herbs. The dung which men make (if the same be not mixed with the rubbish, or dust swept out of the house) is greatly misliked, for that by nature it is hotter, and burneth the seeds sown in that earth: so that this is not to be used, unlesse the ground be a barren, gravelly, or very loose sand, lacking strength in it, which being on such wise, requireth the more helpe of nourishment and fatning, through this kind of dung: yet for lack of the foresaid dungs, the others may be put in use: so that these with the Spade be often changed and dispersed in the ground. Here you may not forget, that a watrie Garden plot requireth the more plenty of dung; but a drie earth needeth the lesser dunging; the one for the daily moisture running in it, being overcold and stiffe, is through the often applying

Gardening has always been a back-breaking business. Here are taking place the seasonal activities of digging and planting.

of the hot dung, resolved and made temperate. And the other dry of it selfe through the heat consisting in it, by much applying of this hot dung, is of the same burned: for that cause the moisture of ground ought to have store of dung, but the dryer, smal dunging. But if no kind of dung can be purchased, then in gravelly grounds, it shall be best to dung the same with chalk: but in chalky places, and over-thick, those dung with gravelly earth: for on such wise Garden plots, shall not onely be caused to be battle and fruitfull, but shall also become faire and delectable, as *Columella* the most diligent and and skilful instructer (of the *Romane* Gardens) witnesseth; let this last instruction of *Pliny* be remembered, that at what time soever you mind to dung a Garden for yeelding of few weeds, see that the wind blow then from the West quarter, and the Moon decreasing of light, and the earth also drie: But for the dunging of a Medow (as before uttered, let the same be done in the increase of the Moon, &c. For by such an observation followed, the plentifulnesse of yield is marvellously much increased: as after the worthy Greeks, the Latine writers of Husbandrie have noted.

CHAP. XI

efore I treat of the sowing of Gardens, it behoveth to admonish you, that it much availeth in a Garden, to frame seemely walks and Allies, for the delight of the owner, by which he may the freelier walk hither and thither in them, and consider thorowly all the matters wrought and done in the Garden, if the disquietnesse of mind hinder not the benefit of the same. The walkes and Allies shall to that end be disposed, that they may serve in the stead of a dunging in those places, as the worthy interpreter M. *Cato* (that cunningly wrote of the ancient Husbandrie) witnesseth. These before considered, let us come unto the matter: Certaine skilful practitioners admonish, that a Garden plot or field, be not sown over all, until the earth before shall be wel moistned with showers. That if these fall in due season and time (then the skilfull Gardeners agree) to be wel liked. If any be otherwise occasioned to sow, as often so it hapneth, then the seeds slowly breake forth, how workmanly soever the seeds may be bestowed in a drie Garden ground, or plough land, as the worthy *Columella* witnesseth: which like matter in certaine Countries is wont to be exercised, where the condition of the aire is on such wise. For what the same is which shall be bestowed in a dry earth, is even the like, as if the same were laid in a house which corrupteth not. But when showers on the seeds (committed to the earth certain dayes before) they after shoot up in one day: yet are these seeds in danger (sown in the meane time) of Birds, and Ants or Pismires, except the seeds be (before the sowing) preserved and defended with those

What is to be considered of every Gardener, after the casting forth and levelling of the beds, with the disposing of the earth.

The garden trodden out into beds and seemly borders is fattened with good dung and finally raked over.

helps which shall after be uttered in the proper place following. Howsoever the occasion & weather serve, the Gardener shal employ his diligence, that the Garden ground or field, which ought to be levelled and sowne in the spring time (that the same may yeeld the proper fruits in the Summer time) be digged and dunged (if need so require to the earth) about the end of harvest, when as yet the cold season and frosts be not approched, nor bitter weather begun. And the same Garden-plot or quarters of the Garden, which the Gardener would in the harvest time have covered with the Sallet, pot hearbs and roots, ought to be turned up in the beginning of the Summer, or in the moneth of *May*, that the clods of earth may through all the cold Winter, and hot Summer weather (speaking or rather here meaning of the greater Gardens) be so dissolved, as the worthy *Maro* skilfully instructeth.

And to these, that the roots of the unprofitable hearbs or weeds may likewise be killed: after the winter or summer time ended, dung then must be orderly turned in with the earth: as in the moneth of *March* (the Moon decreasing) for the spring time, and in the end of harvest for the winter time. And when the sowing time approacheth or draweth near, then shall the Garden ground (as the proper order and manner of every Country is) be diligently raked, weeded and purged, both of the stones and unprofitable roots: after the same, let the earth be dunged and orderly digged, as in the manner afore taught, which through the diligent digging so often repeated, that the dung with the earth by the twice labouring over, be well dissolved and mixed together. After this digging and dunging againe the second time (if the ground needed such fatting) and the earth levelled, may the Garden (about the middst of *February*, but I rather suppose in the month of *March* to be more agreeable, and the Moon especially in her first quarter) be beautified in apt places of the same, with seemly hearbs, before the quarters and beds be workmanly troden out by the Gardener, the instruction of which hearbs shall fully be bettered in the next Chapter.

CHAP. XII

he herbar in the garden may be framed with Ashen poles, or the Willow, either to stretch, or to be bound together with Oziers, or wyers, after a square form, or in arch manner winded, that the branches of the Vine, Mellon, or Cucumber, running and spreading all over, might so shadow and keep both the heat and Sun from the walkers and sitters thereunder. The herbs erected and framed in most Gardens, are to their much refreshing comfort and delight. These two, as the upright, directed by quarters set in the earth, and leaning to the wall, near to which faire Rosemary, or the red Rose, set to run straight up, and the winding in arch manner, framed (as I uttered afore) with the Ashen or Withy poles, to shadow the wals there under. To this fastning the Vine, and sundry herbs which in the growing up, run and spread over the same, as the Briony, Cucumber, Gourd, and divers others, of which hereafter we shall more fully treat. But first I mean to speak of those herbs, which the Gardener planteth and ordereth to run for beauties sake in an upright herbar; after to treat of those which he either soweth or planteth, to run over the winding or arch herbar. The plants to run up and serve comeliest for the straight herbar, ought to be those of a fragrant savour, and that grow or shoot up high, and are spread abroad, which especially framed in a Garden for delight and pleasure, and these properly named wall herbs, in that they are set in a manner leaning to the wall, with the quarters set upright, and plots fastned overthwart, along the which, the Rosemary, the Jasmine, and red Rose in many Gardens, set to grow upright, which in time growing, beautifie an upright herbar, although these cover not the same, through their shorter and lower growing then the herbar; yet the commodity ensueth by the herbar, that the owners friends sitting in the same, may the freelier see and behold the beauty of the Garden, to their great delight. The erection and garnishing of the winding herbar may be best wrought with Ashen poles, in that these may well indure without repairing for

The framing of sundry herbs delectable in a Garden, with the walkes and Allies artly devised in the same.

ten years; but those framed with the Willow poles, require every three years to be repaired.

The owner or gardener that would set Rose trees to run up by the poles of the herbar, ought workmanly to begin and do the same about the middest of *February*, and in the first quarter of the Moon, the beds before wel reared with a stony and dry earth, and not with dung. The Rose trees with their roots, are also to be planted in short and narrow beds diligently raised with a dry earth: But if the Gardener or owner wil, slips may be broken off from the roots, cut in a slope manner at the heads, about a mans foot and a half long, writhed at the ends, and so set in a slope manner, a foot deep into beds, wel reared with a drie earth, and in the increase of the Moon. The old trees new set every fifth year in the wane of the Moon take root the sooner, and yield the more Roses, being pruned and refreshed every year with new and drie earth about the roots, for neither the slips nor old roots joy in a fat clay, or moist ground, but in the drie and stony earth, and to be set in rankes wel a foot distance one from another, in drie beds wel reared up; for bestowed in ranks of such distance between, they prosper the better, and yield more Roses. The seeds of the Rose committed to the earth, do slowly come up, yet so often as you mind to sow the seeds, bestow them a foot deep in light and drie earth, about the middest of *March* with us, and in *February* in hotter places, the Moon then increasing. Here may any truly learn by the instruction of the worthy Neapolitane *Palladius Rutilius*, which are the seeds of the Rose: for a man (saith he) may not think the yellow grains within the Rose flower (being of a golden colour) to be them, but the knobs which grow after the manner of a most short and small Pear, the seeds of which are then ful ripe, when they be perceived brownish and soft, which will be in the moneth of *September*. The owner also may set the Jasmine tree bearing a fragrant flower, the musk Rose, damask Rose, and Privet tree, in beds of drie earth, to shoot up and

Example of lattice-work frames for placing around knots or quarters from a 1616 translation by Gervaise Markham of Charles Estienne's Maison Rustique. *'These knots or other devices may be circumferenced with fine, curious Hedges . . . in sundrie forms, especially good if your ground be little . . . as they take not half so much room as borders . . . made with small Poles and wands bound with wire about two foot high off the ground.'*

spread over this herbar, which in time growing, not onely defendeth the heat of the Sun, but yieldeth a delectable smel, much refreshing the sitters under it. But this Arck-herbar for any kind of Roses, may not be built much above a mans height for the short growth of them. And as this herbar is delectable to the eye, even so laboursome, and with diligence to be tended: for which cause the more number in *England*, plant Vines (for the lesser travel) to run and spread over the upright and square herbs, framed with quarters and poles reaching a bredth. After the herbs seemly performed, in convenient places and walkes of the Garden ground (here meaning and speaking of the large plots) the Allies even troden out, and levelled by a line, as either three or four foot broad, may cleanly be fitted over with River or Sea Sand, to the end that showers of rain falling, may not offend the walkers (at that instant) in them, by the earth cleaving to or clogging their feet. The commodities of these Allies and walkes, serve to good purposes, the one is, that the owner may diligently view the prosperity of his herbs and flowers, the other for the delight and comfort of the wearied mind, which he may by himself or fellowship of his friends conceive, in the delectable sights and fragrant smels of the flowers, by walking up and down, and about the Garden in them, which for the pleasant sights and refreshing of the dul spirits, with the sharpning of memory, many shadowed over with vauting or Arch-herbs, having windowes properly made toward the Garden, whereby they might the more fully view, and have delight of the whole beauty of the Garden. But the straight walks, the wealthy make like Galleries, being all open towards the Garden, and covered with the vine spreading all over, or some other trees which more pleased them. Thus briefly have I touched the benefit of Walks and Allies in any Garden ground; which the Gardener of his own experience may artly tread out by a line, and sift over with sand, if the owner will, for the causes afore uttered.

'In either autumn or the beginning of Spring . . . you shall set Prympe, white Thorne, Eglantine and sweet Bryer, mixt together and as they shoot up you shall wind them within the Lattice-worke . . . they will keepe your Quarters and Knots in great deale more safety because they are not so easy to be runne over or broken downe either by man or beast . . .'

CHAP. XIII

The form of disposing the beds, and apt borders about, with the sowing, choice, and defence of the seeds, and weeding of the beds.

he quarters well turned in, and fatned with good dung a time before, and the earth raised through the dunging, shall in handsome manner by a line set downe in the earth, be troden out into beds, and seemly borders, which beds (as *Columella* witnesseth) raised newly afore with dung, and finely raked over, with the clods dissolved, and stones purged forth, shall be artly troden out, into three foot of breadth, and into what length the owner or Gardener will: but to such a breadth especially troden forth, that the weeders hands may wel reach unto the midst of the same, lest they thus going to the beds, and weeding forth the unprofitable herbs and grasse, may in the mean time tread down both the seeds shooting up, and plants above the earth. To the help of which, let the pathes between the beds be of such a reasonable breadth (as a mans foot) that they passing along by, may freely weed the one half first, and next the other half left to weed.

The beds also ought (after the mind of the worthy Neapolitane *Palladius Rutilius*) to be trodden out narrow, and of a length, as twelve foot long if the plot be large, and six foot broad, and the pathes of these of a seemly breadth, for the easier reaching into the middle of the beds, or at the least freelier, to the furtherance and speed of the weeders. In a moist and watry Garden plot this skilful Neapolitane willeth, that the beds in the same Garden be reared two foot high, for the better prospering of the seeds commit to the earth, and the plants come up. But in a dry ground, the edges of the beds raised a foot high, shall wel suffice. The pathes trodden out between the beds ought to be of good depth and even, whereby the water sprinkled gently forth by a water-pot on the upper face of the beds, and falling into the pathes, may the easier enter into the beds, to the better moistning and

Raised beds from the 1594 edition of The Gardener's Labyrinth.

feeding of the roots of the plants, and the rest superfluous to run the easier into other Allies or pathes needing this moisture, which by this easie running along the pathes, shall proceed a speedier moistning, and far better watering of all the beds, yea the superfluous water in the end, lying stil in the pathes, may through a slope gutter made in the midst of them, be directed forth into a convenient place made for the purpose, of some distance from the beds. And this instruction much availeth to beds in the night time, when as mighty showers happen to fal, which might over-cloy the beds, were it not for the gutters speedily conveying the waters away.

All these instructions conceived, the Gardener or owner may then prepare himself to the committing of seeds to the earth; in which he ought to be careful, that after the bestowing of the seeds in the earth, a clearnesse or mildnesse of the aire may for certaine dayes succeed; for through the aire and weather favouring, and the seeds sowen in warm places, where the Sun long shineth, do they most speedily break and shoot above the earth, so that the seeds be new and good, the age of which in this doing, much availeth to be examined and known. Therefore every Gardener and owner ought to be careful and diligently to foresee, that the seeds committed to the earth (as *M. Cato* willeth) be neither too old, dry, thin, withered, nor counterfeited, but rather ful, new, and having juyce. These notes of the seeds remembred, and the Gardener minded to commit them to the earth, ought afore to regard, that the wind at that instant bloweth not from the North, but rather from the South, or South-west, nor the day very cold; for in such seasons and daies (as all the skilful report) the earth is then fast shut, and hardly receiveth and nourisheth the

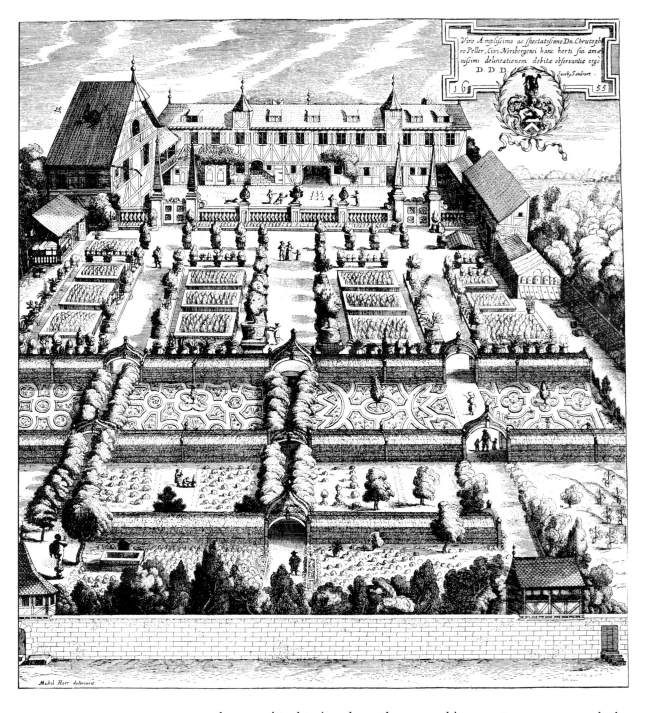

seeds committed to it, where the ground in a contrary manner, doth willingly apply and retain the seeds, bestowed or sown in faire dayes and temperate hot.

CHAP. XIV

he Gardener minding to commit chosen seeds into sundry beds, ought to learn, that the beds lying open to the South, be high raised, through the wel mixing of horse dung with the earth, and after the even raking and levelling to remain a certain time unsowed; then one or two of the beds in the moneth of *March*, and in the increase of the Moon, may he sow with Lettice and Purslane seeds, for these sooner spring up in the moneth of *March* then *February*, to be removed in the beds, after the plants be shot up half a finger high. In those beds may he also sow the Parcely, Rocket, Sorrel, Endive, and divers other Sallet herbs; which after they be somewhat come up, may be thinner set in other beds. Have beside a special regard to your seeds, that they be neither too old, withered, thin, and empty; and the borders of those Beds may you bestow with the seeds of the Hartichock, wel two hand breadth asunder.

In another bed you may sow fine seeds, to have pleasant herbs that may be kept dry for the pot or Kitchin in the Winter time, and those which yield delectable flowers, to beautifie and refresh the house, as the Marioram, French balme, Time, Hisop, Basil, Savery, Sage, Marigold, Buglas, Borage, and sundry others. The Gardener may trie these seeds in beds, lying all open to the warme Sun, as the Orenge, Lemmon, Pomecitron, Pomegranate, the Myrtle and Date, but these ought to be fenced by a succour on the North side, that the cold aire hinder or let not the coming up of them. When the Citron or any of these be well sprung up, the Gardener ought to remove and set them into proper chests filled with light earth, which at will and pleasure may be rolled hither and thither, for the better avoiding of the Suns great heat, and bitter cold aire, by standing under a cover or Penthouse, made for the onely purpose. In another bed being of good length, and placed toward the quick-set hedge, and to run over the Arch-harbour, may the Gardener bestow seeds of the Cucumber, Citron, round Gourd and long: In another bed also, being long and narrow, and deep furrowes at each side made, to set vessels lower then the beds, may the Gardener sow seeds of the sundry kinds of Melons. That the birds and other fowles may be kept from coming to the seeds committed to the earth, the skilful wil, that the white thorne be laid on the beds, but to bestow your seeds in beds rather in the moneth of *March* then *February*, and the Moon increasing, do speedier appear above the earth. But if the Gardener feareth lest the seeds committed to the earth, should be in danger through the bitter cold aire, and Suns heat following (as yearly the like so hapneth) the beds may then be covered with thick Mattresses of straw in such manner, that they hinder not through their weight, the crescent things coming up, which may thus be ordered, in setting first up sundry forked sticks at each corner, and in the sides of the beds, on

The artly disposing of sundry beds, for the sowing and increasing of divers fruits and Kitchen herbs, with the witty defences so be used after the seeds are bestowed.

OPPOSITE *This engraving of 1655 shows a traditional garden with beds reserved for one type of plant only. The more exotic plants were brought out of the greenhouse in fine weather and placed in rows around the beds.*

Citrus fruits were grown in metal-hooped tubs so that they could be moved in and out of doors according to the weather.

Ornamental pots were often featured in gardens of the seventeenth century to add interest where required.

which long rods laid, reaching to each corner, and at the ends, as *Columella* willeth: these done, let him wittily lay on the Mattresses, in covering and defending the young plants from the cold or heat, at that time. But at such times as the aire being clear in the cold season, the Mattresses (when the Sun shineth warme) may be taken off, for the speedier increasing of the Plants springing up. All herbs and roots for the Kitchin, prosper far better by their removing, and thinner setting, through which (by report of the skilful) they yield a pleasanter savour. There are of Greek writers of Husbandry, which wil the sowing of seeds to be done in the increase of the Moon, as from the first quarter until the ful light of the Moon, and she knowing at that time to be under the earth in the day time. Others having devised a perfecter way, do not allow a timely or early sowing of seeds, for which cause they disposed and divided the same sowing of seeds, into two, yea into three or four several times of the day, contenting by this means to avoid the uncertainty of the time to come; herein calling to mind the Husbandly proverb of the worthy *Columella*, which saith, *Have no mistrust in the committing of seeds to the earth.*

It therefore behoveth the Gardener, which hath an earnest care for the purchasing of Kitchin or pot hearbs, to regard and see that the seeds committed to the earth be full and new, the earth artly prepared, the dung in the same laudable, and water as hand for the use of the seeds. For the seeds sound and good, do yeild after the sowing plants of the like goodnesse and vertue: the earth laboured and made apt, will very well keepe and prosper the seeds committed to it; the

dung being good and well mixed with the earth, will cause the earth battler, and to these the looser, whereby water diligently sprinkled on the same, may the freelier and easier enter in, to feed and cherish the roots, and the water serving to the same end, that it may as by a feeding pap, nourish and bring up all crescent things.

P. A. Rysbrack's View of the Orange-tree Garden and Rotunda at Chiswick shows the later development of the orangery in the early eighteenth century.

CHAP. XV

he owner or Gardener ought to remember, that before he committeth seeds to the earth, the beds be disposed and troden out, into such a breadth and length, as best answereth to every plant and root, in that the beds to be sowen for the Navew roots, ought to be troden out large and long; next to which may the beds for Coleworts and Cabbages be joyned of a sufficient breadth: to these next may you place beds of a reasonable breadth for the Rapes and Turen roots: then for a seemly division in the Garden, may he tread out by those an Alley of three foot broad: next to which, if the Gardener will, may he dispose sundry beds together for divers kinds of hearbs, as the Arach, Spinedge, Rocket, Parcely, Sorrel, Beets, Speradge, Chervil, Borrage, Fenel, Dill, Mints, white Poppy, and sundry others. Next joyning to these, may the owner or Gardener place an other Alley of three foot broad, by which, frame beds for the Leeks and Cives: and to the next, may the Gardener joyne' beds for the Onions and

The workmanly casting forth, dividing, and preparing of beds for the most hearbs and roots of the Kitchin.

Cause's engraving of 1676 showing the way in which citrus fruits in pots can be transported from place to place according to the season.

Chibouls; by these next, the Scalions and Garlick in two beds disposed. Then level out by these, an Alley of three foot and a half broad, to which the Gardener may adjoyne many beds about for borders, serving as well for the keeping in of the savours, as for hedges, and pot-hearbs for the Winter. After these, it shall be right profitable to levell a bed, onely for Sage, another for Isop, the like for Tyme, another for Marioram, a bed for Lavender, another for Rosemary and Southern-wood, a bed for Savery and Isop, beds for Costmary, Basill, Balme, and running Tyme: yea a bed for Camomile; for the use of Benches to sit on, and a delectable Labyrinth to be made in the Garden (if room will so serve) with Isope and Tyme, or the Winter Savery onely. In the Garden besides, to sow and plant divers Physick hearbs, and pleasant flowers, shall be to great use and commodity, in that these beside their delectable sight, yeild a commodity to our bodies, in curing sundry griefs as well in women as men; for which cause, it shall be necessary to sow beds of Physick hearbs next to these, as the blessed Thistle, the Romane wormewood, the Sperage, hearbe Mercury, Gentian, Dittany, hearbe Fluelline, Harts tongue, Buglosse, Selfe heale, Liver-wort, Lungwort, Stecados, Valeriane, Spiknard, Lionsfoot, Mugwort, hearb Patience, *Angelica*, Bittony, and many others, of which in the second part shall particularly be uttered, and their Physick benefits to be employed many waies.

Hovenden's map of All Souls, Oxford 1585. Note the similarity with Thomas Hill's own designs for knots (see illustration above).

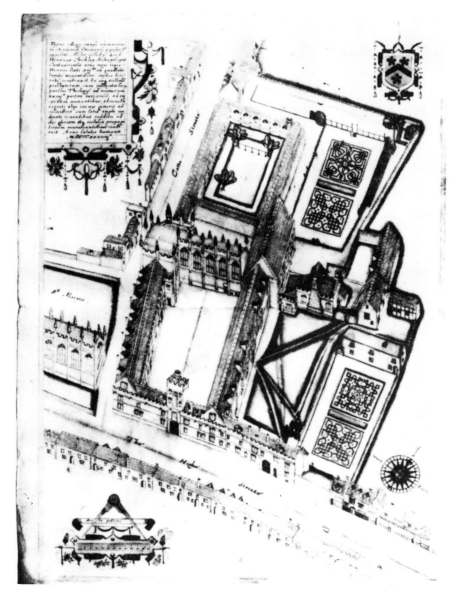

From Estienne's Maison Rustique. *'The way and maner to stretch the lines, to make a quarter with borders, and to make a border with squares, broken and crossed thorow the middest'.*
'You shall have in your hand many measures of small cord, many cord re-reeles and dibbles . . . and stretch your line to draw and cast the shape of it . . . to dispose them such as may delight the eie . . . You shall not draw up your line . . . until you have marked out all your border or at the least the one side.'

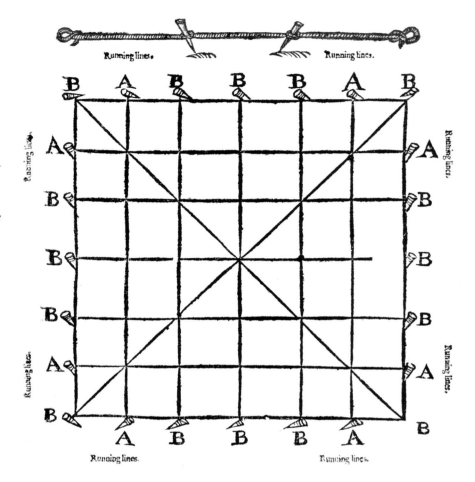

CHAP. XVI

The rare inventions and defences for most seeds to be committed to the earth, that these be neither endamaged of Birds or creeping things.

ll worthy writers agree, that in vaine the Husbandly Gardener shall travell, yea and all other, if the seeds bestowed in the earth happen after to be endamaged either of wormes, and other creeping things, or otherwise scraped up and wasted by birds, or else harmed by any other injury, whether the same be wrought within or without the earth, for which cause, that the owner or Gardener may avoid these injuries, it is high time that he employ a care and diligence in the conceiving of these remedies and secrets following. If seeds to be committed to the earth, are a little time before the bestowing, steeped in the juyce of Housleeke or Singreen, they shall not onely be without harme preserved from Birds, Ants, field Mice, and other spoilers of the garden herbs, but what plants shoot up of these, shall after prove the better and worthier, as I observed the like, found noted both in the Greeke commentaries (of matters of the field) and

Latine Authors of Husbandry; which to be most true, although experience instructeth and approveth the same, yet this many times happeneth in sundry Countries, that small store of the herb can be found to supply the turne, by reason whereof the Gardener must be forced to exercise a sparer way after this manner, in steeping of the herb for a night in a good quantity, and the same to sprinkle sufficiently on the seeds, whereby they may all the night draw and drink in the substance of the herb, as the worthy *Columella* instructeth.

And for lack of this herb altogether, (the said Author reporteth) that the Gardener may use instead of it, the soot cleaving on the chimney, which gathered a day before the bestowing of the seeds in the earth, and mixed for a night with them, doth the like defend the seeds in safty.

The Greeke writers of husbandry (and after them *Plinie*, and the worthy Neapolitane *Palladius Rutilius*) report, that those seeds may be preserved in safety from all evil and Garden monsters, if the bare head without flesh, of either Mare or she Asse (having been covered with the Male) be buried in the Garden, or that the middest of the same fixed on a stake set into the earth, be erected.

The worthy *Plinie*, further reporteth, that there is a garlick growing in the fallow field (named *Allium*) which on such wise boiled, that the same wil not grow againe, and strawed on the beds sowne, doth in such manner availe, that Birds after wil not scrape up the earth, nor spoile the seeds bestowed in them. And such which have eaten of this, are taken (as being astonished) with the hand. The wel practised *Africanus* unto the same matter instructeth, that if a quantity of Wheat or Barley be boyled or infused in wine, and mixed with

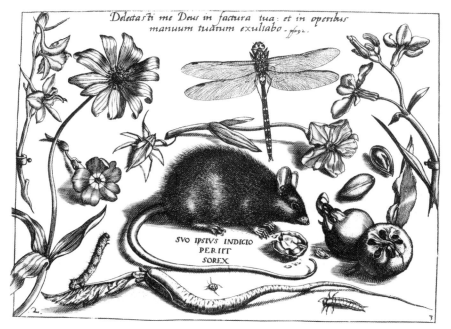

Study by George Hoefnagel, 1592.

Neeswort, as either the black or white, and the same sprinkled abroad by the pathes of the beds round about, doth on such wise, defend the seeds sown from the injury of birds. But those being in a manner dead by eating of this, or at the least starke drunk, he willeth then to hang up by the legs on a long rod sticked in the earth, to the terrour and fearing away of all other birds coming to the place. Nor this worthy Authour omitteth the rare practice of the decoction of river Crevices, with which if the Gardener shall sprinkle his seeds before the sowing, Birds will never after (a matter to be marvelled at) approach to the Garden beds; yea the plants beside, which are sprung or shot out of these, shall indure and continue safe and free from all the injuries of creeping things. There are certaine skilful practitioners, which affirme to have availed mightily in driving away birds, by the only sprinkling of this decoction above taught of the plants come up, which matter hath of many been experienced above a hundred times, so that the same were wrought at a certain period and time of the Moon. Sundry practitioners mixed the bruised leaves of the Cypresse tree, with the seeds for a night, and the same mixture on the morrow they bestowed in the earth, being afore wel wrought and turned in with dung. For on such wise the plants sprung out of these, were delivered from all manner of gnawing or creeping things. Others skilfully practised, used the dry shavings or fillings, either of the Harts horne, or Elephants tooth, which they mixed with the seeds for a day, committed them after to the earth, or they otherwise sprinkled, the seeds to be sown with the water of the infusion and mixtion of these for a night.

CHAP. XVII

The witty helps commended of the ancient for the Garden seeds, to be employed as wel before as after the sowing, that these be not harmed by outward nor inward injuries.

he singular Poet *Virgil* counselleth, that the seeds to be committed to the earth, be afore sprinkled and moistned with the water of *Nytre* infused, or the Brine made of the same.

The Greek *Apuleius* willeth, that seeds (before the sowing) be sprinkled and moistned with Wine, for on such wise handled, the plants springing and shooting up, weaken the less, yea being feeble, they shall mightily be holpen with water and brine mixed and sprinkled on them.

There are certain Greek instructers of Husbandry (both of *Pliny*, *Columella*, and the Neapolitane *Palladius Rutilius*) allowed and commended, which wil, that the roots of the wild Cucumber be infused for one whole day and a night in faire water, and with the same, through the often sprinkling, so to moisten wel the seeds, the next day those seeds covered over with a blanket, they wil, the next morning be committed to the earth, affirming the seeds thereby to prosper the better, and these for a certainty to be preserved from all

Fert Æstas flores, terramque virentibus herbis
Vestit, dans auibus cantum, syluisque decorem.

*Study by George Hoefnagel,
1592.*

evil annoyances. The self same doth the skilful *Apuleius* wil, that a few Lentels be also mixed with the seeds in the sowing of them, for as much as the same pulse by property availeth against the harmes of winds. This Author further willeth, that for a safety of the seeds bestowed, a speckled Toade, named of the Greeks *Phrynum*, be drawn by a line in the night time round about the Garden or field, afore the earth be laboured, or diligently digged and dressed of the Gardener: and the same after inclosed in an earthen pot, to be buried in the middest of the Garden or fallow field, which at the present sowing time approached, shall be digged forth, and thrown or carried from that place, a great distance off, lest the Plants (after the seeds sown) growing up in that place, may prove and become bitter and unpleasant of smel.

The *Egyptian* and *Greek* instructors of Husbandry report, that the seeds after the bestowing, wil remain ungnawn or bitter, and free of harm by creeping things in the Garden, if the seeds shall be committed to the earth when the Moon possesseth her half light, or is a quarter old. It might be thought an obliviousness, to have overpassed the Physick experiment of the singular *Democritus*, both for the seeds and plants, diligently (of the skilful Neapolitane *Palladius Rutilius*) after this manner: Bestow and close over (saith *Democritus*) of the Sea or River crevises, no fewer than ten in number, into a glass body filled up with water, the same set abroad in the aire, let so stand to be sunned for ten daies together, the feeds that you would after have to remain in the earth unharmed, sprinckle and moisten with the same water for eight daies together, after these eight daies ended (as *Rutilius* instructeth) do in like manner with that water, until the plants after your desired mind be wel sprung up, at which experiment thus handled, you wil greatly marvel; for out of these seeds, what plants shall be sprung and shot up, wil not only drive Beasts and Cattel from the eating of them, but all other creeping things of what condition they be, from the gnawing and biting of them, of which matters shall further be treated, in the proper Chapters a little after, and for other defences and helps of seeds as occasion offereth in the places shall be uttered.

CHAP. XVIII

The laudable instructions of the ancient, in the nature and election of sundry Seeds, with the apt times commended for the sowing of most Kitchin herbs.

he singular *Columella* instructeth, that all seeds bestowed in the Garden, for the use and benefit of the Kitchin or pot, ought rather to be in the increase of the Moon, as from the first, unto the sixth day; forasmuch as all seeds committed to the earth, in the decrease or wane of the Moon, either slowly break and shoot up, or else so weakly increase, that these after serve to smal purpose. It many times also hapneth (as the worthy *Varro* reporteth) that although the seeds bestowed in the earth, be done in the increase of the Moon the seeds besides having a juyce, weighty, ful, white meal in them, and in no manner corrupted or too old, yet these notwithstanding are hindered through some evil constellation, which of the skilful is named an influence of heaven, were the Gardeners diligence never so much, so that it is not impertinent to the matter here to recite what the worthy Neapolitane *Palladius Rutilius* reporteth of the Garden ground, which saith, that a Garden plot, placed and lying under a fresh and sweet aire, and moistned gently by some spring or sweet water running by, is in a manner battel and ready enough, whereby the same requireth but a smal instruction and diligence, to be bestowed in the sowing of it. The bestowing of seeds in a moist earth, the beds afore shorter cast, ought to be done in the warme season of the Spring, as in *May*, and the Moon increasing, for seeds on such wise handled, prosper the better, through the warm and dry time following. But if occasion moveth you to commit seeds into a dry ground, and that water be far distant, then dig the Allies of the beds deep, and in a slope manner, for the better leading of water from beds sufficiently moistned, to others lacking moisture; and to these such a dry earth agreeth to be sown in the harvest time, the ground before wel moistned with showers, herein not forgetting the choice of seeds, nearest agreeing to the natures of these two earths, with the furtherance of the Moon at time of the sowing. If the Gardener mindeth to commit seeds to the earth in the Summer time, let the same be done in the increase of the Moon, in the moneths of *July* and *August*. In the harvest time about the middle of *September*, and in *October*, the Moon in those moneths in her first quarter: for the time againe of committing seeds to the earth, let the same be done in the moneths of

February and *March*, the Moon at those times increasing of light.

The seeds which ought especially to be sown in the earth, about the end of harvest, as about the middle of *September*, and in *October* the Moon at those times increasing, that these may all the Winter endure, and be strengthened in the ground, are the Endive, Onions, Garlick, Scalions, the great Garlick, young Leek heads, Coleworts, Mustard seed, and such like.

The Garden ground naturally cold, or all the day received but a weake comfort of the Sunne, through his short presence or tarrying there, or else in cold Countries, as at *Yorke*, and farther North. In such places I say, the bestowing of many seeds better agree to be done about the middle of the Spring, or in the moneth of *May*, in warme and calme daies, the moone then increasing of light.

But the seeds to be committed to the earth in those Countries and places in the harvest time, ought rather to be done sooner, or before the time with us, where the seeds otherwise to be bestowed in hot Countries and places in the spring time, require far timelier to be done, as in the beginning of the moneth of *March*, and the seeds to be sowen in those places in the harvest time, to be bestowed much later.

During the tempests of winter, the gardener of 1626 prays that his work will come to fruition.

The seeds that at will of the Gardener may be committed to the earth, either in Harvest, or Spring time, chiefly for the Kitchin or Pot, under a gentle aire, and in a battle ground, are these; the Coleworts, Navew, Artichoke, Endive, Lettice, Dill, Rocket, Coliander, Parcely, Fennell, Radish, Parsnip, Carret, and sundry others. Yet these by the report of the skilful, come better forward, being sown in the moneth of *July*, the Country there hot; but in the Country temperate, the seeds ought rather in the moneth of *August*; and in the Country being cold, in the moneth of *September*. Those seeds committed to the earth in warme and calme dayes, prosper far better then those being sown in hot and nipping cold dayes: for that the warme comfortably draw up the plants, whereas the hot daies (in a contrary manner) doe drie, and the bitter cold shut the earth.

The seeds which the Gardener minds to bestow in the earth, ought not to be above a year old, and that bruised have a white meale within and full, for otherwise being over old, or withered, they will neither grow, nor profit at all. The fresher and newer that the seeds be at time of the bestowing in the earth, as the Leek, the Cucumber, and the Gourd, so much the sooner these breake, and appeare above the earth: contrary-wise, how much the older the seeds shall be, as the Parcely, Beets, Organy, Cresses, Peni-royall, and Coliander, so much the speedier do these shoot up, and appeare above the earth, so that the seeds before the sowing be not corrupt.

CHAP. XIX

Certaine precepts of the skilful in our time, for the sowing of many delectable flowers, and tender hearbs, with the observations of the Moone, in these and in other matters necessary.

The latter writers of Husbandrie report, that these tender Hearbs, and pleasant flowers, as the Marjoram, Savery, hearb Fluellin, Buglosse, the blessed Thistle, the hearb Angelica, Valeriane, Balme, Annis, Dill, Fenel, Organy, Mints, Rue, or hearb Grace, Sperage, Arach, Spinach, Beets, Endive, Borage, Rocket, Taragone, Parcely, Sorrell, Endive, Strawbery, Lettice, Artichoke, and sundry others, the Marigold of all kinds, Rose campion, the red and white, the Flower Armoure, the Flower Petilius, the Columbine white and blew, sweet Johns, the Pinck, Hearts ease, the Piony, red Lilly, hearb Sticas, or Lavender gentle, Batchelers-button, the Gelly-flower of all kinds, the Carnation, and many other, ought rather to be committed to the earth in the spring time, and sown in the moneths of *March* and *April*, for they speedier come forward, then bestowed in the moneth of *February*, herein considering the state and diversity of the time. The seeds also of the tender herbs committed to the earth in an apt time, and the moon in her first quarter, do the speedier shoot up, being specially sown after showers of raine, on sunny and warme places, (as lying open all day to the Sun) which on such wise do the soonest and speediest breake, yea and appeare about the earth. For

All the activities of March, April, and May are put together in this one engraving of 1570 after Pieter Bruegel.

which cause, a diligent care must be had in the bestowing of tender seeds, that the winde then bloweth not from the North, nor done in cold and close dayes: for these both include the seeds in the earth, and hinder their growing and shooting up.

Seeds bestowed in hot places, doe sooner yeeld their stems and leaves yea these speediest give their seeds. Such time use in the sowing of your seeds, as may be both mild and warme, in that warm daies following speed more forward the seeds bestowed.

As touching the most seeds committed to the earth, they ought rather (as afore uttered) to be new, not revealed, but full, bigge, weighty, faire of colour, fatty or having a juyce, which broken, give a white meale and not dry powder; for the seeds that after the breaking yeild a dry powder, do well declare them to be corrupt, and serving to no purpose.

The seeds thus tryed afore, and bestowed at that time in the earth, when showers fell a day or two before, and a temperate day at the sowing of the seeds, do very well prosper the growing, and procure these to shoot up far speedier, in that a cold aire at the sowing, and a

Establishing an orchard in 1638.

day or two after is known to be harmefull to seeds, through the including of them in the earth, and hindering in their growth and shooting up.

If necessity forceth the Gardener to bestow any seeds or plants in a salt earth, let these be either set or sown about the end of harvest, whereby the malice and evill quality of the ground may be purged, through the showers falling all the winter.

If the owner or Gardener mindeth to bestow young trees in this ground, let sweet earth or River sand be turned in with the same.

The Greek writers of Husbandry (after whom *Columella*, and *Rutilius*) will that all the kinds of pulses, as Peason, Hastings, Vetches, Tares, and such like, to be sown in a dry earth, saving the beanes, which rather joy to be bestowed in a moist ground.

What seed the Gardener mindeth to commit, in a well dressed earth, let these be bestowed from the first day until the full light of the Moon, (well nigh) for that seeds sown in the wane of the Moone come up thin, and the plants insue weake of growth. Such trees as the Husbandman mindeth to build withall, let those rather be cut down after the consent of the skilful in the last quarter of the Moon, (she shining at that time) of small light, yea near to her change, and under the earth.

In the cutting downe and gathering of Corne (as *Macrobius* willeth) for the longer preserving of it, and the straw dry (so that the same be done in a dry season) doth better agree, being in the wane of the Moon.

Such crescent things as the Garden (or Husbandman) mindeth otherwise to sel, ought to be cut, and gathered in the ful Moon, whereby the greatnesse thereof, such things may yield a better sale, and be delectabler to the eye.

Such things as the Husbandman mindeth to preserve a long time moist, as Apples, Pears, wardens, and such like, let them (after the mind of the skilful) be rather gathered near the ful of the Moon.

For the committing of seeds to the earth, although the ancient Husbandman prescribe proper moneths and daies, yet may every person herein keep the precept, according to the nature of place and aire, so that these diligently be considered, how certain seeds there are, which speedier spring up, and certain which flower spring up above the earth.

CHAP. XX

he singular *D. Niger* learnedly uttereth, that the more of estimation the seeds and plants are, with travels thereabout bestowed, so much the circumspecter ought every Gardener and husbandman to be; and the more instructions and help the Gardener may attaine, and the greater danger he may therein avoid, the more careful ought he and all others to be.

The daily experience is to the Gardener, as a Schoolmaster to instruct him, how much it availeth and hindreth, that seeds to be

The commended times to be observed, with the annoiance and incommodity to be eschewed in the bestowing of seeds and plants in the earth.

Picking the fruit on a fine day. From a fifteenth-century manuscript of Pietro de Crescenzi.

sown, plants to be set, yea Cions to be grafted (in this or that time) having herein regard, not to the time especially of the year, as the Sunne altereth the same, but also the Moons increase and wane, yea to the sign she occupieth, and places both above and under the earth.

To the aspects also of the other Planets, whose beams and influence both quicken, comfort, preserve, and maintain or else nip, wither, drie, consume, and destroy by sundry means, the tender seeds, plants, yea and grafts, and these after their property, and vertue natural or accidental.

Herein not to be forgotten, the apt choice and circumspection of the earth, with other matters generally required in the same, for which cause (after the mind of the skilful Astronomers) and prudent experimenters, in either committing seeds to the earth & planting, or other like practise to be used about the seeds, plants and young trees, these rules following are to be understood and kept (which they have

Activities in spring (RIGHT) *and autumn* (FAR RIGHT) *with their signs of the zodiac, from* The Shepherds Great Calendar, *late fifteenth century.*

left to us for our commodity) in eases of importance, and where the occasion may be imployed.

When the Moon and *Saturne*, are either threescore degrees of the *Zodiack* asunder (which distance in heaven) is named of the skilful, a Sextile aspect, it is then commended to labour the earth, sow, and plant, marked after this manner. *

But when these are 126 degrees asunder, which properly is named a Trigon, or trine aspect thus noted △ for the more part, then is that time better commended for labouring the earth, whether it be for tilling, gardening, sowing, planting, and setting, or cutting of Vines.

When the Moon and *Saturne*, are wel a quarter of the Zodiak distant, which is 90 degrees (named of the skilful a quadrate aspect) thus commonly marked □ then is denied utterly to deal in such matters.

The Moon being six signs distant from *Saturne*, so that he occupieth

the like degree in *Taurus*, as *Saturne* in *Scorpio*, or the *Moon* otherwise in like degrees of *Gemini* to *Saturne* (right against) in Sagitary, this aspect together is disallowed of the expert Astronomers, and noted after this manner. 8

The Moon possessing her ful light at those times, is alike denied of the skilful; yea the Moon being near to that Section, named of most Astronomers the Dragons taile, is in like manner disallowed for sowing of fine seeds, and setting of dainty plants. Here uttering precepts general as we now do.

But the Moon approached near to that Section, named the Dragons head, the same time for doing the like is very well commended, all things before supposed agreeable. But to be brief, and to knit up other observations, answering to the Moons place especially, learn these ensuing.

The Moon increasing and running between the 28 degree of *Taurus*, and the 19 degree of the sign of *Gemini*, sow fine seeds, and plant dainty herbs, your earth afore prepared, and aire answerable.

But the Moon found between the 28 degree of *Gemini*, and the sixt of *Cancer*, (although the increase) yet bestow no dainty seeds in your earth prepared for the purpose.

From the sixt degree of *Cancer*, unto the 19 degree of the same sign (so that the Moon increase) both labour the earth, sow fine seeds, and plant dainty herbs, herein regarding the condition of the aire.

From the 28 degree of the sign *Leo*, unto the 11. degree of *Virgo*, your seeds and plants of value sow and set, the warme aire and Moon aiding thereto.

From the 11 degree of *Virgo*, unto the 24 degree of the same sign, commit seeds to the earth, and set up your dainty plants, so that the wind then bloweth not from the North, nor the aire cold.

From the 24 degree of *Virgo*, unto the 7 degree of the sign *Libra*, labour the garden ground, and sow your fine seeds, so that the Moon increase.

From the seventh degree of *Libra* unto the ninteenth degree of the same sign (the Moon answering thereto) sow and plant.

From the sixt of *Capricornus*, unto the ninteenth degree of the same sign (both the Moon and aire aiding thereto) sow your fine seeds and dainty plants set.

From the four and twentieth degree of *Pisces*, unto the seventh degree of *Aries*, the Moon increasing of light, and aire calme, bestow your seeds and plants in the well dressed earth, prepared for the only purpose.

These precepts of the prudent experimenters, wel born away of every careful Gardener, the seeds and plants no doubt, shall prosper and increase the better.

CHAP. XXI

he learned *Pliny* worthy of memory, uttereth a special note and rule of the ancient observers, to be learned of every careful Gardener, in the bestowing of seeds: that if he be occasioned to commit seeds into a moist earth, or the seeds to bestowed are of a great moisture, then shall the Gardener commodiously chuse the end of the Moons decrease or wane, and near to her change.

In a contrary manner, the Garden ground of the driest, or the seeds very dry, then in committing such seeds to the earth let the Moon be increasing, and drawing near to her full.

To the better furthering of the Gardeners travels, he ought afore to consider, that the Garden earth be apt and good, wel turned in with dung, at a due time of the year, in the increase of the Moon, she occupying an apt place in the Zodiack, in agreeable aspect of *Saturne*, and wel placed in the sight of heaven. All these thus aforehand learned, and with diligence bestowed, procure the plants the speedier to grow, and wax the bigger, if afore weighty, ful, &c. as before uttered in the nineteenth Chapter, for otherwise this care and pains bestowed about the seeds and plants, nothing availeth the Gardener.

Certaine instructions more curious to be learned of every skilful Gardener, in the bestowing of seeds and dainty herbs in a well dressed earth.

A Tudor diagram showing how a tree can be budded.

The yearly Almanacks do marvellously help the Gardeners in the election for times, for sowing, planting and grassing, but especially in observing the Moon, about the bestowing of plants, as when the Moon increasing, occupieth *Taurus* and *Aquarius*. But if it be for the setting of young trees, let the same be done in the last quarter of the Moon, she then being in *Taurus*, and in a conjunction with *Venus*, for so these speedier take root in the earth, and the Gardener planting in either *Taurus* and *Aquarius*, or *Virgo* and *Pisces*, must as carefully take heed alwaies, that the Moon is not evil aspected of *Saturne* and *Mars*.

In the planting also of young trees, let the same be done from the middle of *October*, unto the middle of *March*. In the sowing of seeds, in a wel dressed earth, let the Moon run at those times in *Taurus*, *Cancer*, *Virgo*, *Libra*, and *Capricornus*.

But this diligently learn, that the seeds and plants increase the better, if any of these signes shal be ascending in the East-angle, and

An engraving of 1526.

*Thomas Hill commended
requesting 'the counsel of the
skilful' to determine the best
times to sow seeds.*

that *Mars* neither behold the Ascendent, or the Moon by any aspect,
but shall be weakly standing in a weak place of the figure at that time.

Here might many other rules, as touching the particular favour,
and hinderance of the Stars be uttered, but that it is not my intent in
this Chapter to be tedious in words, or dark in sense. For which cause,
let these few rules content the Gardener, who by exercising of them,

*A Tudor gardener at work on
the three stages of cleft
grafting. From Mascall's
treatise of 1569.*

and through an instructer, may invent other rules more particular.

Yet I fear me, that the common sort of men wil suppose these rules to extend somewhat above their capacity, which for zeale I bear unto my Country, moved me notwithstanding to utter and put such matter into their heads, procuring them thereby (that where the daintinesse and value of the seeds, and plants so require) to request the counsel of some skilful, that both may make plain these precepts, and instruct them in other rules alike, if need requireth.

To conclude, the Gardener must here suppose all matters on his part to be fully and duly first prepared and wel appointed, and then to attend, or diligently take heed to those times afore uttered for the working of the Planets and Stars, in the bestowing of seeds and tender plants in the earth.

CHAP. XXII

In what space of time seeds committed to the earth, in the increase of the Moon, commonly shoot up and appear above ground.

lorentius (a Greek writer of Husbandry) cunningly uttereth, that the naturalnesse of the ground, the clemency of heaven, the favour of the weather, and age of the seeds, procureth that the seeds being bestowed in the ground, do either speedier or later shoot up into plants. For which cause, the dainty seeds committed to the earth in a faire and warm day, the place hot or lying open to the Sun, and the seeds new, do far speedier shoot up, then those that being sown in a contrary season, place, and ground.

All seeds sown, do evermore appear above the earth at one certain time in a manner, for which cause the Gardener ought to have regard unto the proper times answering to the bestowing of seeds, and gathering the fruits or yield of each seeds.

The Spinage, Rocket, Basil, and the navew seeds, break and appear above the earth, after the third day sowing, if a warm aire succeed.

The Lettice seeds bestowed in a wel dressed earth, do break and appear above ground by the fourth day following, if the clemency of aire ayde thereto: the Cucumber and Citrone seeds bestowed in the increase of the Moon, and showers of raine falling the same or the next day following, procure them to appear the fift day after.

The seeds of that sightly hearbe, named the flower Armour, being sowne in the increase of the Moone, and the aire favour, doe breake and appeare above the earth by the seventh or eight day following.

The seeds of the hearb Dill, bestowed in the earth, in the increase of the Moon, do (for the more part) appeare by the fourth day following.

The seeds of the Garden Cresses and Mustard, committed to the

A late seventeenth-century English embroidery showing a garden teeming with flowers and insects.

Careful watering has always been an essential part of successfully sprouting seeds.

earth in the increase of the Moon, do commonly appear above the ground by the fift day after.

The Leek seeds (bestowed in the ground) in the Summer time, are seen above the earth by the sixt day following, but in the Winter time in well dunged beds by the tenth day after.

The seeds of the hearb Rocket, committed to the ground in the increase of the Moon, appear by the eight day following.

The seeds of all kinds of Coleworts, bestowed in well dressed beds, are evermore seen by the tenth day following, if the cold aire hindereth not.

The seeds of the great Leeks bestowed in well dunged beds, appeare many times by the ninteenth, but oftner by the twentieth day following.

The Coliander seeds, bestowed in well trimmed beds, and in the increase of the Moon, are commonly seen above the earth by the five and twentieth day: but the young plants latter appear, if the seeds bestowed are new.

The seeds of the Organy and Savery, bestowed in light earth, and the Moon increasing, do appear above the ground by the thirtyeth day following.

The Parcely seeds committed to the earth, and the increase of the Moon, do commonly break and appear above ground, by the fortieth day following, although they are not many times seen before the fiftieth day.

Thus have I briefly uttered a true and pleasant instruction, both for the age of seeds, and skil of the Gardener in sowing of them. For as I have above-said, the Leeke, the Cucumber, and Citorne seeds do speedier come up, being new seeds: in a contrary manner, the seeds of the Parcely, Beets, Spinage, Cresses, Savery, Organy, Peny-royal, and Coliander, the elder that these are (before the bestowing in the earth) the speedier the seeds break and appear above ground.

The seeds in like manner of the Cucumber, steeped in milke or luke warme water for a night, and committed to the earth, under a warme aire, do far speedier break, and appear above ground. The like may

The tools used by the seventeenth-century gardener to produce the fine tilth suitable for sowing and planting. Sketched by John Evelyn for his projected Elysium Brittannicum.

*Also by John Evelyn, a
fascinating range of
implements, cloches, frames,
barrows, watering machines,
and seed beds. 1659.*

the Gardener conceive to be done with the seeds of the Artechoke,
and many other hearbs, of which shall particularly be uttered in the
proper places hereafter.

The third moneths sowing, or rather in *May*, to such dwelling far
North, or where snow lyeth long, there (this bestowing of seeds)

better agreeth, especially where the quality of Summer is known to be moist.

But in other Countries (this like) by a seldome hap answereth, seeds three moneths old committed to the earth in harvest time will better agree, being done in hot Countries, the Moon herein considered.

The Gardener in his well trimmed earth, (the time aiding) may commit to the ground all worthy and excellent kind of seeds, plants, slips, kernels, and such like: but these for a trial bestow in the beds in your Garden.

So that in any new kinds of seeds, not assayed or proved before, the Gardener may not throughly hope that these will prosper in his ground.

These seeds committed to the earth in moist places, do speedier shoot up (the Moon helping) then bestowed in dry ground: for which cause, election used in sowing of good and full seeds (in either ground) much availeth.

The seeds or sets bestowed in shadowy places, although the earth be well laboured before, do rarely or very seldom prosper, and yeild their flower.

The plants grown to their flower, may at that time (after the mind of the Neapolitane *Palladius Rutilius*) be little or nothing handled, for doubt of corrupting their flower, or the sooner shedding of them.

CHAP. XXIII

 fter the seeds being workmanly bestowed in the beddes, the Gardeners next care must be, that he diligently pull up, and weed away all hurtful and unprofitable hearbs, annoying the Garden plants comming up.

What care and diligence is required of every Gardener, in the plucking up, and cleare weeding away of all unprofitable hearbs growing among the Garden plants.

But about this exercise in weeding of the beds, there is a disagreement among the writers of Husbandrie. For certaine denie that the raking doth profit the plants any thing at all, in that by the rake the roots of the Garden plants are so uncovered, and the plants with the same felled, and caused to lye flat on the ground, which if cold weather ensue, are utterly killed with the nipping aire, for which cause, they better thought of that weeding and cleansing exercise, by pulling up with the hand, so that the same were done in due order and time.

Yet it pleased many husbandmen in time past to rake up the weeds in beds, yet not after one manner, nor at all times alike, but according to the usage of the Country, the skill, and condition of the weather: for which cause, in what manner soever this exercise shall be taken in hand, that weeding shall need or be required in these places, the Gardener shall not attempt or beginne the weeding of beds with the hand, before the plants well sprung up, shall seem to cover their proper beds, and that in this high growth, the plants shall be mixed and joyned one to the other, according to the nature and forme in their growth.

In this plucking up, and purging of the Garden beds of weeds and stones, the same about the plants ought rather to be exercised with the hand, then with an Iron instrument, for feare of feebling the young plants, yet small and tender of growth.

And in the weeding with the hand, the Gardener must diligently take heed that he does not too boisterously loose the earth, nor handle much the plants in plucking away of the weeds, but the same purge so tenderly, that the roots of the young plants be not loosed and feebled in the soft earth: for occasion will move the carefull Gardener to weed dainty hearbs, being yet young and tender, lest grosse weeds in the growing up with them, may annoy and hinder their increasing. Therefore the young plants in some readinesse to be taken in hand, ought not to be stayed until their strong and big growth, but weeded in the mean time, for doubt of the conveniences above uttered. But

Ovid's nymph, Pomona, confined her favours to her garden until the wily god, Vertumnus, in the guise of an old woman, won her over to the wedded state. David Teniers I (1582-1649).

the common hearbs for the Kitchin, the Gardener shal not begin to weed before they be grown strong in root, and big shot up. And this learn, that if the earth be loose and soft at the time of weeding the dainty plants you may not then loose and pull up weeds, but in a soft and tender manner: and yet fine hearbs require all times to be weeded, so that showers of raine have well softened the earth a day before.

The walking or treading often about the beds of the little and tender plants shooting up, looseth much the soft earth about them, yea this so settled down the ground by the helpe of showers of raine falling, that the weeds growing up in those beds, are caused the harder to be plucked up. And sometime the roots of the weeds in the plucking up with the hand are left behind, through this fastnes caused of the earth.

Here remember, that you never take in hand or begin the weeding of your beds, before the earth be made soft, through the store of rain falling a day or two before.

Here conceive, that the clipping, plucking away, and pressing down of sundry hearbs with Tiles or other weighty things, after they be grown to some greatnesse, is to great purpose, for so much as this causeth them to keepe the longer green, and to yeild the thicker, bigger, and fairer turfs, besides the letting of the hearbs, that they grow not up into seed, and to give these a pleasanter savour, then the same that before they possessed in their growth simply.

As by a like means and ordering, hath the Lettice, Cabbadge, and Colewort, may be caused better and more pleasant of taste, then the leaves simply growing, without any such manner of ordering.

In the like condition do the Radish and Navew roots grow the fairer and bigger, if divers of the green leaves (after some growth) be handsomely clipped or broken off.

But of the apt ordering of these two last, in causing their roots to be far bigger then customable, and pleasanter in taste, shall more fully be uttered in their proper Chapters hereafter, in the second part of this treatise.

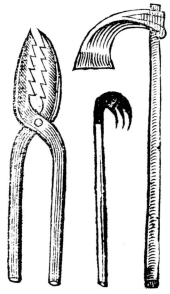

Contemporary weeding implements.

CHAP. XXIV

he beds being furnished with seeds in due age of the Moone, requireth diligence (if the aire sufficiently moistneth not) in the watering of them, lest the ground being very dry of the proper nature, may through the drith for the lack of raine, cause both the seeds and tender plants shoot up, to perish and drie.

For which cause every Gardener ought carefully to consider the condition and property of the earth of his Garden, whether of it self the same be very moist or over dry, which two extreames learned, he

The commended times for watering of the Garden Beds, and what manner of water ought necessarily be used to plants, with the latter inventions of divers vessels aptest for this purpose.

Thomas Hill's example of 'a great Squirt' to water the garden gently as if with drops of rain.

may with more diligence bestow paines about the watering of the Garden beds, so often as need shall require.

And for that the seasons in a manner, sufficiently instruct every owner and Gardener, when to water the plants come up, it shal not be (of my part) a new instruction to utter unto them, the daies and times necessary to water the plants, seeing the youngest of any discretion know that the beds chiefly require watering after a drought, or when many hot dayes have chanced together, as the like especially commeth to passe in the summer time, about the Cosmick rising of the Canicular or dog Star, which with us commonly happeneth about the seventeenth day of *July*. And this watering of the beds, ought rather be done (as *Pliny* witnesseth) in the morning, soon after the Sun rising) and at the evening when the Sun possesseth a weak force above the earth. The reason this Author alleadgeth of the same, is, that by watering at the hot time of the day as at noon, the water then made hot by heat of the Sunne, would so burn the young and tender roots of the plants. And in this watering of the beds, the Gardener must have a speciall care and regard, that he moisten not the plants too much, lest cloying them too much with water, they after wax feeble and perish. The water best commended for watering of the plants, is the same drawn or gotten out of the River, or other narrow stream ebbing and flowing; or else sweetly running one way, through the helpe of Springs falling into it. But if the Gardener be forced to use Wel-water, drawn especially out of a deep Well, or the water out of some pit: he ought then to let the same drawn up, stand for two or three daies together, or at the least for certain hours in the open aire, to be warmed of the Sun, lest the same being new drawn up, and so watered or sprinckled forth on the beds both raw and cold, may feeble and kill the tender young plants comming up.

A late fifteenth-century clay watering pot.

The age also of the plants, shall greatly direct the Gardener to know how much and how small he ought to moisten them at each time needfull, for the tender young plants new come up, require a lesser watering, and the same gently where the hearbs more grown, wil joy to be plentifully moistened with the water temperate warm. And this water ought gently to be sprinkled forth on the beds, with a watering pot, and by other meanes, which after shall be demonstrated, that the roots of the young hearbs may alike drink in of the water, and not to be cloyed through the over fast, or too much moisture sprinckled on them, by which doing, these the rather retaine the spirit vanquishing, procured to passe thorow the exhalation of the earth. For which cause, the beds at one instant shal not fully be watered, but as the earth and plants drink in, so gently sprinckle forth the water, in feeding the plants with moisture, as by a brest or nourishing Pap, which like handled, shall greatly prosper the tender plants comming up, where they otherwise by the hasty drowning with water, are much annoyed, and put in hazard of perishing.

To the water standing in the Sunne, if the owner or Gardener mixe a reasonable quantity of dung, after his discretion, this mixture no doubt will be to great purpose, for as much as the same gently watered or sprinkled abroad, procureth a proper nourishment to the tender plants and young hearbs comming up.

The cold as well as the salt water, is known to be enemy unto all kinds of plants, yet *Theophrastus* reporteth, that the salt water is more proper for the watering of certain plants, then any other.

The common watering pot for the Garden beds with us, hath a narrow neck, big belly, somewhat large bottom, and full of little holes, with a proper hole formed on the head to take in the water, which filled full, and the thumb laid on the hole to keep in the aire,

The watering pot described by Thomas Hill.

may on such wise be carryed in handsome manner to those places by a better help aiding, in the turning and bearing upright of the bottom of this pot, which needfully require watering.

The watering pot best to be liked, and handsomest for this turn, both for the finely sprinckling forth, and easie carriage of water in the same from place to place in the Garden, is that much used in the chiefest Gardens about *London*, and in divers parts of *England* now known, whose form is after this manner, the body wholly of Copper, having a big belly and narrow neck, a strong handle of the same, mettal workmanly fastned to the belly and head, to carry the pot if need be to place in the Garden: but for a more easinesse and quicknesse in carriage of the pot upright and ful, is an other strong ring or handle fastned artly to the lips of the pot, much like to the Barbers water-pot carried abroad, that serveth to none other turn, saving for the easie carriage of the pot ful of water to needful places: but this other handle especially serveth to sprinkle forth the water by the long pipe ful of little holes on the head, that some name a pumpe, which reacheth from the bottom, unto the head of the pot, for the handsomer delivering forth of the water, the handle in the mean time guiding this long pipe of the pot, until all the water be spent.

Careful watering in a garden depicted by Crispin de Passe, 1614.

The Gardener possessing a Pump in his ground, or fast by, may with long and narrow troughes wel direct the water unto all beds of the Garden, by the pathes between, in watering sufficiently the roots of all such herbs, which require much moisture. But for a plainer understanding of this, I have here demonstrated the form to the eye.

There be some which use to water their beds with great Squirts, made of Tin, in drawing up the water, and setting the Squirt to the brest, that by force squirted upward, the water in the breaking may fall as drops of raine on the plants, which sundry times like squirted on the beds, doth sufficiently feed the plants with moisture.

A watering pot of 1620.

The owner or Gardener, enjoying a Pond with water, in his garden ground, or a ditch of water running fast by, so that the same be sweet, may with an instrument of wood (named of most men a skiff) sufficiently water all the beds of the Garden, with great ease and expedition.

Such plants which come speediest forward, through much moisture bestowed on them, as the Cucumber, Mellon, Gourd, and sundry others, the Gardener may with far greater ease and travel water after this manner, in taking Wollen cloathes or Lists, and these like tongues cut sharp at the one end, which lay to the bottom of the pot, filled with water, the sharp end hanging forth, wel four fingers deep, and the pot leaning somewhat forward, that these may through the continual dropping, hastily speed the increase of the above said plants, so that to each plant a like pot prepared be set, which manner of doing, is termed filtring.

CHAP. XXV

he Husbandman or Gardener, which would have plants grow unto a greater bigness then customable, ought to remove after four or five leaves be wel come up, and set them again, as out of one bed bestowed into another, and like from one border into another. Although the owner may (at all seasons) dispose plants, at his will and pleasure, yet is it better commended, that all plants be changed into other earth prepared when showers of rain have wel moistned and softned the same.

The plants also removed, and set again into a fat earth wel laboured and dressed, needeth besides, as *Columella* witnesseth, no other amendment by dung.

The skilful Neapolitane (*Palladius Rutilius*) in his worthy work of husbandry reporteth, that when the Gardener hath bestowed sundry kinds of seeds in one bed together, which after the diligent watering be so risen, that four or five leaves of divers plants are sprung above the earth, such then after this Authours consent, may wel be removed and set again (into beds workmanly prepared) a certain distance

At what times divers plants sprung up, ought to be removed and set again, as out of one bed or border into another, with the breaking or slipping of sundry sets from old bodies, which with skil require to be bestowed in the earth.

A mid-sixteenth-century (1542) gardener hard at work using a mattock to transplant into a raised bed.

asunder, being such plants, that (before the setting) require to have tops of the leaves, and ends of the roots cut off, whereby they may the freelier grow up broad in tough or big in roots.

Those kinds of seed, which after the committing to the earth, and diligent watering, need not, after certain leaves sprung up, to be removed, may the owner or the Gardener bestow (as *Rutilius* witnesseth) in the beds the thinner, the Moon herein remembred.

The worthy *Columella* (in instructions of the Garden) willeth the owner or Gardener, having occasion to pull up plants, and set them again in beds, and that the ground the same time (for the lack of raine, be over drie and hard) to moisten and soften well the earth a day before, with water sprinkled forth, by a watering pot, serving onely to that use.

And certain of these, which require to be set a good distance asunder, the worthy *Rutilius* willeth to clip off the tops of the young leaves, and the ends of the roots to cut away, before the bestowing again in beds workmanly prepared, as like the Colewort, Cabbadge, Lettice, great Leeke, Navew, and Rape.

Again, a good distance asunder, are the Cucumber, Gourd, Mellon, Artechoke, *Nigella Romana*, and sundry other, which this placed in beds artly prepared, may the readier and handsomer be weeded, and cherished by the earth digged about, so often as need shall require; whereby the plants, through help of diligent watering, and furtherance of the Moon in setting, are after procured to increase the better, and delectabler to the eye.

The young sets for the Garden (of pleasant delight and smell) may the owner or Gardener also bestow in borders at all seasons, (although better commended to be done in the spring time) in breaking off the slips or branches of one years growth, from the bodies of old stocks, and in wreathing the ends about, so to set them a good depth into the earth, the Moon at that time drawing near to her change, and known to be under the earth, which much furthereth the sets in the sooner taking of root.

But the skilful *Columella* rather willeth, to cleave the end of the branch or slip beneath, in which cleft an Oat grain to be thrusted or put, and in the setting deep into the ground, to bestow Oat graines round about the same, (the Moon then near to her change) rather than any dung.

As the young hearbs which the Gardener mindeth to remove, need not (saith this *Columella*) to be striked about the roots with any dung, but rather that the ends of their roots (before the setting again) be cut off, as I above uttered.

The Marigold, Dazie, Columbine, Primrose, Couslip, sweet Iohn, Gilly-flowers, Carnations, Pincks, and sundry other delectable flowers, are procured to increase the bigger, fairer, and doubler, if the owner or Gardener do often change these into beds, workmanly prepared, the Moon at those times considered, to be increasing of light, and that a diligence bestowed in the often watering.

Thomas Hill's illustration of planting, demonstrating the use of the dibble.

As touching the pulling up of sundry dainty hearbs of pleasant savour, and that these to be set again in beds (orderly prepared) after the course of the Moon, with a care and diligence to be bestowed particularly on most plants of the Garden, shall at large be uttered in the second part of this treatise, where we purpose to treat of many laudable and weighty matters besides.

The plants (which after certain leaves spring up) need not to be removed into other beds, are the Spinage, Arach, Dill, Sperage, Sorrel, Chervile, Parcely, and divers other of like sort.

CHAP. XXVI

Particular Rules for the sowing, setting, watering, and ordering of several Plants, Roots, Flowers, and herbs for Gardens.

aving digged and prepared your Garden (as is aforesaid) into Beds or Borders; I wil now shew you the best order and manner for setting and sowing of the chiefest Plants, Hearbs and Flowers most now in request.

First, in the setting of Hearbs or Flowers, be sure that you chuse no stalk or slip that hath blossoms or buds on it, or those which are spingled, for such will hardly ever take or grow.

When you set any Hearb, Flower, or Plant, you must the next day a little moisten the ground in the morning, and so keep the ground moist, until they be wel rooted by watering.

The best watering which is certain, (except your ground be new made ground, with half dung) is to make a hole with a Dibble a little from the herb or plant, a slope to the root, and so water the root under ground, for water rotteth and killeth above ground.

And whatsoever you sow, cover it with earth, but so thin as you can, for if they be too deep set or sown, most seeds, kernels, and such like, wil never come up.

For setting of any thing, be sure to make the earth very wet, then half a foot over lay on dry mould, making it so close (with beating it with your Spade) as you can, then set in your hearbs or plants, thrusting the earth very hard to the root.

Hearbs for works may be watered, but plants must not be wet above ground, (as is before said) for rotting.

Never water but in a morning, except in *June* or *July*, and then you may water about four of the clock in the afternoon.

For setting, sowing, or planting, it is best when the weather is warm, and the ground neither too wet nor too dry at the top, but so moist as it will stick to your shoes as after a frost: And for the time of the Moon, I hold the second day before the new Moon to be the best for most things; but for flowers, a little after the change, or new Moon.

The ground which you will sow at the spring, must be digged at *Michaelmas*, and good dung then trenched the digging.

The best time for sowing is in *February, March*, or *April*: But for

Detail of planting from a late fifteenth-century illustration of a fourteenth-century gardening treatise by Pietro de Crescenzi.

setting of Hearbs, *March*, and the beginning of *April* is best; And those Hearbs which spring out of the ground in *February*, must be set in *February*.

CHAP. XXVII

In the midst of *April*, or in the beginning of *May* (as the Moon shall happen to be in the wane) dig a ditch about a yard deep, and lay some three quarters of a yard of Horse dung therein; then cover the dung over a foot thick with good earth, laying your seeds along on the earth dry, and cover them an inch thick with light earth, and every night (until *May* be past) cover them with a wet cloth or straw, to keep away the frost, and uncover them in the day time: And note, that when the Cucumber hath three leaves, you may then remove them to other places, if you please. The Pumpion seeds should be set a finger deep in the earth; and the Cabbadges should be removed when they are a handfull high.

Parsnep seeds may be sown in *October*, in the wane of the Moon; but if they prove not, sow more seeds in *February* following; and to make the roots the bigger and fairer in dry weather tread down the tops and leaves of them.

Carrots are to be sown in the latter end of *April*, or the beginning of *May*.

Turneps groweth best in a sandy earth, and should be sown at the time that Carrots are: But if you will have them for Lent, sow them in *August*, at the wane of the Moon.

Onyons must have a rank fat ground half dung, sow them in *February*; you may sow Onyons seeds, and Lettice seeds, and Radish seeds mingled together in one plot, for Sallets at the same time in a hot ground: set Onyons for Scallions, and to seed in *October*.

Garlike desireth a temperate ground, not too ranck, and it is good setting it in *February* or *October*.

Leeks liketh a rank ground, and would be sowed in *October*.

Radish desireth such ground as the Onyon doth, sow it in *February*, and all Summer, every moneth before Woodseer, in the wane of the Moon for fear of seeding, and you shall have them alwaies fresh and young; but after Woodseer you may sow them at any time of the Moon.

Skerrots must be set in the wane, about the latter end of *September*, or beginning of *October*; for all roots should be sowed in the wane of the Moon.

Lettice sown in *August* will live all Winter, but if you sow them in *March*, they will be so bitter that they cannot be eaten.

Parsley should be sowed about the beginning of *August*, and it will be fresh in the spring of the year, and it loveth the shade: The seeds of

Here followeth the ordering of the Kitchin Garden, for Plants, Hearbs, Roots, &c. And first for Cucumbers, Pumpions, Musk-millions, Cabbadges, and Gilly-flowers.

Labours in a seventeenth-century French kitchen garden.

Parsley and Marjarom will lye six weeks in the ground before they come up.

Isop may be sown in seeds in *April*, but they will not last; the roots that are young are good to set, but the slips are best.

Marigolds may be sown in *August* for the spring, you may remove the Plants about two inches long, they will grow the bigger.

Alexanders is sowed in *March* or *April*, you may remove the roots, and they will grow the next year.

Borage and *Buglas* are sowed in the spring, and dyeth that year.

Succory and *Endive* are sowed in *March* or *April*, remove them before the spindle, and they will be better.

Peny-royal, the roots parted, or the branches set into the ground, being moist will grow.

Mints, either the roots set, or the branches being cut in divers peaces and set in the earth, being wet will prosper.

Savery sowed in the spring commonly dyeth, but being removed it will live in Winter.

Tyme is sowed or set in the Spring, and both seeds, Slips, and roots will grow, keep it from seeding, and it will last three or four years.

Tansie may be sowed in *March* or *April*, the roots being removed wil prosper wel.

Bloodwort may be sowed in the Spring, or the roots being new set wil last long.

Dandelyon may be sowed in *March* or *April*, and may be ordered as the former.

Sage is best to be set in Slips in *April* or *May*, if you would have it last long, suffer it not to seed, but if you please you may sow the seeds in the spring.

Cardus Benedictus must be sowed in the spring, for it will dye in Winter.

Wormwood is best to be set in Slips, it will last three or foure years.

Clary is to be sown in the spring, it seeds the second yeare and then dies.

Fennel may be sown in the spring or fall, or you may set the roots, it will continue many years.

Sweet *Marjoram* may be sown in *April*, but they wil dye in winter, but if you set the Slips they will prosper.

Artichokes come of young Plants taken from an old stock; the best time to plant them is in *March* or *April*, two dayes before the full Moon, (yet some plant them in August;) Set no plants, if you may have choice, but those which have the bottom knobs whole, neither pluck any plant from the stock till it be strong, and if the bottom knobs be pulled off and broken, it will hardly grow. And when you would take the Plants from the stock, dig the earth away half a foot deep round about the stock, and pull the earth clean from the stock; then thrust your thumbs between the stock and the Plant, and slive them off, keeping the bottom whole and unbroken. When you would set them, take a Spade and dig a hole, into which put straw ashes

mingled with earth wel wet with water; and then make a hole a little deeper where you will set them, spreading the roots of the plants, and put the wet stuffe to them very close, and cover it an inch with dry earth, setting them no deeper then they grew in the ground before: And let them be set some two foot one from the other in rows, placing the next row against the middle of the other; also, when you water your young Artechokes, make make a trench about them, wetting the ground temperately, not dirt wet, nor wet not the leaves, or any part of them above ground: After raine, when the earth dryeth again, tread the earth close to the young Plants, that the wind get not to their roots.

The ground which Artechokes loveth, is a fat warm earth, that hath been made fat with dung turned to present earth, for dung of it self is too hot, breeding wormes, which will spoile the roots; and they desire to enjoy the presence of the Sun all day, and be sure to weed them wel. You must gather your Artechokes (cutting them almost a foot from the ground) when their top beginneth to open a little; and with your foot break off the stalk left on the ground, treading it aside on both sides, about the latter end of *August*; it will breake off at a joynt at the ground, then take away the stalk, and pul away all the leaves at the roots: The stalks being so broken, cast a little earth on the top of the root, and this will mak it shoot out again with young, which by

Plants were often distilled for their scent as shown in this painting by Lucas Van Valkenborgh: Spring, 1595.

October following will be great and strong-leaved; And these be the good plants which you must set in the Spring: And note, that the two leaves next before the strong Plant, set about the middle of *April*, will beare as soon as the plant set in *February*. And if you mean to have great and good Artechokes, suffer but one to grow upon each stalk from the root.

Pease and *Beanes* for the Garden must have their seed changed every yeare, if not, the increase will be very smal, and grow lesse and lesse, for in three years, the great Rounseval and great Bean will be no bigger then the wild ones, do what you can to your ground, if you set or sow them which grew there before; and so likewise it is with Corn, if the seed be not changed.

If you set Pease in *February*, set them an inch and a half deep, but if you set them in *March* or *April*, set them but an inch deep; but be sure you set them in the wane of the Moon, some six or seven dayes before the change, or else you will have a great Cod, and but smal Pease; and let them be set from eight inches asunder: And to have Pease long, and have them often, set them in several plots, some in *February*, some in *March*, and others in *April*: A quart of Pease will serve to set a good plot of ground; Pease and Beanes will prosper well being set under any Trees; and being sown in temperate wet weather, they will appear above ground in ten or twelve dayes, but being set in cold weather, it will be a moneth, or longer before they will appear.

CHAP. XXVIII

Expert and certaine rules, for the sowing, planting and setting of most delectable Flowers and Hearbs in use, for adorning a Summer Garden, or Garden of pleasure and delight.

he life of man in this world is but a thraldom, when the Sences are not pleased; and what rarer object can there be on earth, (the motions of the Celestial bodies excepted) then a beautifull and Odoriferous Garden plat Artificially composed, where he may read and contemplate on the wonderfull works of the great Creator, in Plants and Flowers; for if he observeth with a judicial eye, and a serious judgement their variety of Colours, Sents, Beauty, Shapes, Interlacing, Enamiling, Mixture, Turnings, Windings, Embosments, Operations and Vertues, it is most admirable to behold, and meditate upon the same. But now to my Garden of Flowers and sweet Hearbs, and first for the Rose.

Roses are of several sorts and Colours, as White, Red, Damask, Province, Musk and Sweet-bryer, &c. Of all the Flowers in the Garden, this is the chief for beauty and sweetness: Rose-trees are commonly planted in a plot by themselves, (if you have roome enough) leaving a pretty space betwixt them for gathering: Now for to get and set your plants, you must do thus, In the latter end of *January*, *February*, or beginning of *March*, (at the increase of the Moon,) go to some old Rose-trees, (but not too old) and you shall find long young

Suckers or Branches, which spring up from the root of the tree the last year; dig a hole so deep, that you may cut away those Suckers close to the root, (but take heed of wounding the tree,) then fill up the hole again with earth very close and hard; These Suckers must be your plants for young Trees, If the Suckers have too many branches cut them away, also the tops of them, and they will take root the better: Then where you intend to set them, dig holes in good ground at least a foot deep, and set them a good depth, treading in the earth hard about them, leaving a little trench neer them for watering, till they have taken root: Your Provast Roses wil bear the same year you set them. You may if you please, plant Strawberies, Primroses, and Violets amongst your Rose-trees, and they wil prosper very wel.

Gilly-flowers, Carnations, or *July-flowers*, (so called, because in *July* they are in their prime and glory;) these for beauty and sent are next the Rose; they are of several curious Colours, and smelleth like to Cloves, and therefore of some are termed Clove-July-flowers;

Jacob Van Walscappelle (1644-1727), Flowers in a glass vase.

these are to be set of young Slips without shanks, taken from the old body or root; and when you set them, leave one joynt (next to the leaf) at the top of the ground, so that the ground be above the top of the middle joynt, for if you set any part of the leaves within the ground, your Gilly-flower heads wil never prove. Earthen pots are good, which have holes in or neer the bottom, in which pots plant your July-flowers, and in dry weather, twice a week in the Summer time set them in a Tub of water for three hours, or more, but let no water come to the top of the pot, but the rain, the pot wil suck up sufficient moisture at the bottom holes; you need never take in your pots but in frost.

Stock-July flowers are very sweet, and are of several Colours, they seed plentifully, which you may sow, otherwise you may set the Slips, and they will prosper very wel.

Wall-July-flowers, or Wal-flowers, usually growing on Walls; for they delight to grow in Lime or Morter, they will sometimes seem dead in Summer, and be green and bear flowers in Winter, they beare store of seed, which you may sow or set the Slips; If you wil have them grow upon a wall, dig little holes between the bricks or stones with an old knif, and put in the seeds and they wil grow there.

Tulips are very beautyful flowers, but have no sent, they adorn a Garden wel, or the house; their roots are like Onyons, which you must set in *January* if there be no frost; and after they have done bearing, about *Michaelmas* take up the roots out of the ground, which wil be double, and keep them dry in a Box or Paper against the next year.

Primroses, so called, being the first flower in the spring, they are very sweet, growing both single and double; when the roots grow too great, in the spring part them in two, or three parts, and set them again, though they be flowered they wil grow.

Cowslips are dainty sweet flowers, they grow both single and double, if the roots grow broad, you may sever them as you did the Primrose.

Violets is a timely flower, and very sweet, you must get some few roots and set them in the spring, the roots wil soon grow and spread themselves abundantly.

Harts-ease or *Pansies*, they are in shape almost like a Violet, they shed their seeds and dye, but come thick up the next spring.

Lavender is wonderous sweet both leaf and flower, the Slips are best to be twined and set about *Michaelmas*.

Daffadowndillies is a timely flower, good for shew, their roots will grow double as the Tulip, which being parted must be new set.

Marigolds shew pleasant, and a reasonable sent, you may sow them of seeds, or set young Plants.

Daseys be red, white, and mingled Colours, they do make a pretty shew in a Garden in the spring, their roots growing too thick or broad, are to be parted, and new set.

Flower-deluce sheweth wel in a Garden, the roots are to be severed and new set, which being dryed smelleth sweet.

Lillies that are red shew pleasantly, but have no sent, their roots grow as Garlike double (but bigger) which being parted and new set, wil grow again.

White Lillies, their roots are not like the red, yet they must bee parted, the flower hath a very sweet sent.

Turks-Caps, they are almost in Colour like the red Lilly, and their roots are to be parted, and set as the Lilly.

Crocusses must be used and set as the Tulip, if you set it in your Borders, it will make a pretty shew in the spring.

Lupines commeth of seeds set in *April* or *March*, it beareth a dainty flower, and the green leaves are of a strange shape, it beareth Cods like small Beanes, in which are the seed.

Tulips from Crispin de Passe,
Hortus Floridus, *1614.*

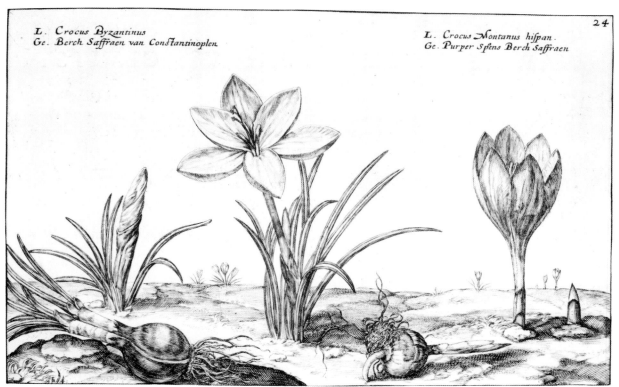

Holly-hocks are white and red, you may sow them of seeds, or plant the root.

Pyonie must have the roots parted and set, the green leaves spreadeth very broad, it beareth a great beautifull red flower, bigger than a Rose.

Monks-hood is a very pretty shaped flower, it must be sowed of seed in the spring.

French-mallows maketh a handsome shew, they are to be sowed of seed in the spring.

Poppey hath a very faire flower, and of a pretty colour, it must be sowed of seeds in the spring.

Saffron flowereth about *Michaelmas* when other flowers fade; it is to be set of roots, which ought to be removed every third year about *Midsummer*.

Batchelers Buttons come of seed sowed in the spring, or the roots may be planted.

Sweet-Sisley hath a pleasant sent, you may sow the seeds, or part the roots and set them.

Rosecampions may likewise be sowed of seed, or the roots planted.

Flowers of the *Sun* groweth very high, and beareth a great yellow Flower as big as the crown of a hat, it openeth and shutteth with the Sun (as the Marigold) and seeds must be set in *February* or *March* about half a finger deep.

Strawberies are white, red, and green; but the best Strawberies are gathered out of the wood, which have roots wel bearded; set them in *January, February*, or in *August*, three inches one from the other, in the beginning of the last quarter of the Moon; it is good planting them among your Rose-trees (as is said) for they naturally delight to grow in shady places.

CHAP. XXIX

Here followeth the order of sowing and setting of green and sweet hearbs for the Summer Garden.

*A*ngelica groweth high and broad, and lasteth long, you may sow it of seeds in the Spring, or the roots may be removed after the first year.

Lovage groweth much like to Angelica, and is to be ordered in the like kind.

Fennel is to be sowed of seeds, or the roots set either in the spring or fall.

Annyseeds commeth of seeds sowed, but it dyeth the first year, and so doth Coriander.

Elicampane may be sown of seeds, or divide the root and set, this hearb will endure long.

Isop may be sowed of seeds, or you may part the roots, or set the Slips.

Tyme may be sowed of Seeds in *April*, the roots may be parted, or set Slips.

Savory is to be sowed of seeds in *April*, and will hardly grow in Winter, unlesse the roots be removed.

Mints, peeces of the roots new set, or the stalks being cut in severall peeces, will prosper very wel, being set in moist ground.

Penny-royal is to be ordered as the Mints, it is good to set in the edges of your beds, or Borders, so are Dasies.

Camomel is also good for the edges of Borders, and it may be set in banks to sit on, either the roots parted, or the peeces set into the

Herbs have long been cultivated for their medicinal properties. This is an illustration of a herbalist's garden from a medieval gardening treatise.

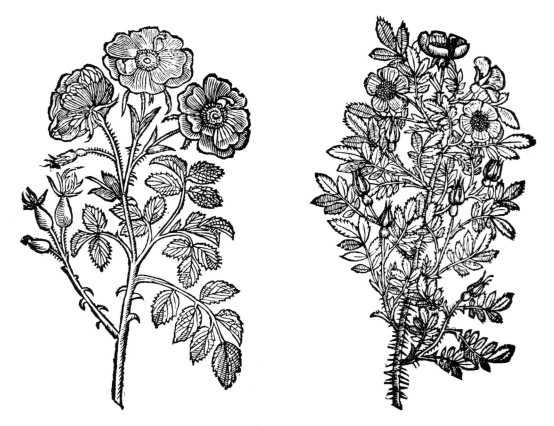

The double eglantine and the brier rose from John Gerard's Herball, 1597.

ground will grow.

Coast-mary may be sowed of seeds, or the roots parted and set in *March* is best.

Fetherfew is to be sowed of seeds in *March* or *April*.

Oculus Christi is best to be sowed of seeds, or you may remove the young Plants, and new set them.

Sage may be sowed of seeds, but the best way is to set the Slips in the spring.

Tansie may be sowed of the seeds in the spring, or you may remove the roots.

Herb of *Grace*, or *Rue*, the best waie is to set it of Slips, is green most part of the year, and thrives best in the shade. *Sothern-wood* is to be ordered as the *Rue*.

Marjoram is to be sowed of Seeds in April, and the Slips are to be set in July.

Dutch-Box groweth green most part of the year, it is prettie for Works or Borders; you may part the Roots and set them.

Rosemarie is a tender herb, it is best setting of it in April; or in the end of March you must set such as hath no blossoms, and as you take it from the branch; and by no means do not slive or tear your Slips, but cut them off a little from the bodie, leaving some few leaves behinde on the piece, and then it will grow again, otherwise it hurteth the bodie, and it will never grow there again.

CHAP. XXX

 efore you set your Rosemary Slips in *April*, or *March*, wrap the bottom end or slip with Clay, about the bignesse of a walnut, and so put it into the ground, and it will grow the better: And about *Midsummer* following, take it up again, being well rooted, or otherwise get some that is rooted out of some other Garden, though it be half a yard (or more) in length, then make close to your wall (where you intend to plant your Rosemary) a trench, of what length you please, and about a foot deep, and as much in breadth: In this trench set your Rosemary Roots; then fill the trench with water almost to the top, and put in your earth by little and little: in this manner you may remove a good pretty Tree in *May*, (which is late to remove any tree.) In this sort I have set Rosemary, which in two years have spread and covered a Wall, and grown almost two yards in height. I have also known Bowers and Arbours made all of Rosemary, which was wondrous sweet and pleasant.

Bay-trees wil come of the Bay-berry being set in the spring, or you may plant the young Suckers which spring from the root.

Honeysuckles or *Woodbine*, you may get them in Woods or Hedges in the fields, but dig deep enough to have their roots, prune them, and plant them against a Wall or Pale, which will yeild a most comfortable sent; these must be taken up and planted, in *January, February*, or beginning of *March*.

Hedges, or *Quick-sets* in your Garden, may be made either with the Suckers of Gooseberries, Currans, Privet, or Haythorn, and planted in *January* or *February*, at the increase of the Moon.

Eglantine, or *Sweet-bryer*, is to be set of Suckers also, and in those moneths as the former; they will grow of the red Hips which they beare, but it will be long before they come to any bigness.

In *August*, four dayes after the change, or three dayes before the full Moon, cut all your Hearbs within a handfull of the ground, then will they get head against Winter, and it will preserve them the better from hard weather; and in the end of *September*, sift earth or good mould upon them, to cover the roots well, otherwise the frost and rain will beat the earth from their roots, that your hearbs will be in danger of killing. And such Hearbs as you intend to keep against winter, cut often, to keep them from seeding, (for seeding doth kill most hearbs) and so they will live the better in winter: Also, cut your hearbs seldom in the wane of the Moon.

To have your Flowers great, remove them once in three yeares, the second or third day before the full Moon, and so plant them in

To have a wall of Rosemary of age it height quickly.

*A splendid hedge in a garden
of 1627.*

August, as in *March*, the weather being warm and the ground wet.
Also, the tops of the leaves set in *April* or *May*, the ground being wet
will grow.

To dry hearbs for Broth, or for Chests.

Dry them in Platters in the Sunne in *August* in their Flowers, as
winter Savory, Tyme, Marjoram, Peny-royal, Mints, Balme,
Rosemary tops, Marygolds, Lavender, Rose-leaves, &c. Gather

In this woodcut, sweet-smelling herbs are being used either to produce perfume, or are dried and placed in chests to keep the clothes fresh. Title page from Das Kreüterbuch oder Herbarius, *1534.*

them as you dry them, when you see the morning fair and hot, and the hearbs dry.

CHAP. XXXI

he best and worthiest roots of hearbs, for the more part, to be gathered in apt places when the leaves are beginning to fall off, and the fruits or seeds already shed, so that the season be faire: for done in a rainie time, thy roots be caused the weaker, and filled with rude moisture.

The flowers in like manner are to be gathered, as the Borage Buglosse, and all others of like sort when they be wholly opened, and before they feeble, except the flowers of the Rose, and Jacemine, which ought to be gathered for the better and longer keeping, before they be much, or rather but little opened.

The leaves and whole hearbs are to be gathered, when these be come to their full growth and perfection.

The fruits, as the Mellone, Cucumber, Cytrone, and Gourd, when these appear yellow, and be come to their perfect growth and perfection.

The seeds in like condition are to be gathered, when they be wel ripened, and before the seeds shed on the earth, but those which remaine after the hearbs thorow dried, ought to be rubbed forth with

The laudable instructions of the wise, in the gathering and preserving of the great number of Kitchin hearbs and roots, with the times aptest for the like doing by all flowers, dainty hearbs, and roots to the use of Physicke.

Carefully picking and collecting the blooms, as depicted on the title page of The Grete Herball, *1526.*

the hands, and kept unto the time of sowing.

Here remembring that the seeds ought to be gathered in a clear season, and in the wane of the Moon.

And this for a general rule observe, that all those to be gathered, as the hearbs, flowers, roots, fruits, and seeds are to be done in a faire and dry season, and in the decrease of the Moon.

The hearbs which the owner mindeth to preserve, are afore to be clean picked and clensed, and dried in the shaddow, being a place open towards the South, not moist and free from smoke, and dust.

These after are to be put in Leather bags, rather then into Canvas, the mouths at the hanging up fast tied, and into wooden boxes of the Box-tree, to the end the hearbs may not lose their proper vertue, as we see those persons to do, which preserve dainty hearbs for the winter time. So that the Apothecaries in mine opinion are very negligent, which hang up the Physick hearbs in their open shops and ware-houses, through which the vertue of these not only breath away, but the hearbs charged and clagged with dust, copwebs, dung of flies, and much other filth.

The Flowers ought not to be dried in the Sunne, nor in that shadow caused by the Sun at noon, nor in any chamber or high place above, forasmuch as these through their softness and tenderness do lightly of light occasion, breath away their proper vertue, but especially through the sharpe heat of the Sun, and heat of the aire, unlesse it be our Rose of the Garden, which to be preserved for a long time, requireth to be dryed in a high place, standing open to the Sun at noon, or that the Sun beames enter unto, and yet touch not the Rose leaves.

From a German treatise on plants of 1587 with illustrations showing, not only the plant, but also indicating astrological speculations on the apt times for sowing, planting, and picking. (Cervaria faemina from Thurneisser, Historia sive descriptio plantarum, 1587.)

Pounding the herbs to release their essential oils. From the Hortus Sanitatis, c. *1497.*

The better way for drying flowers, is to lay them in a temperate and darke place, free from moisture, smoke, and dust, and to stirre them to and fro, that these in the drying corrupt not, but to be either close kept in bagges, or continually covered over well, that these in the meane time lose not their colour, nor natural savour.

After being wel dryed, these ought to be close stopped in a glazed earthen vessel.

The finer seed are to be preserved in the leather bags, or in earthen vessels, having very narrow mouthes, or else in glass bottles, or gally glasses very wel stopped.

But the seeds of the Onions, Chibols, and Leekes, as also of the Poppy, are to be preserved in the huskes and heads.

For the preserving of roots, the owner ought to learn and exercise two meanes, the one for keeping them fresh, and the other for the round roots, as the Navew, Radish, Carrot, and others of like sort, and for to preserve them drie.

The way and meanes to keep and preserve roots fresh, is to bury them in a Seller, in either Gravell or Sand, well turned upon them, or in a Garden ground reasonably deep digged, even so deep as the Gardener doth for the Radish and Navew in the Earth, to enjoy the commodity of them for the greater part of the Winter: to preserve roots dry, the owner or Gardener (after the plucking of roots out of the earth) ought to wash them very clean with Conduit or Spring water, after to cut away all the small and hairy roots; which done, to dry them in a shadow place free from the beames of the Sunne, as being somewhat dark, if so be these are slender and thin of rinde, as be the roots of the Fennel, Succory, Parcely, Endive, Borrage, Buglosse, Sperage, and sundry others like; but if the roots be thick of rinde, of a grosse essence and bigge, then may the owner lay them to dry in the Sunne at Noonday, as the root of Gentiane, the Earth Apple, Brionie, Raponticke, *Aristolochia*, or any others like.

After that these be well dryed, and like prepared, ought the owner to hang them up in some Garret or open room a high, being sweet and dry (through the Sunnes daily shining on the place at noon) or open to the North, where nothing damaged by smoke, nor dust, nor that the Sun beames may harm in any manner, even as that ancient and singular Physitian *Hippocrates* instructeth, who willeth the hearbs, flowers, and roots, so wel fresh as dry, not to be bestowed in any manner, in an open place, to be dryed of the wind, but rather close stopped in Glasses, Earthen pots, and square boxes of wood, to the end that these lose not their vertue, which otherwise they might soon do by lying open to the wind.

All the field plants, flowers, and roots, are stronger in nature, but in substance inferiour to the Garden plants, &c.

Among the wild plants, those growing on the mountaines or high hils, do excell the other in property.

Among all plants those also are of a stronger nature, which shal be of a livelier colour, better tast and savour.

A sixteenth-century woodcut demonstrating the use of the hand as a sundial.

The force besides of plants do indure (for the more part) unto two or three years.

The hearbs which a man would use for the Kitchin, ought rather to be gathered with a Knife, somewhat above the earth, when these are shut up unto their perfect growth, as the Beets, Succory, Arach, Borrage, Marigold, Colewort, Endive, Clary, Rocket, Basill, Marjoram, Lettice, Parcely, Mercury, and many others.

When the owner mindeth to use certain hearbs; hot of quality, he ought to gather them for the more part, rather fresh then dry; but if his intent be rather to heat lesser, then seeing the moisture of the green, doth much mitigate the heat consisting in it, for that cause is he willed rather to gather the hearbs for Physick before they begin to alter their colour.

This for a general rule note, that all flowers, hearbs, and roots, ought carefully to be gathered in a dry faire season, and not in cloudy, misty, nor rainy weather. The roots beside are not to be gathered, but after the fall of the leaves, and those specially from the middle of *September*, unto the beginning of the moneth of *November*. But flowers are chiefly to be gathered from the middle of the moneth of May, unto the beginning of *July*, and after.

And for the fruits of sundry hearbs, these properly are to be gathered, according to the diversity of the hearbs.

CHAP. XXXII

The worthy remedies and secrets availing against Snailes, Canker wormes, the long bodied Mothes, Garden fleas, and Earth wormes, which vitiate and gnaw, as well the pot-hearbs, as trees and fruits.

 here is none so dul of eye-sight (as I beleeve) who not thorowly perceiveth and seeth, how that the Garden riches be diversly annoyed, and harmed by divers creeping worms and beasts, as wel above as under the earth, and that through the same occasion, often procured to feeble and wast, and unlesse speedy remedies shall be exercised, that these in the end do fall down and perish.

For the pestilent company of these increase, and are seen many times to be so many or great in number, that by no devised meanes, neither by fire nor Iron Engin (from the Garden grounds or fields, in which these once shal be lodged or abiding) can either be driven away or destroyed: therefore I shall do herein a most grateful matter (as I suppose) both to Husbandmen and Gardeners, if against this pesti-ferous annoyance and destruction, I shal utter and teach those worthy remedies, that both the ancient and latter men by great skil invented, and noted in their learned works.

From words to come unto the matter, I think it time to treat: And first, that singular *Africanus* among the Greek writers of Husbandry reporteth, that Garden plants and roots may wel be purged and red of the harmfull wormes, if their dens or deep holes be smoked, the winde aiding, with the dung of the Cow or Oxe burned.

That worthy *Pliny* in his first book of Histories writeth, that if the owner or Gardener sprinkleth the pure mother of the oyle Olive without any salt in it, doth also drive the wormes away, and defend the plants and hearbs from being gnawne of them. And if they shal cleave to the roots of the plants, through malice, or breeding of the dung, yet this weedeth them clean away. The plants or hearbs wil not after be gnawn or harmed by Garden Fleas, if with the naturall remedy, as with the hearb Rocket, the Gardener shal bestow his beds in many places.

The Coleworts and all pot herbs are greatly defended from the gnawing of the Garden Fleas, by Radish growing among them. And the worthy *Anatolius* in his Greek instructions of Husbandry affirmeth the like, so that some bitter fitches be also bestowed with the Radish in beds. And this seed committed in bed with the Radish and Rape, doth greatly availe, as the ancient witness of experience. The eager or sharp Vinegar doth also prevaile, tempered with the juyce of Henbane, and sprinkled on the Garden fleas. To these, the water in which the hearb *Nigella Romana* shal be steeped for a night and sprinkled on the plants, as the Greek *Pamphilus* reporteth, doth like prevaile against the Garden fleas.

If from creeping things the Gardener would defend the seeds committed to the earth, from being gnawn or harmed, let him steep

An etching by Wenceslaus Hollar of Six insects, a caterpillar and a snail.

those seeds for a night (as I afore uttered) before the sowing in the juyce of the Sengreen or Houseleek, which seeds also the Gardener shal preserve ungnawn, if he bestow of them in the shel of that Snaile, which I suppose to be the same, named the Tortuise, as the former Author *Anatolius* writeth: in which place I may not omit the same practice of the skilful *Palladius Rutilius*, who reporteth, that the noisome vermine or creeping things wil not breed of the pot hearbs, if the Gardner shal before the committing to the earth, dry all the seeds in the skinne of the Tortuise, or sow the hearb Mint in many places of the Garden, especially among the Coleworts. The bitter Fitch and Rocket (as I before uttered) bestowed among the pot hearbs, so that the seeds be sown in the first quarter of the Moon, do greatly availe us: as unto the Canker and Palmer wormes belongeth, which in many places worke great injury both to the Gardens and Vines, may the owner or Gardener drive away with the Figge tree ashes sprinkled on them and the hearbs.

There be some which sprinckle the plants and hearbs with the Lic made of the Fig-tree ashes, but it destroyes the worms, to strew (as experience reporteth) the ashes alone on them.

Study by G. Hoefnagel, 1592.

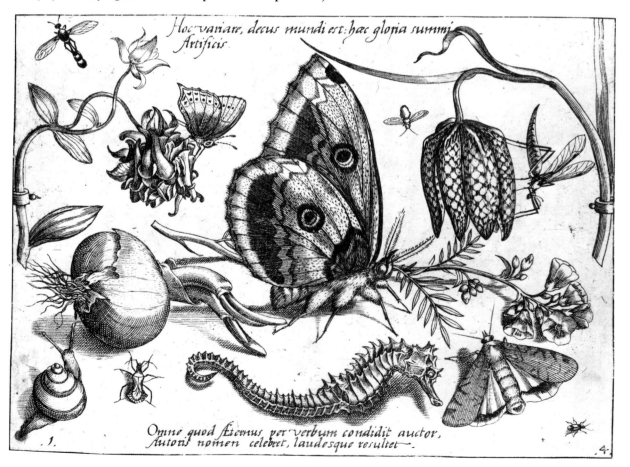

There be others which rather wil to plant or sow that big Onyon, named in Latin *Scilla* or *Squilla* here and there in beds, or hang them in sundry places of the Garden.

Others also wil, to fix river Crevisses with nailes in many places of the Garden, which if they shall yet withstand or contend with all these remedies, then may the Gardener apply to exercise this device, in taking the Ox or Cow Urine, and the mother of oyle Olive, which after the wel mixing together, and heating over the fire, the same be stirred about until it be hot, and when through cold, this mixture shall be sprinkled on the pot hearbe and trees, doth marvellously prevaile, as the skilful *Anatolius* of experience reporteth.

The singular *Pliny* in his practises uttereth, that those harmful worms, touched with bloody rods, are likewise driven away.

The worthy *Palladius Rutilius* reporteth, that if the owner or Gardener burn great bundles of the Garlike blades without heads dryed, through all the Allies of the Garden, and unto these the dung of Backos added, that the savour of the smoke (by the help of the wind) may be driven to many places, especially to those where they most abound and swame, and the Gardener shall see so speedy a destruction, as is to be wondred at.

The worthy *Pliny* of great knowledge reporteth, that these may be driven from the pot hearbs, if the bitter Fitch seeds be mixed and sown together with them, or to the branches of tree, Crevisses hanged up by the hornes in many places, doth like prevaile. These also are letted from increasing, yea they in heaps presently gathered are destroyed, as the Greeks report of observation, if the Gardener by taking certain Palmer or Canker worms out of the Garden next adjoyning, shal seeth them in water with Dil, and the same being thorow cold, shal sprinkle on the hearbs or trees, that the mixture may wet and soke thorow the nests, even unto the young ones, cleaving together, that they may tast thereof, wil speedily dispatch them. But in this doing, the Gardener must be very wary, and have an attentive eye, that none of the mixture fall on his face or hands. Besides these, the owner or Gardener may use this remedy certain, and easily prepared, if about the big armes of trees, or stems of the hearbs, he kindle and burn the stronger Lime and Brimstone together: or if the owner make a smoke with Mushromes growing under the Nut-tree, or burn the hoofs of Goats, or the gum *Galbanum*, or else make a smoke with the Harts horn, the wind aiding, by blowing towards them.

There be also some which infuse the Vine ashes in water for three daies, with which they after sprinkle abundantly, both the hearbs and trees. Many besides make soft the seeds, steeped before their committing to the earth, in the Lic made of the Fig ashes.

The Husbandmen and Gardeners in our time have found out this easie practise, being now common every where, which is on this wise; that when these, after showers of raine are cropen into the warm Sun, or into places standing against the Sun, may early in the morning

shake either their fruits and leaves of the pot herbs, or the boughs of
the trees, for these are yet stiffe through the cold of the night, are
procured of the same the lightlier and sooner to fall, nor able after to
recover up again, so that the Palmer worms thus lying on the ground,
are then in a readinese to be killed of the Gardener.

    If the owner mind to destroy any other creeping things noyous to
hearbs and trees, (which *Palladius* and *Rutilius* name, both Hearb
and Leeke wasters) then let him hearken to this invention and device
of the Greek *Diophanes*, who willeth to purchase the maw of a
Wether sheep new killed, and the same as yet full of his excremental
filth, which lightly cover with the earth in the same place, where these
most haunt in the Garden; for after two dayes, shall the Gardener
find there that the Moths with long bodies, and other creeping things
shal be gathered in divers companies to the place right over it, which
the owner shall either remove and carry further, or dig and bury very
deep in the same place, that they may not after arise or come forth;
which when the Gardener shal have exercised the same but twice or
thrice, he shall utterly extinguish, and quite destroy all the kinds of
creeping things that annoy and spoile the Garden plants. The
Husbandmen in *Flanders* arme the stocks, and compasse the bigger
armes of their trees with wisps of straw handsomely made, and
fastned or bound about, by which the Palmer worms are constrained
to creep up to the tops of the trees and there staied, so that as it were
by snares, and engins laid, these in the end are either driven away, or
thus in their way begun, are speedily or soon after procured to turn
back again. As unto the remedies of the Snailes particularly belongeth, these may the Gardener likewise chase from the Kitchin
hearbs, if he either sprinkle the new mother of the oyle Olive, or soot
of the Chimney on the hearbs, as if he bestowed the bitter fitch in beds
among them, which also availeth against other noisom worms and

creeping things, as I afore uttered, that if the Gardener would possesse a green and delectable Garden, let him then sprinkle diligently all the quarters, beds, and borders of the Garden, with the mixture of water, and powder of Fenny-Greek tempered together, or set upright in the middle of the Garden, the whole bare head without flesh of the unchast Asse, as I before wrote.

That worthy man *Julius Fronia*, reporteth that all Kitchin hearbs may greatly be holpen, if among them the hearb Rocket shall either be sown or planted. But an intollerable injury shall be wrought to the Husbandly Gardener, if the Goose dung dissolveth in brine, be sprinkled on the Kitchin hearbs, as these worthy writers *Democritus, Fronia*, and *Damageron* in their chosen precepts of the Greek Husbandry left noted to our age.

CHAP. XXXIII

 orasmuch as the Moles in many places of Garden grounds through their casting up, and hollowing of the same, the seeds afore bestowed in beds they on such wise uncover, and the plants in like manner turn up, and unbare of earth, to the great grief and paine of the careful Gardener, in daily renuing and repairing of their former labours, for that cause hath he just occasion to travel and busie himself in searching out, & devising by all skilful means, in what manner he may surest and best prevaile against this harmful blind beast. And that I may do a most grateful matter so all Gardeners in the same, I wil here utter all such singular practises, as either the worthy Greeks or Latins have uttered and noted to be available against them.

The skilful inventions and helps against the Garden Moles, Ants, Gnats, Flies, and Frogges, everting, harming and wasting, as well Kitchin hearbs, as trees and fruits.

First, the skilful *Paxanius* hath left in a writing, that if the Gardener shall make hollow a big Nut, or bore a hollow hole into some sound piece of wood being narrow, in filling the one or the other with Rosen, Pitch, Chaffe, and Brimstone, of each so much as shal suffice to the filling of the Nut, or hollow hole in the wood, which thus prepared in a readiness, stop every where with diligence all the goings forth, and breathing holes of the Mole, that by those the fuming smoke in no manner may issue out, yet so handle the matter, that one mouth and hole be onely left open, and the same so large, that wel the Nur or Vessel kindled within, may be laid within the mouth of it, whereby it may take the wind of the one side, which may so send, in the savour both of the Rosen and Brimstone into the hollow Tombe, or resting place of the Mole: by the same practise so workmanly handled, in filling the holes with the smoke, shall the owner or Gardener either drive quite away all the Moles in that ground, or finde them in short time dead.

There be some that take the white Neeswort, or the rind of

ABOVE *and* OPPOSITE *Ants, woodlice, flies, and a slug and snail from the* Hortus Sanitatis, c. *1497.*

Cynocrambes beaten and farced, and with the Barly Meale and Egges finely tempered together, they make both Cakes and Pasties wrought with Wine and Milk, and those they lay within the Moles denne or hole. *Albertus* of worthy memory reporteth, that if the owner or Gardener closeth or diligently stoppeth the mouths of the Mole-holes with the Garlike, Onyon, or Leek, shal either drive the Moles away, or kill them through the strong savour, striking or breathing into them. Many there be, which to drive away these harmful Moles, do bring up young Cats in their Garden ground, and make tame Weasels, to the end that either of these, through the hunting after them, may so drive away this pestiferous annoyance, being taught to watch at their straight passages and mouths of the holes comming forth. Others there be also which diligently fill and stop up their holes with the red Okar or Ruddel, and juyce of the wild Cucumber, or sow the seeds of *Palma Christi*, being a kind of *Satyrion* in beds, through which they wil not after cast up, nor tarry thereabouts. But some exercise this easie practise in taking a live Mole, and burning the powder of Brimstone about him, being in a deep earthen pot, through which he is procured to cry, all others in the mean time as they report, are moved to resort thither. There are some besides, which lay silk snares at the mouth of their holes. To the simple Husbandmen may this easie practise of no cost suffice, in setting down into the earth a stiffe rod or green branch of the Elder tree. The worthy *Pliny* which hath left to memory skilful practises reporteth, that the mother of the Oile Olive alone, sprinckled on the heap of Pismires or Ants, killeth them. This author also writeth, that the Pismires are wicked annoyners to trees, which the Gardener or Husbandman (saith he) may force to foresake and leave, if he strike the nether parts of the trees round about with the powder of the Ruddel, and Liquid Pitch or Tare mixed together: and hang also by the place, the fish named of the worthy *Rutilius* after the Greek writers of Husbandry, *Coracinum*, and of *Ruellius, Graculum*, for on such wise handled, they will resort and gather all into one place, whereby the Husbandly Gardener may the speedier destroy them. Others there be, which with the power of the Lupines and oyle Olive tempered together, do bestrike the lower parts of the trees and plants, for the letting of them in creeping up. Many kill them, as I afore uttered, with the onely Mother Oile Olive. The skilful Neapolitane *Rutilius* reporteth, that if the great company of Pismires or Ants have deep holes in the Garden ground, those may the owner chase away, or kill in the ground by stopping the mouthes of the holes, with the heart of an Owle. If they creep abroad, then sift all the Allies where these runne with bright asher, or else score the ground thick together with the red Okar or white Chalk, or make long strikes with oyle on the earth. Further he writeth that the husbandly Gardener may drive away Pismires, if on the mouthes of their holes he sprinckle the powder of Organy and Brimstone beaten together, or burn the empty shels of snailes, and with the ashes of the same, stop abundantly the mouthes of their dens and holes. In which device, this *Rutilius* omitted the Storax, that of *Paxanius* the Greek, out of whom he borrowed this conclusion, is added. The words of *Paxanius* be on this wise: If the owner, saith he, shall burn certain Ants or Emots in the middle of the Garden, the others of the savour will creep away. To these, it about the mouths of the Emots holes, the careful Gardener shall smeare the grosser Turpentine, the Emots or Ants wil not after come forth, and these he may expell or drive away from their proper resting place, or dwelling together, if the shelly coverings of Snailes, burned with *Storax Calamita*, and beaten to powder, or the ashes sifted, he shall after sprinkle on the heape of the Pismires. And the owner shall thorowly destroy the Ants, if he sprinkle on them the juyce of *Cyrenaicum*, dissolved and wel mixed in Oile. This Author further reporteth, that the Emots wil not creep on the plants or tree, if the husbandly Gardener shall diligently sprinkle the bodies and stems of them, with the powder of the bitter Lupines and mother of Oile, wel mixed or boiled together. The self same matter shall the Gardener performe, if he compasse their holes with white and clear wool or bombast, or that he marke on the ground long strikes, or forme round circles with white Chalk or red Okar, all those waies especially that these most often haunt, or compasse their holes with Organy, as I afore uttered: for by the like doing, as he affirmeth, the Emots after wil not onely leave the creeping up on the plants, but refuse also to ascend over the rings made with white Chalk about the bodies of trees. There be others which report, that the Emots wil not creep to that hony pot set on the ground, about which the like circles with Chalk or red Okar shall be formed, yea though the same were left uncovered, yet is it known to many, that the Ants are marvellous desirous of honey, and other sweet things.

The skilful Neapolitane *Rutilius* willeth, that the diligent Husbandman anoint or bestrike the stemmes of Plants, and the bodies of trees, with the red Okar, Butter, and liquid Pitch mixed well together. There be certain of the Greek writers of Husbandry, which wil the thicke Ivie Garlands to be bound about the bodies of Trees and Vines, that by the same skilful device, the Ants lodging under the shadow of these, as then pledges, they slay and kill.

There be many which report, that the like may be wrought and done with the Buls gaule, mother of Oile, and liquid Pitch, smeared about the bodies of trees. The singular *Pliny* reporteth, that the Sea mud or ashes, stopped diligently into the holes, is a most sure remedy against the Emots, so that the places be not moist or watery. But with the surest practise and remedy of all, are the Pismires killed with the hearb *Heliotropium*. Some suppose that the water in which the crude Tile shall be infused for a time, to be enemy to them. The Gardener may drive away Gnats, if he sprinkle on the beds and plants, the decoction of Organy in Vineger, as that skil- *Democritus* in his Husbandry hath noted. To these the owner may sprinkle on the Plants, the infusion of Rue in water or use the decoction hearb Fleabane, or else make a smoke either with Brimstone, or Cummine, or the drie Oxe dung, or the gumme *Bdellium*. The learned *Pliny* uttereth, that the Gardener may drive these away with the smoke of *Galbanum* burned; and that worthy Neapolitane *Rutilius*, of experience affirmeth, that if the owner either sprinckle the new mother of Oile, or Soot of the Chimney on the plants, it likewise driveth them away. That skilful Greek *Beritius* hath left in writing, how the Gardener may drive the flies far off with this fearful device, if mixing the powders of the Hellebore or Neeswort, and Orpiment with Milk, the same be sprinckled on the plants and place where the flies most haunt, it either hastily driveth them away, or kills them sooner after. The self same wil the common Allum beaten with Organy, and tempered with milk prevaile against the flies: for what plants and hearbs shall be sprinkled with this mixture, will not after be resorted unto, or touched or flies: The Bayberies with the black Neeswort beaten together, and infusing it in milk or water and honey mixed, doth like profit: for this mixture sprinkled on the plants and places where the flies most haunt, doth after as it were by a poyson hastily kill the flies, or otherwise force them to flie speedily away, never to return.

As touching remedies against the Frogges, which in Summer nights are wont to be disquieters to the wearied Husbandmen, through their daily labour, by chirping and loud noise making, let the Husbandman exercise this helpe or secret, borrowed of the skilful Greek *Africanus*, which is on this wise: Set on some bank (saith he) a Lanthorne lighted, or other bright light before them, or on some tree (fast by) so hang a light, that by the brightness of the same light, it may so shine upon them, as it were the Sunne, which handled on this wise, wil after cause them to leave their chirping and loud noise making: a practise tried by many of latter years.

The skilful Greek *Beritius* reporteth, that if the Husbandman bury in some banck fast by, the gaul of a Goat, the Frogs wil not afterward gather to that place.

CHAP. XXXIV

The rare practises and secrets, both of the ancient and latter writer of Husbandry against Serpents of the Garden, and any others, venoming as wil men as the Kitchin hearbs, trees, and fruits.

lorentius (a singular and diligent interpreter of the matters of the field) wrote, that Serpents in the Garden ground or elsewhere wil not lodge or abide, if the owner sow or plant in borders about, or in apt corners of the Garden, either the Worm-wood, Mugwort, or Southern-wood, which if these shall some where happen to haunt, then may the Gardener (as he writeth) drive them incontinent forth of the ground, if he make a smoke either with the Lilly roots, Harts horn, or Goats hoofs.

The skilful *Rutilius* uttereth, that all Serpents be forced out of the ground by every sower savour, and stinking smoke, flying abroad

Detail of a frog from a series of manuscript paintings of fruit drawn by John Tradescant the Elder in the first half of the seventeenth century.

A marginal illustration from The Hours of Anne of Brittany, c. *1510.*

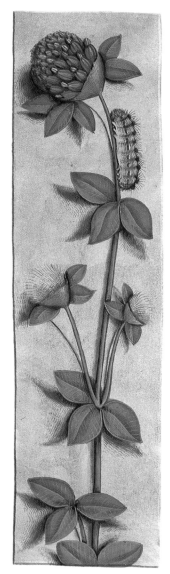

with the wind.

The learned *Democritus* affirmeth that the Serpents assuredly do die, if the Gardener strew or throw Oken leaves on them, or if any spitteth fasting into their mouth gaping or wide open.

The wel practised *Apuleius* writeth, that these stricken but once with a tough reed or willow rod, are mightily astonied, but giving them many strokes do recover and wax strong again. *Tarentinus* (a skilful writer of the Greek Husbandry) denieth that any can be harmed of a Serpent, if the person afore be anointed with the juyce of a Radish, or that he hath eaten of the Radish, which matter *Athenæus* and *Galen*, (with many other worthy Authors) ascribe to the Orenge or Lemon, and they confirm the same with a pleasant History.

The former *Florentius* uttereth another singular practise, against Serpents of the Garden, to be wrought after this manner: Lay (saith he) the fat of the Hart in the Garden earth, or else bury the Centory root, or the Geat stone, or else the Eagle, or Kites dung, and the Serpents wil refuse the ground, or at least not come near the place, and every venemous worm wil be driven away, if the Gardener by taking *Nigella, Pellitory, Galbanum*, of the Harts horn, Hissop, Brimstone, *Peucedanum*, and the Goats hoofs, shall diligently bring these to powder, and infusing the whole for a time in the strongest Vinegar, shall after make little bals of the mixture, with which thorow dried cause a savour and a smoke. For through the savour of these matters spersed in the aire, all creeping vermine will either hastily (for the great fear) forsake the ground, or die there incontinent. The same Author *Florentius* reporteth, that the Serpents may like be gathered on a heap into an old deep poudering Tub, as fish in a wele or bow net, if the same be deep set about that place of the Garden or Field, where these most lurk and haunt, for after the speedy resorting of these to the brink of it they fall willingly on, not able after to recover themselves out. *Pliny* writing of the withie named *Siler*, reporteth this, that the Serpents refuse both the tree and fruit, for which cause, the Husbandmen made them staves of the wood to carry about with them. But this by a most certain experience or triall, proved and confirmed, that by making a smoke with old shooes burned, the Serpents incontinent speed away, or these onely flie out of the Garden ground, field, or house, but such as are entred into men, by dead sleep in the Summer, in sleeping open mouthed, or with open mouth, in the field, do like come forth with the said smoke. Which matter *Marcus Gatinaria*, a famous Physitian, confirmeth, who reporteth, that the like happened to a certain man in his time, to whom after infinite medicines and most effectuous remedies were ministred, and none of them prevailed, at the last this imployed, fell out most luckily, and wonderfull of all others, in burning the leathers of old shooes, and receiving both smoke and savour of a Tunnel into the body. For as soon as this hideous beast (which was a mighty Adder) felt the savour of this smoke, he was seen to the standers about to come out at the fundament, to the mighty astonishment and wonder of all the beholders. And this worthy secret easie to be prepared, I thought here good to place, that the same, a like case hapning, might be profitable to every person. But in this place is not to be omitted, that Serpents greatly hate the fire, not for the same cause, that this dulleth their sight, but because the nature of fire is to resist poyson. These also hate the strong savour far flying, which the Garlike and red Onions procure. They love the Savin-tree, the Ivy, and Fenell, as Toads do the Sage, and Snakes the hearb Rocket: but they are mightily displeased and sorest hate the Ash-tree, insomuch that the Serpents neither to the morning nor longest evening shadows of it, will draw near, but rather shun the same, and flie far off. As a like manner *Pliny* reporteth, was on a time proved, by inclosing a Serpent, within the large circle made of green Ash-tree leaves, in the middle of a quick fire made, to the terrour of the Serpent, for that end to prove whether she had rather run over the circle, then draw near to the fire, which neverthelesse (the fire kindling more and more) at the last rather crept to the fire, where she perished, then by any meanes would draw near to the circle of the Ash-tree leaves. Yet here learn, the marvellous benignity of nature, which permitteth not the Serpents to come forth of the earth, before the Ash-tree buddeth forth, not to hide them again, before the leaves fall off. The singular Poet *Virgil* saith, that the smoke made of Rosen or *Galbanum*, doth hastily chase and drive the Serpents away.

These hitherto uttered, for the driving away and killing of Serpents. But here was almost forgotten, that the leaves of Fern, do chase away the Serpent: for which cause many skilfull thinke it profitable, either to sow or straw the Fern in such places where the

Serpents haunt. The Neapolitane *Rutilius* addeth, that if the leaves of the same be turned, they (with the savour onely) will fly or creep hastily away, yea and force them to change their lodgings, far from the Garden ground or field.

Here a doubt may be made, whether the same be to purpose here to recite, that the worthy *Albertus* reporteth of the round *Aristolochia* with the field Frog, and a certain proportion of writing Inke diligently laboured, and mixed with these, to make the Serpents immediately to quaile as dead, if any of the mixture be written withall, and thrown before them.

But I think it high time to come unto the remedies, which are both ready and easie to be prepared.

If that any shall be smitten of a Serpent, unless he have a Fever, and drinketh a certain quantity of the juyce of Ash leaves, with pleasant white wine, and applyeth also of the fresh leaves to the place bitten, shall in short time see a worthy secret, greatly to be marvelled at, and by happy successe proved of many.

Here briefly to conclude, if the Gardener bestoweth the fresh Elder flowers where the Serpents daily haunt, they will hastily depart the place, yea these by report (artly bestowed in the Garden ground) do in short time destroy the the Mothes, the Canker worms and Palmers breeding in trees.

The other helps and remedies necessary to be uttered in this Chapter, shall in apt places be declared in the second part, where we purpose to treat particularly of most hearbs growing in the Garden.

CHAP. XXXV

 liny reporteth, that if slips of the green *Heliotropium*, be set round about the place where the Scorpions frequent, that they will not after creep thence. But if the owner either lay or strew upon the Scorpions, the whole hearb, they incontinent (as he affirmeth) die.

That skilfull writer *Diophanes* (in his Greek commentaries of Husbandry) uttereth, and the like many other, that the fresh Radish, either laid or strewed on the Scorpions, killeth them incontinent.

To these, if any anointeth the hands circumspectly with the juyce of the Radish, he may after handle Scorpions, or any other venemous thing without danger.

This Author further addeth, that a smoke made with *Saudaracha* and Butter, or the fat of a Goat, will drive away both them and other venemous things, and by burning one Scorpion, all the other flie forth of the ground.

If any boileth the Scorpion that stung him, or any other in Oile, and anointeth the sore place with the same, it shall greatly availe.

The like commeth to passe, if he may kill and bruise the same on

The laudable devises and cunning helps against the Scorpions, Todes, Garden-mise, Weasels, and all other greater beasts, wasting and corrupting as wel the Kitchin hearbs as fruits.

the stinging; but perilous will the same stinging be, if he refraine not the eating of Basil all that day of the stinging. *Florentius* reporteth, that the juyce of the Fig tree leaves dropped on the stinging, mightily availeth.

The learned *Pliny* affirmeth, that the ashes of the Scorpion drunk in Wine (if the fit of the Fever be not upon the person) to be a singular remedy, as the pouder of worms burned, to persons having Worms, or to beasts the like ministred, and any bit-of a mad Dog, if the haires of the same be burned and drunk, do greatly availe.

The Toades (as the Greek and Latin professors of Husbandry write) may be driven forth of the Garden ground, with those remedies that the Serpents: for which cause, the remedies and helps against them to repeat, I think here superfluous.

Then, as now, one of the simplest ways of keeping the mice at bay is to have a cat. This one is being distracted from its duties by the attentions of its owner. Detail from a painting by David Teniers II (1610-90).

The Mice (as the learned *Apuleius* writeth) wil in no manner harm or waft those seeds commited to the earth, which before the sowing are steeped a time in the gall of an Oxe.

They will be killed in the ground, if the Gardener shall stop their commings forth with the fresh leaves of *Rhodophanes*.

There be (of the Greek witers of Husbandry) which will, that like portions of the wild Cucumber or Henbane, or the bitter Almonds and black Nosewort be orderly bruised, and tempered with Meal, the same after wrought into bals with Oile, to be laid at the holes of the field and house Mice. *Pliny* writeth, that the seeds (before the bestowing in the earth) infused either in the gall of a Weasel, or the ashes of him committed to the earth with seeds, doth like defend them from being harmed of Mice, yet the plants springing out of these are greatly misliked, for that they then give the savour of such a ranck beast, so that the seeds are better commended to be steeped afore in the gall of an Oxe.

The skilful *Africanus* uttereth, that the Gardener may either kill or drive away Weasels, if he mixt salt Armoniack with wheat paste, and lay of the same in such place where these most haunt. Others there be, which wil the careful Gardener to get one alive, and cutting off both taile and testicles, to let him passe again, for by that means others (perceiving the like sight) wil depart the place, the easie experience of which matter, wil after bring a credit to thee in the same. Por the driving away of the greater beasts, conceive these remedies following, that if the Garder shall water the seeds bestowed with the olde Urine, in which the ordure of a Dog shall be infused for a time, they shall after be defended in the growing up, from the spoile of great beasts.

The self same doth the worthy *Democritus* affirm to come to pass (as I afore uttereth) if that the owner take to the number of ten River or Sea Crevisses, and in putting them into an earthen pot full of water, he set the same in the sun for ten daies, to be wel heated and vaporated through the hot beames, which thus handled, let him sprinckle on the beds and plants, that he would have defended from the aire and great beasts: yet may he not water the younger plants, but every third day, until these be grown up stronger. The skilful *Africanus* and other worthy writers of Husbandry report, that if either the *Pionie* or hearb *Personata* be buried, or otherwise sowen about bancks or borders in the Garden or field, are after (as by a secret protection) preserved, that neither the great nor smaller beasts wil after spoile the plants there growing. But if the Husbandman would have his trees preserved from being sore eaten and wasted of the greater beasts, then let him exercise (after the mind of *Pliny*) this easie practise, in casting or sprinckling on the leaves, the water in which Oxe dung hath been dissolved, so that he be sure those times that rain will fall within a day after, to the clean purging again of the branches and leaves of that savour, a matter in very deed wittily devised for the purpose.

Henbane and hart's-tongue. From an early sixteenth-century Tudor pattern book.

CHAP. XXXVI

The skilfull practises and remedies against Haile, Lightnings, and Tempests, beating downe and spoiling the Kitchin hearbs, trees, and fruits.

or the Hail, which for the more part destroyeth both the labours of the Oxen and men, conceive these few remedies following: That if the Husbandman would avoid the same danger at hand or ready to fall, then let him draw about the the ground (whether it be Field, Orchard, or Garden) the skin of a Seale, or Crocodil, or *Hiena*, and hang it after at the entry or comming in of the place, as the worthy *Philostratus*, in his Greek commentaries of Husbandry, hath noted. Others there be, which seeing the haile at hand, by holding up a mighty glass, do so take the image of a dark cloud, directly over the place, to the end the object by the same remedy (as *Rutilius* reporteth, may offend) whereby as doubled it may give place the other, and on such wise be speedily averted and moved away.

There were some (as *Philostratus* writeth) which with the right hand drawing the Marish Tortoise on her back, laboured so about the Garden ground or field, and returned to the place where they began, they so laid her upright in the furrow made with her back, and shord clods of either side, that she might not fall, neither to one nor the other side, but abide steady upright, to the end she might so behold the big and thick clouds, directly over the place. And the same at such times they exercised in the sixt hour of the day or night. Certain others (seeming to be of greater skill) when the hail approached, did spread over every space in the Garden or field, white Vine, or fastened in some place right against the Tempest imminent alive Owl, with the wings spread abroad, which two remedies also much avail against the lightnings an hail, as saith the singular writer of Husbandry *Junius Columella*, in his little treatise of the Garden.

To utter here the popular help against Thunder, Lightnings, and the danger out hail, when the tempest approcheth through the cloud arising, as by the loud noise of Guns shot here and there, with a loud sound of Bels, and such like noises which may happen: I think the same not necessary nor properly available to the benefit of the Garden.

The famous learned man *Archibius*, which wrote unto *Antiochus* King of *Syria*, affirmeth, that tempests shall not be harmful to plants or fruits, if the speckled Toade inclosed in a new eathern pot, be be buried in the middle of the Garden or Field. Others there are, which hang the feathers of the Eagle or Seales skin, in the middle of the Garden, or at the four corners of the same.

For these three, as by a certain secret property (and for truth) by a marvellous regugnancy do resist the Lightnings, and that of these (the abovesaid) in no manner to be harmed or blasted, is to memory of the posterity committed, and by the experiences or trials of many skilful men confirmed. Wherefore *Tiberius Cesar* (as reporteth *Suetonius*) was wont to weare a Garland of Bayes, and to cover his proper tent all

OPPOSITE *An engraving of 1610 shows the botanic garden founded at Leiden by Charles l'Ecluse in the late sixteenth century. Note the correct orientation of the garden and the presence of favourable southerly winds. It might be wondered whether the curiosities engraved below the picture are objects of study or talismans used to ward off inclement weather.*

over with Seale skins, as such times as Thunder and Lightning hapned, supposing himself to be defended from these, which he marvellously feared. *Pliny* reporteth that *Bulbus* (not for the smalness onely of his body) escaped the force of lightning, but through a secret and naturall repugnance doth this availe against the stroke of lightning.

CHAP. XXXVII

o most men it is manifest, that there are two kinds of celestial injures, the one that men name tempests, in which the Hail, Storm, and such like are meant.

These (when any happen) are named a mightier violence and working of heaven moved forward, as *Pliny* reporteth, by the fearful stars, which be *Virgilia, Hyades,*

The laudable devices and helps against frost, blasting of trees, mists, and rust, which be enemies as wel to Garden hearbs as fruits.

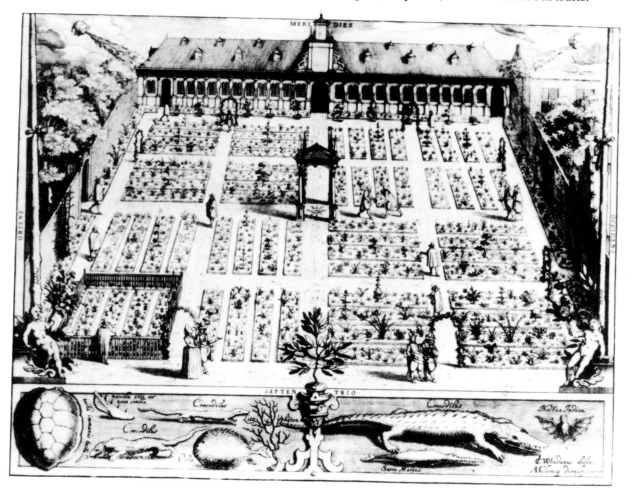

A late sixteenth-century stained-glass window showing the month of March when the weather is at its most unpredictable.

Canicula, Arcturus, Fidicula, Hædi, Orion, Aquila, and sundry others, carefully observed of the writers of Husbandry and Physick, and of men most diligently noted.

The other kind is wont to happen, the aire being calm and quiet, and in fair nights, no feeling to be discerned, but when the same is to come to passe and wrought, which bewailed calamity is one while wont to be named rusty; an other whiles burning, and an other whiles blasting, that to all crescent things is a sterility, and at one word a destruction, so that all is caused by heaven, and wont especially to happen in the Spring time. The blasting and burning of the blossoms of Apple-trees, the flowers of Vines and Corn, are caused through the injury of frosts happening in the night, and not as many report, to be wrought through the Suns sharp heat, burning hastily up the dew, or the moisture entring in, and corrupting the heads of Corn. The same also wasting the tender buds, plants, and branches is commonly named burning, for that it burneth and consumeth in places so black as any shale. The blasting besides of the tender blossoms of Trees and Vines, is named sideration, for that this especially is caused through the blast and striking of some constellation. To these we add the rust, as a mighty enemy to fruits. The worthy *Pliny* reporteth, that the rust and burning, be caused only of cold, which happeneth in the night time, and before the Sun rising, so that the Sunne is not worker of these. And the time when the like succeedeth, is known to be, after the mind of sundry skilful writers of Husbandry, at the change or ful Moon, some stars then on the first bignesse aiding in the rising or setting. The suspected times, and daies of the rust, for judging of the good and evil success of fruits is known in April, according to the

The planting of vines and arbours, from a late fifteenth-century manuscript of a treatise by Pietro de Crescenzi.

falling out of St. *George* and St. *Markes* day, and the ninth day of May, for the calmenesse and clearnesse of the aire. This celestial sterility doth neither happen nor cannot every year, for the proper courses of the stars, both in the descending and ascending in heaven, with the radiations or aspect one to another. In the which working, who cannot but wonder, and for the same honour and reverence the marvellous benignity and goodness of almighty God towards mankind? Yet of the constellations afore mentioned, and the others which are infinite in number, the diligent antiquity onely feared three of these greatly, and observed them for that cause, as the diligent *Pliny* noted, and to memory committed. First the constellation *Virgilie* for the fruits, the constellation *Aquila* for the Corn, and the constellation *Canicula* for the gathering of fruits, so that these for the same cause were named the judicial stars, to foreknow the seasons by. In whose dayes of the first appearance, if the aire clear and calme sent down a kindly and feeding juyce to the earth, then was it a sure note to them, that such things sown, would grow and increase prosperously. Contrary-wise, if the Moon at those times sprinckled a dewie cold on the plants and crescent things, then as a bitternesse mixed contrary to the sweet nourishing and juyce, the same so slew and killed the tender things, shot forth appearing above the earth. But to come to the matter, there is neither frost, hail, storm, nor tempest, so harmful to certain fields or Garden grounds, through which they at any time cause the sterility and penury of Victuals, as the rust and burning heat do, for these falling and working in open Countries, procure for the more part through their harms a publique calamity and present death, to the avoiding of which, shall here be uttered these skilfull remedies, invented of the ancient writers of Husbandry. If the carefull Gardener would withstand the force of frost and rust approching, then let him burn store of chaffe if such plenty by there or near at hand, but for lack of the same, may he use the dry weeds plucked up out of the Garden or Field, and the bigge Thistles, or other wast fruits in many places of the same, especially toward that way which the wind then bloweth, for on such wise handled, *(Diophanes* in his precepts of Husbandry writeth) that the evil nigh or at hand is averted. The self same practise may be used against thick and dark Mists. *Beritius* in his Greek precepts of Husbandry giveth warning, that the Husbandman or Gardener diligently mark, whether the same be gathered in the aire, which ready to fall, let him then burn incontinent the left horn, of the Oxe, with either Cow or Oxe dung, making with them a mighty smoke round about the Garden ground or field, but the smoke especially directed by the wind, in fleeing against it. The worthy *Apuleius* wrote, that the smoke of three river Crevisses, burned with the Oxe or Goats dung, or with chaffe to be a most sure help and remedy against the like, that if the same be already fallen, I mean the rust, the Gardener may recover the harm after this manner, as the skilful *Beritius* reporteth, in taking the roots or leaves of the wild Cucumber or *Calocynthis*, which after the bruising and infusing in water for a night, sprinckle and wet the places wel taken with the rust before the Sun rising. The like may the Gardener work and do, with the *Fig* or Oke tree ashes, sprinckled in the place endamaged with rust.

All seeds of the Garden or Field are defended, as reporteth *Anatolius*, from all injuries and Monsters, if the Husbandman or Gardener before the committing of seeds to the earth, doth infuse them for a time in the juyce of the wild Cucumber.

If the Gardener or Husbandman, as *Apuleius* witnesseth, shall stick and plant round about the Garden ground or field, many slips, stocks, and branches of the Bay-tree, these wil after availe against the rust, for into them all the harme of the rust passeth and entereth, as the like many times hath been observed of the skilfull, which very often is wont to happen in the dewie Countries, Vallies, and in places where big wind of a sudden doth many times blow. Thus much for the rust being enemy to fruits. Against the burning heat which peculiarly is wont to happen to Vines. The learned *Pliny* willeth the Husband-men to burne three live Crevisses, or to hang them alive on the Tree or Vine.

The Greeks (as certain Latin writers have noted) did sow Beanes as well within as without the Garden Ground or Field, to avoid by that means the frost falling, or at least to availe against the frost.

These instructions for the workmanly handling and ordering of a Garden plot, shall at this present suffice, and like the remedies, against the harms and injuries that commonly annoy, whereby all seeds and plants bestowed in the same, may with gladsome chear to the Gardener prosper and increase, which the gentle Reader shall conceive to be borrowed out of the works both of the old and new writers of Husbandry, as wel Greeks as Latins, that by great study and painful labour, searched and observed the most of these, or else not attempted of any part, to be published and made common to all men. Besides these you shall well conceive, that the better part were confirmed in our time, by the experience of sundry skilfull men in the matters of Husbandry, and by earnest sute purchased, which to be brief, being thankfully accepted, the Author hath his due reward; And so an end of this first part of the Gardeners Labyrinth. *Vale*.

THE CHAPTERS CONTEINED IN THE SECOND PART.

ABOVE *Betony and bugloss from an early sixteenth-century Tudor pattern book.*

LEFT *A vigorous climbing gourd from a stained-glass window of 1631, at Christ Church, Oxford.*

BELOW *Mallow and mint from an early sixteenth-century Tudor pattern book.*

FINIS TABULÆ.

Seventeenth-century painters delighted in depicting these probably idealized colossal vegetables and fruits. This painting is anonymous but in the style of the Northern French School, and is dated 1607.

The Second Part of the
Gardeners-Labyrinth,

Uttering such skilful Experience, and worthy secrets, about the particular sowing and removing of the most Kitchin Herbs, with the witty ordering of other dainty Herbs, delectable Flowers, pleasant Fruits, and fine Roots, as the like hath not heretofore been uttered of any. Besides, the Physick benefits of each Herb annexed, with the commodity of waters distilled out of them, right profitable to be known.

LONDON,

Printed by *June Bell*, and are to be sold at the East-end of Christ-Church, 1651.

Tradescant's Orchard from the first half of the seventeenth century. The May Cherry. A grasshopper, a fly, a snail, and a butterfly.

Tradescant's Orchard from the first half of the seventeenth century. The Blue Grape.

Artichoke watercolour study by Jacques Le Moyne de Morgues, c. 1568.

here in my first part I have fully satisfied (as I trust) the expectation of the Husbandly Gardener and owner in all such matters, which may appear needfull or requisite to be learned and known, for the better aid, in possessing of a commodius and delectable Garden: in like manner I purpose to aid the carefull Husbandman or Gardener, after the possibility of my skill in this second part, with such skilfull helps and secrets, as are required about the artly sowing, and particular bestowing as wel of the kitchin, as other dainty Herbs, pleasant Fruits, delectable Flowers, and fine Roots, which at large I purpose to utter in the same, and likewise the Physick benefits to each herb I add, with other matters profitable, to the end the owner or Gardener may with better good will be moved to bestow an earnest care and diligence about the often removing, as well of dainty flowers and herbs, with the clipping pressing down, breaking away, and cutting away the ends of the roots, that these may grow the thicker and bigger both in herb and root. All which instructions and rare secrets, are part borrowed out of the worthy works and treasures of the Greek and Latin professors of Husbandry, and part purchased by friendship and earnest sute, of the skilful observers and witty searchers in our time of laudable secrets in Garden matters, serving as well for the use and singular comfort of mans life, as to a proper gain and delight of the mind.

The like of which already uttered, may the owner both see and know by that plant, which in Gardens every where, as well those in the Countrey as in the City, is placed none so common, none more plentifull, nor oftener used among Kitchin Herbs, then this familiar pot-hearb, named the Colewort, which by a diligence of the husbandly Gardener, may wel serve in the coldest Winter, in the stead of other pot-hearbs, so that this herb by good reason, known to be not onely profitable for the pot, but to the uses of Physick right necessary, hath moved me the rather to begin first with the Colewort, in uttering what rare and diligence is required about the sowing, often removing, clipping and dressing of the same, being before bestowed in beds workmanly prepared.

CHAP. I

 he worthy *Marcus Cato* in his Husbandry preferred the Colewort before all other pot-hearbs, and the learned *Pliny* in like manner ascribed a principality to the same of all Garden herbs, for which cause, I purpose here to treat first of this herb, that many of the Latins also for the mighty stem and armes like branches named the Colewort. Such is the nature of this plant, that the same refuseth no condition of aire, for which cause it may be committed to the earth in any time of the

What helps and secrets are to be learned in the sowing and often removing of the Colewort.

year. This plant desireth a fat earth, and wel turned in with dung, but the clayie, gravelly, or sandy, this refuseth, except a flood of rain water shall now and then help.

The Colewort prospereth the better, being placed toward the South, but this standing open to the North, not so wel encreaseth, although both in tast and strength it overcometh in the same place, for though the cold aire and frosts, the herb is caused the tenderer and pleasanter.

The Colewort joyeth on a hill side, or the ground steeping down, it delighteth in dung, and increaseth by the often weeding, as the worthy *Rutilius* hath noted: when six leaves shal be sprung up, or but five, the same then must be removed, but in such manner handled, that the root afore the setting again, be anointed with soft Cow dung, which ought to be ordered in a warm day, if it be Winter, but in Summer time, then at such time as the Sun shall be going down in the West.

The most ancient of the Greeks divided the Colewort into three kinds onely, as the crisped, which they named *Selinoidea*, for the similitude of the leaves of Parcely, the same of them *Lean*, for the broad leaves issuing or growing forth of the stem, for which cause, some named it *Cauloden*. And the same which properly is named *Crambe*, growing up with thinner leaves, both single and very thick. The Colewort becommeth the bigger, through the earth daily turned light about the body. And particularly to write, the common Coleworts, which they name the long or green, ought to be sown from the middle of August, or from the beginning of September, that these may be grown up into big leaves to serve in Winter and in the Lent time. The husbandly Gardener or owner may plant young Celeworts in October, and set them again in December, to possesse the leaves in the sharp Winter, and the seeds in June and July, and to make them also grow as big tuft, as in the other seasons of the year, and as tender or rather tenderer, although not so delectable.

The Colewort may be caused both big and pleasant, if thrust into a hole, you set unto the leaves in earth, that no part of the stems be left bare, for doubt of perishing; and as the same groweth up in heigth, and the earth shrinking from it, so continually raise the earth high up to the body, and cut away the outward leaves, so that no more then the top of the leaves may appear above the earth. The Colewort often weeded about, and workmanly dunged waxeth the stronger, and causeth the Colewort to be of a greater increase, and tender of leaf.

The red Coleworts naturally grow through the abundance of hot dung, or through the watering or wel moistening of them with the Lees of wine, or else by the planting of them in hot places, where the Sun daily shineth a long time together.

Never take the tops of the Romane, crisped, nor the other for your turn and use, but alwaies the thick leaves downward, from the heads or tops.

A cabbage from Fuchsius Fuchs De historium stirpium, *1542, (one of the leading botanical works of the period).*

All the sorts or kinds or Coleworts may be planted at all seasons, so that the times and earth be neither too cold, no too hot. When you mind to set them again in holes made with a Dibble, cut away the ends of the roots, lest in the setting into the earth, they fold or bend to the ground, which harms them greatly, and onely those of a big growth are to be set again, which although they slowly take root, yet are they caused the stronger. And the roots of these, neither desire any soft dung, nor river mud to be anointed or laid about them, or to be set in a soft earth, in that they joy and prosper in a ground meanly dry, although the outward leaves wither, untill that time a sweet rain falling, recover their strength. Some water the younger Colworts with salt water to cause them grow tender, &c. as afore uttered.

Colewort greatly availeth against drunkennesse; of which it is now a common exercise among the Egyptians, that greatly love wine, to boil the Colewort with their meats, that in eating of the like prepared, they may so avoid the annoyance of wine after drunk. *Paxamus* (a Greek writer of Husbandry) reporteth, that if any poure a little quantity of wine by drops, into the liquor of the Colewort boiling, the same after seetheth no more, but quailed in strength, is corrupted and changed in liquor. By a like a man may contrary gather, that the person which would drink plenty of wine, without being overcome with the same, ought to eat afore a quantity of the raw Colewort with meat. But for this matter, hear the sentence of the singular man (*M. Cato*) who willeth the person purposed to drink much wine at a feast, and to dine or sup freely, to eat afore supper, as great a quantity of the raw Colewort as he wil with good Vinegar, and being also set down to supper, to eat five leaves raw, these then wil cause him to be as one that had neither eaten or drunk, whereby he may drink as much as he wil, through the marvellous repugnancy of the herb with wine, as afore uttered, and like noted by *Agrius*, in the worthy work of *M. Varo*.

The Colewort in like manner, ought not to be planted nigh to the Organy, Rue, or Sowes bread, for the drying quality consisting in them, so that these either sown or planted nigh to the Colewort, and other very moist herbs, do generally hinder, and cause them to wither. A like matter worketh the Lavender, set in beds near to moist herbs, through the heat consisting in it, as the Radish doth, which through the proper tartnesse or sharpness being in it, burneth any moist and tender plant growing nigh to the same.

This also is worthy memory which *Athenæus reporteth, that in Athens* (in time past) the Colewort was wont to be prepared with meat for women with child, instead of a certain defensative against annoyances.

There is also made of the Ashes of Colewort, infused in water, a salt, in that the same possesseth a Nitrous substance (as afore uttered) through whose benefit, if this be meanly boiled, and taken in broth (as we shall hereafter write) doth loose the belly.

CHAP. II

What worthy instructions to be conceived, in the sowing and ordering of the Beete for the Pot.

he Beete more often eaten at poor mens tables, ought to be bestowed in a most fat earth, and sowen at any season, but rather the seeds to be committed to the earth about the middle of December, and unto March, and like in August, to possesse seeds, which may endure for three years. The seeds ought rather to be thick then thin sown in beds, and shot up to some growth, as that four or five leaves be sprung above the earth; then in Summer time, the plants are to be removed, if the beds afore were moistned or wet with showers, as the singular *Columella* writeth: but if the ground be dry in harvest time, then to remove them where showers lately fell and softned the earth.

The Beet loveth or joyeth to be often digged about, and to be fed with much dung, for which cause the young plants to be set again, ought after the ends of the roots cut off, and the tops of the leaves clipped, to be striked or anointed about with new Cow-dung, and then bestowed in beds a good distance asunder, which after the plants be more grown up, to be diligently weeded about, and the unprofitable weeds thrown away, for by the meanes they grow the fairer and bigger, being as I said, bestowed in fat earth and wel dunged.

The Beet may be caused to grow big and broad, as *Sostion* in his Greek instructions of Husbandry affirmeth, if before the Beet shall be grown up into a stem, and shot forth in stalks, the owner lay upon the head a broad Tile, Potsheard, or some other thing of weight, to presse the top gently down, for by that practise or meanes in the weighty bearing down, the Beet is caused to spread into a breadth with the leaves.

The Beet becommeth the whiter and far greater, if the Husbandly Gardener anoint or cover the root with new Oxe or Cow dung, and that he cut the root and top of the young Beet, as the Leeke handled before the setting, and after a bigger growth to presse it down, as afore uttered. To have the beet grow red, water the plant with Lees, or set the same in a hot place, where the Sun daily shineth long. The Beet rosted in embers, taketh away the stinking smell and savour of Garlike eaten, if the same be eaten upon or after the Garlike, as the Greek *Menander* hath noted. This is marvellous to heare by the seed of the Beet, that it yeildeth not the whole perfection or perfect seeds in the first year, but an increase in seeds somewhat more the second year, and in the third year a full perfection from the first sowing: And *Pliny* reporteth, that the Beet speedier commeth forward with the old seed, then with new: for which cause, the matter demanded of a skilful Gardener, reporteth of experience, that the seeds of the Beet to sow, ought not to be gathered before the Beet had borne a third yeare, after the first sowing: of which seeds sown in due time of the Moon, the best Beets come; and this not to be forgotten, that when the taste of wine, through the Colewort (as afore uttered) is corrupted in the Vessel, the same again by the savour of the Beet, as through the leaves put into it, is recovered. These hitherto of the Beet.

CHAP. III

here are two kinds of this Blete, as the white and the red or black, both at this day very wel known, through their growing as common in the Field or Garden. The stalks and leaves of the red wax so red in the growing, that they appear as dyed with a Scarlet colour, but after a further growth, in time these from that colour are changed into a purple, and at length wax black to the eye, of which the same also is named of some the black Blete. The root besides of this herb in the breaking appeareth so red as any blood.

The white Blete possesseth or rather sendeth forth branches and leaves like to the Beet, and the same without sharpness or biting, being unsavory, and each is of the same condition, that it speedily springeth in the Garden, as *Pliny* reporteth.

And the white or red Blete may be sown in any earth, but rather in a wel dressed ground, in the moneth of March, as the skilful Neapolitane *Rutilius* willeth, which strongly grown in the earth, or fully come up, continueth and yearly renueth of it self, without any proper sowing, so that in time this so taketh root by the seeds yearly falling, that the Gardener after can hardly weed the same out of his ground if he would: wherefore this once sown in a fertile earth, prospereth many years by the yearly yield and falling of the seeds, and requireth neither raking nor weeding about it, as the worthy *Palladius* reporteth.

What rare helps and secrets so to be learned, in the sowing and setting of the Blete.

CHAP. IV

he Garden Orage for the pot, ought by the agreement of the skilful, to be sown in the moneth of March and April, and in the other moneths following unto Harvest, the apt seasons and times herein considered. But in some places are seeds bestowed in moneth of December, in a wel dressed and dunged earth, and the plants better prosper being thin sown. These also may be sown by themselves in beds, and together with other herbs, and they alwaies desire to be cut or broken off with an iron instrument, that they cease not yeilding forth of young. The Orage joyeth in the often watering, if the season and ground be very drie. The seeds of the Arage ought diligently to be covered, incontinent after they are bestowed in the earth, and the

What diligence and skill is required in the sowing and setting of the Garden Orage.

roots of the herbs to be often digsted under, and left hollow of earth, that the roots may grow within the stronger.

This herb is supposed to grow the greater, being not removed at all, and for that cause the plants thin bestowed in beds, do evermore joy and increase the better. The plant in like manner increaseth and becometh the sooner great, through the often and diligent weeding exercised about the same. To be brief, this plant after the mind of *Rutilius*, requireth to be watered all the hot and drie seasons, unto the time of Harvest, in that the same delighteth and increaseth the faster, through the daily moisture bestowed on it.

CHAP. V

What singular skill and secrets is to be known in the sowing, removing and setting again of the worthy hearb named Sperage.

he field or Garden Sperage, joyeth in a fat, moist, and wel dressed earth, and the hearb grown up to height, hath by every leaf growing forth, a red berry hanging down, in which a seed is, that the hearb in the sowing commeth of.

The seeds to be committed to the earth, as the worthy *Dydimus* in his Greek instructions of Husbandry reporteth, ought to be bestowed in the spring time, into little holes of three fingers deep in which the owner or Gardener may put two or three seeds together, wel half a foot distant one from the other, which thus bestowed, require after no more travel nor care for the first yeare, saving the digging about, and plucking up of weeds growing among them.

But for the sowing and increase of the Sperages, it shall be to great purpose and commodity, to heare the witty precepts and instructions of *Marcus Cato, Columella, Pliny*, and *Palladius* like agreeing.

The seeds (say say) as much as three fingers can take up at one time, may the owner or Gardener workmanly put, and lightly cover, in earth both fatted and well dunged, and in very little furrows, so straight made as a line, which on this wise handled, will by the fortieth day after grow so inward in the earth, that the roots shot forth, will clasp and fold one another, as if they joyned together in one, and for the same named of the ancient Gardeners earth Spunges. If the places in which you purpose to commit the seed shall be drie, then these laid on soft dung, lying alow in the furrowes, shall on such wise be ordered and covered, as if they lay or were bestowed in little Hives. But in a contrary manner shall the owner or Gardener work and do, in continuall moist places, for the seeds in like places shall be bestowed on high ridges, workmanly raised with dung, that the moisture may lesse annoy the plants in the growing, which onely ought to be fed or watered with the moisture passing by, and not still to abide in that moisture, to be cloyed with it. The seeds on such wise bestowed, will yeild a Sperage in the first year, which the owner or Gardener shal then break or cut off beneath. But if the owner assay to pull at it near

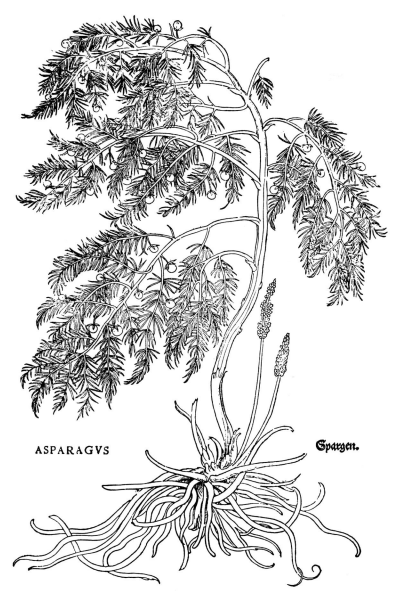

ASPARAGVS   Spargen.

*Asparagus from Fuchsius
Fuchs* De historium stirpium,
1542.

the ground, the smal roots (as yet tender) and weak in the earth, may
happen to rise and follow with the whole Spunge, which therefore
workmanly broken off, ought thus to be fed and nourished in one
proper place, growing still for two years with dung and diligent
weeding. In the other years following, the Sperage shall not be
broken off by the stalk, but plucked up by the root, that the same may
so open the eyes of his branching, for except the plant be handled on
such wise, the stems broken off, wil not increase the eyes of the
spunges, but rather grow as blind, so that these wil not suffer the
Sperage to yeild or send forth the proper increase. The same shall the

Gardener preserve, of which he gathered the feed, and burn after the crops and knobbed ends or joynts of the same herb. After this, about the winter time, shal the owner lay or bestow on the spunges, both ashes and dung, which the learned M. *Cato* rather willeth to be sheeps dung. There is another manner and way of sowing by spunges onely, which after two years ought to be removed into a sunny and wel dunged place. The like furrows ought to be made wel a foot distant one from the other, and not above twelve fingers deep, in which the tender and young spunges are to be set, that lightly covered with earth, they may easily spring and shoot up. But in the spring time, before they shall come up or appear above the ground, the Gardener or owner with a forked iron, commonly named a Dibbel, shal so loose the earth, that the end of it may appear out, and the root of the herb loosed from the ground, may by that means increase to a more bignesse.

The same *M. Cato* willeth the plant to be raked and diligently weeded about, but so handled in the digging about or weeding, that the roots of the plant be not loosed, or in the weeding by it be otherwise feebled in the treading down.

In the winter time the little grove of Sperages shall be covered over with thin and light mattresses or straw, lest it should be bitten and greatly endamaged with the frosts and cold aire, which in the spring time shall be opened and uncovered again, and fed with dung about the roots that the plants may the speedier come forward and increase, through the comfortable feeding of the dung and moisture, orderly done.

The worthy *Dydimus* (in his Greek instructions of husbandry) reporteth, and after him the learned *Pliny*, that many Sperages do spring up thorow the hornes of wild Rams broken into gross pouder, and these strewed along in little furrows, and after the light covering with earth, often watered, which although it seemed not credible to the worthy *Diosoorides*, and that he much misliked the reason of the same, yet if the Gardener or owner shall make a proof or trial, he wil after confesse (I dare affirm) this experiment to be most true.

There be which more marvellously report, even that the whole hornes of Rams, not broken asunder, nor cut into smal pieces, but onely bored thorow in many places, and then bestowed in the earth, to bring forth or yeild in short time Sperages, which if the owner would prossesse of them for all the yeare to feed on, when he gathereth the fruit, must then in the digging about (as the said *Dydimus* writeth, open those roots, which scatter and spread in the top of the Turf, for the young plant thus ordered, will speedily send forth new tender stems, and yeild Sperages, which lightly boiled in water and fresh broth, and to the same both salt and oyle, or sweet butter orderly mixed, and a little quantity of Vinegar poured upon, wil after yeild a singular delight to the eaters thereof.

But in this place I think it necessary to be remembered, that the Sperages require a smal boiling, for too much or long boiled, they

An asparagus plant from Hortus Sanitatis, c. *1497.*

become corrupt or without delight in the eating.

Of which the worthy Emperour *Drusus*, willing to demonstrate the speedy success of a matter, was wont to say, the same should be sooner done then the Sperage boiled.

As touching the making of the sauce or pickle, the tendes stalks sprinkled with salt, and wrought up in round heaps, ought so to be let alone to sweat in the shadow, after to be diligently washed with their own liquor, until they be sufficiently abated, and cleared of the moisture in them, at the least clensed from the pickle, and in the laying on of a weight (after such manner) pressed forth. Then poure into an apt vessel two parts of Vinegar, and one of the pickle, which workmanly thickened with drie Fenell seeds, in such manner as the tender stalks and leaves may wel be pressed down and covered in the same, and that the liquor reach up unto the top or brim of the earthen pot.

CHAP. VI

 his plant aptest for the Lent time (for that the same is oftner or more common used in that season) may in any good ground be bestowed, for it commeth up very wel in every place. And the seeds are to be committed to the earth in the monethes of September and October, to serve for the Lent ensuing, for that it is the first Pot-herb which is found in Gardens about the Lent time. But in the monethes of December, January, February, and March, for all the Summer following. And this plant very wel indureth the extremity of times and seasons, as the cold, frosts, and snow. And although Spinage commeth wel up in any ground, yet the earth ought to be diligently laboured before, and the same to be somewhat moist. The Plants after the comming up, which appear by the seventh day after the sowing, need no weeding to be done about them, but onely to clip off the tops of tender leaves, whereby they may grow up the comlier and fairer to the eye. If the Gardener would have the bed of Spinage indure a long time, and to profit, he ought to cut half the bed along at one time, and the other half at an other time. This pot herb (after the tops cut off and thrown away) ought to be sodden without water, in that the same (in the seething) yeildeth much moisture, for contented with the liquor, it refuseth any other broth added, so that this otherwise sodden, loseth the kindly and naturall juyce of the same, and besides too hastily drowned or overcome with the same. This being very tender after the seething, ought to be finely chopped with a wooden knife, ortherwise stamped and turned often in the beaten of it, which wrought up into round heaps, and fryed in the sweetest oile or butter, must so be prepared with a quantity of Verjuyce and Pepper bruised, that it may the more delight the tast.

What skill and and observation to be followed in the sowing, and ordering of the Spinage.

CHAP. VII

What skill and diligence is required in the sowing and ordering of the Garden Sorrell.

he Sorrell of the Garden, although it will well enough come up in ground, not dressed, yet the seeds evermore bestowed in laboured earth, not dunged at all, in the moneth of April, and to be much and often watered, until they be welcome, in that the same especiall joyeth being placed near the water.

And the Gardener minding to possesse the seeds of the Sorrel, ought after certain leaves come up, to remove the plants, in letting them grow unto the full ripeness of the seeds, which after the thorow

Marigolds from John Gerard, The Herball or Generall Historie of Plantes, *1597.*

drying, to be kept unto the sowing time. The Sorrel come up, neither wel abideth frosts, cold, nor overmuch moisture: and to have the beds of Sorrel continue seemly to the eye all the Summer thorow, let the owner or Gardener cut the tops of the Sorrel three or four times in the year.

The like diligence may be imployed in the sowing and ordering of the Garden Pimpernel.

CHAP. VIII

 he Borage and Buglosse, or Longde-beefe serving for the pot, when the leaves are yet tender, and the flowers for Sallets require to be sown in the moneth of August, and in September, to serve the winter time, and in the moneth of April (the Moon increasing) for the Summer time, in that the seeds (especially of the Buglosse) prosper not so wel to be sown at any other time, for so much as it joyeth to be placed in a warm and Sunny place, the earth afore diligently laboured and dressed. These may the owner or Gardener remove (after certain leaves sprung up) at any time of the year, and to be placed in beds, either alone, or in Borders, round about the new beds of other herbs. The seeds both of the Borage and Buglosse, require to be gathered in a manner half ripe, to the end they fall not out of their huske. And the whole herb with the seeds of either, ought to be laid in some high place, open to the warm Sun, that they may ripen the speedier, which ful ripe, rub tenderly between the hands the seeds forth on a linnen cloth or sheet, and these may you keep for two years.

What skill and diligence is required in the workmanly sowing and ordering of the Borage and Buglosse.

CHAP. IX

 he Marigold named of the Herbarians *Calendula*, is so properly tearmed, for that in every Calend, and in each moneth this renueth of the own accord, and is found to bear flower, as wel in Winter as Summer, for which cause, the *Italians* name the same the flower of every moneth: but some term it the Suns flower, or the follower of the Sun, and is of some named the Husbandmans Diall, in that the same sheweth to them, both the Morning and Evening tide. Other name it the Suns Bride, and Suns herb, in that the flowers of the same follow the Sun, as from the rising by the South unto the West, and by a notable turning obeying to the Sun, in such manner, that what part of heaven he posesseth, they into the same turned behold, and that in a cloudy and thick aire like directed, as if they should be revived, quickned, and moved with the spirit of him. Such is the love of it

What skill and secrets to be learned in the sowing, removing and setting of the Marigold.

known to be toward that royall Star, being in the night time, for the desire of him, as pensive and sad, they be shut or closed together, but at the noon time of the day fully spread abroad, as if they with spread armes longed, or diligently attended, to embrace their Bridegroom. This Marigold is a singular kind of herb sown in Gardens, as well for the pot, as for the decking of Gardens, beautifying of Nosegaies, and to be worn in the bosome.

The seeds of this flower, are commonly bestowed in a husbandly and wel dressed earth, but this rather done by the counsel of the skilful in the increase of the Moon, whereby the flowers may grow the bigger and broader. But to procure the flowers to grow the doubler, bigger and broader, the owner ought to remove the plants often, and to set them in new beds, lying in Sunny places, herein considering at those times of removing, that the Moon be increasing so nigh as you can.

Besides, some wil, that many seeds be put together into one hole, in the first quarter of the Moon, and to be sundry times watered in the first comming up of them, unlesse the moisture of the aire otherwise help.

These after certain leaves sprunk up, if they be often removed and clipped by due course of the Moon, yeild a better, broader, and a fairer flower, and they yeild alwaies more flowers in the harvest, then in the spring time.

CHAP. X

What skill, industrie, and secrets is to be learned in the sowing and ordering of the Parcely.

he Parcely in the bestowing in the earth, requireth small labour and diligence, and loveth a stony and sandy Earth, so that the same needeth smal fatning, whereby it may wel agree to be sown in shadowie places, near to the hedge or harbour in the Garden, and this especially requireth much watering, for the speedier shooting up. The old seeds, if we may credit *Theophrastus*, do sooner come up, yea and the elder seeds are better for the turn: the plants shot up, do endure a long time without sowing any more, in such condition, that the owner or Gardener shal not need to sow or set of the plants again for five years after. The Parcely when it hath grown a yeae, it sendeth up or beareth stalks and seeds, and a yellowish flower. The new seeds of the Parcely committed to the earth, do most slowly come up in beds, in that these not before the fortieth, yea fiftith and sixtith day after the sowing, do not for the more part appear, as the learned *Pliny* reporteth; yet this ease and commodity ensueth, that once sown and come up (as above uttered) it yearly increaseth of the own accord, without renuing for many yeares. The seeds, as the worthy Nea-politane *Rutilius* witnesseth, joy in any earth, and as wel in the cold as warme places, saving the seeds in the first comming up require much moisture, through which watering they come so speedily strong, that after no aire nor ground hindereth them. Both the seeds and plants (as *Columella* instructeth) may prosperously be bestowed to increase the speedier, near to springs and little running waters. If the owner or Gardener would have the leaves grow very broad, then let him attend to the words of the worthy Greek *Florentius*, who willeth to take up of Parcely seeds at one time, as much as can handsomely be holden between three of the fingers, and these after the tying up in a thin or wel worn linnen cloth, to be set into a shallow hole with dung handsomely mixed in the earth, which on such wise handled, wil after come up and grow with so large a leaf, for the Increase of all the seeds wil then be joyned, and shot up together in one blade, as the worthy *Rutilius* hath noted, and before him the singular *Columella*. But the Parcely shall grow biggest, (as the worthy *Florentius* reporteth) if the owner by digging about the roots, bestow chaffe about them, and after the covering with light earth, do water them wel and often. The Parcely may the Gardener cause to grow crisped in leaf, if he thrust and bestow the seeds a little before the sowing in a ball stuffed with them, which broken somewhat with a staffe, and as they were spoiled, commit them (as *Columella* willeth) to the earth.

Or the Gardener otherwise with lesser pain may procure them to grow crisped in what manner soever they be sown, if he turns on the bed and plants a round stone, or big roller, a soon as the plants be somewhat grown up above the earth: and the like may the owner do with the plants come up, if he tread them often down.

The best commended time for committing of seeds to the earth, is from the midst of May, unto the Summer solstice in June, in beds thick together, and to be often watered, for that these speedier increase and come forward, through the heat in the same season. If the owner or Gardener would have the seeds sooner break and shoot up, let him infuse the seeds for a certain time in Vinegar, which bestowing in a wel laboured earth, fill half the beds with ashes of the Bean cods. After the seeds are thus sown, water them often and lightly with a smal quantity of the best *Aqua vita*, and soon after the sprinckling and moistning of the beds, cover the beds over with some piece of woollen cloth, to the end the proper heat ministred breath not away, for by that meanes the plants within one houre wil begin to appear, so that the owner must then take off the cloth, and sprinkle or moisten the plants appeared oftentimes, whereby they may the sooner shoot up in a high stemme or blade, to the wonder of the beholders. To *Florentius*, do *Junius, Columella, Pliny*, and *Rutilius* agree, that there are two kinds of the Parcely, as the Male and Female, the Male (as they describe it) hath blacker leaves, and shorter root: but the Female possesseth crispeder leaves, and hard, a big stem, in tast sower and hot: but neither of these two doth *Dionysius* and *Chrisippus* the Physitian, allow to be eaten with meat, as *Pliny writeth:* Although the same much used in *Plinies* time, as at this day, both in broths and sauces, for a better delight and appetite.

They report that by the often eaten of the Female blades, worms engender in the body, and that the Female eaten, doth procure the woman barren, as the Male the man. And further, the Parcely eaten of a woman with child, doth cause the births to have the falling sickness; yet they affirme the Male to harm less, so that for the same it was not altogether misliked nor condemmned of the ancient, among the wicked fruits. Therefore it is not to be marvelled at, if the late Physitians do advise and warn persons, having the falling sickness, and women with child, not to eat the Parcely: to these, the Greeks forbad Nurses, and women with child the eating of Parcely with meat, although an other occasion may also ensue of the same, that it may hinder womens milk-springs, and extinguish the comming of milk, besides that, this procureth the eaters of it unto the venereal act.

Certain report, that the sick fishes in Ponds, are mightily recovered and made lusty through the Parcely in them.

There is nothing that doth like sweeten the mouth, as the fresh and green Parcely eaten, so that the herb often eaten of them which have an unsavory and stinking breath, and sendeth forth an odious smel to be abhorred, doth in short time marvellously recover and amend the same: A matter very commendable and necessary, both for maidens and widows to deceive their wooers, by the chewing and bearing about of the green and fresh blades, whereby they may so remove for the present, the strong smel of the breath, yawning or otherwise issuing forth, and by the customable eating, send forth a sweeter breath.

Sundry in times past, preserved the blades of Parcely into a pickle unto us, which received or contained two parts of Vinegar, and a third part of Brine.

CHAP. XI

What skill and diligence is required, in the sowing and ordering both of the Garden and wild running Tyme.

he Garden time, although it seem better to agree, to be placed nigh to Bee-hives (for the commodity of honey) then in Gardens, yet our purpose is here somewhat to write of the same, in that this is so carefully bestowed in Gardens, as well for the commoditie of meats, as for the decking of Garlands. There are found to be two kinds of it, the one white with a woody or hard root, growing on little hils, which is accounted the worthiest.

The other as well in kind as flower black, which *Ætius* (in meats) disalloweth, for the same inwardly received, lightly putrifieth, and increaseth cholerick humours.

The Tyme of the Garden growing bushie and full of slips, is seen to shoot up two handfuls high, being most sweet and delectable of savour, and decked with a number of smal leaves, bearing also purple flowers, tending to a whiteness, and the tops after the form of Ants

Serpillum Creticum.
Wilde Time of Candy.

*Wilde time of Candy from
John Gerard's* Herball.

bending in body. The garden Tyme better commeth forward, being bestowed in a lean and stony ground: for which cause it neither desired a fat nor dunged earth, but joyeth to be placed in a sunny and open place. This wel enough prospereth, being bestowed in beds, either in seed or plant, but this speedier commeth forward being onely set, yea this increaseth, being set again with the flowers bearing, as the singular *Theophrastus* witnesseth. The owners of hives have a perfect foresight and knowledge, what the increase or yeild of honey will be every year, by the plentiful or smal number of flowers growing and appearing on the time about the summer solstice: for this increaseth and yeildeth most friendly flowers for the Bees, which render a colour and savour to the honey.

The said *Theophrastus* writeth, that the flower of Tyme spread abroad, is destroyed and dieth, if a bigge shower of rain happen to fall.

The worthy Neapolitane *Rutilius* in his Husbandry instructeth, that the whole plant is to be rather set then sown, about the middle of April in a wel laboured earth, lying open to the Sun, and that the same may prosper and come the speedier forward.

He willeth the owner to water the plants of Tyme, or to moisten them all a day with water finely sprincked on the beds, in that the Tyme so fast drinketh in. If the owner or Gardener would possesse the seeds, he must diligently gather the flowers, (in which the seeds are contained) and not labour to separate the one from the other.

The running Tyme joyeth to be set or sown near to springs of water, as by a Wel or Pond, for on such wise bestowed in the earth, the same yeildeth the fairer leaves: this neither requireth a fat nor dunged earth, but onely to be bestowed in a sunny place, and joyeth in the often removing. The running Tyme doth many times proceed or come of the Basill, rudely or without care bestowed in the earth.

CHAP. XII

What skill and diligence is required in the sowing and ordering, both the Mints and Holihoke.

he Garden Mint desireth to be bestowed, neither in a dunged nor fat earth, but rather in an open and Sunny place: yet this best joyeth in a moist place, or by some well. And where the like is not, the Mint in that ground ought to be often watered in the first bestowing in the earth, or this otherwise in short time withereth and dyeth.

The Mint ought to be set in the root or whole stem, in Harvest, or in the Spring time. The owner or Gardener lacking, or not having the Mint seeds to sow, may in stead of them, use or bestow in his ground, the seeds of the field or wild Mints, in setting the sharper ends of the seeds down-ward, thereby to tame and put away the wildnesse of them. This plant well grown up, needeth not after to be renued or sown every year, in that once sown or planted, it after commeth up yearly of the one accord, and for the delectable savour which it enjoyeth, much desired and used both in broths and Sallets.

But this plant after comming up, may in no case be touched with any iron instrument, in that the same soon after dyeth. This plant flourishing in the Summer, becommeth yellowish in the winter time.

This Holihocke or greater Mallows of the Garden, as *Ruellius* out of the learned *Theophrastus* affirmeth, doth often shoot up into the form of a tree, and waxeth so great, that the stems or body of it may serve to the use of a staffe, which sendeth forth big stalks and leaves both large and round.

The flower of this plant for the proper time flourishing, is named the winter Rose, in that this plant yeildeth flowers like to the Rose, from the beginning of Harvest unto the winter time, which flowers both of the red and white, lesser then the fading or vanishing Rose, longer endure and enjoy force.

This Rose of the ancient Greeks was named *Moloke*, in that the leaves (*Columella* reporteth) turn about with the Sun, which at Noon time of the day are fully opened. The ancient Romans did also name it the sown or garden Mallows. The common people in time past greatly pleased with the beauty of the same, named it the beyond sea Rose. For in comliness, neither of them giveth place to the Rose, which if the same joyned a savour, it were not inferiour to the Rose, seeing in colour they be equall in bearing of the red carnation and white, so that in savour the Rose onely excelleth.

This for the worthy comelinesse and beauty, to be set in windows, is at this day diligently sown and set in Gardens.

The worthy *Rutilius* (in his treatise of the Garden) instructeth, that the seeds to be committed to the earth, ought rather to be bestowed about the middle of Aprill, in a well dunged and fat ground, and to be often watered, until the plants be well sprung up.

The skilfull *Columella* in his Husbandry uttereth, that this rather joyeth to be bestowed in a fat earth, wel turned in with dung, and that moist dung laid about the roots of the young Plants, in the setting again, which the said Author willeth to remove, after four leaves as wel shot up above the earth.

This learned *Columella* writing of the Holyhoke, reporteth that the flower (as the Marigold) openeth at the rising of the Sunne, full spread at the Noon time, and closeth again at the going down of the Sun.

Mentha cruciata, sine crispa.
Crosse Mint or curled Mint.

Mint from John Gerard's Herball.

CHAP. XIII

he Herbarians write the Artechoke to be a kind of Thistle, of them named, the Thistle of the Garden.

The Artechoke which before grew wild in the fields came by diligence (for the benefit of sale) to be carefully bestowed in the Garden, where through travell, brought from his wildnesse, to serve unto the use of the mouth and belly. The Artechoke growing with thick scaly eares, in forme to the pine apple, and sufficiently known to most persons, joyeth in a loose and dunged earth, yet the same better commeth forward, being bestowed in a fat ground, and by that meanes defended from Moles, as the worthy *Rutilius* reporteth, but sown in a fat earth after their growth, be not so lightly digged up of an Enemy. The said *Rutilius*

What care and skill is required in the sowing and workmanly ordering of the Artechoke.

willeth the seeds of the Artechoke, to be committed to the Earth in the moneth of March, the Moon then encreasing of light, and that in beds well dunged, and workmanly prepared, which bestow in the earth half a foot asunder, yet these not deep put, and in such manner deale with the seeds, that taking so many up, as you may handsomely with three fingers thrust or set those unto the middle joynts in the earth, covering them lightly with loose Earth, which if hot weather happen to ensue, the Gardener with diligence must water the plants for a time, for the plants on such wise handled, will yeild a tenderer fruit and fuller head, as the worthy *Varro* reporteth, yet may not the owner hope or look for fruits or heads, to come to their full growth and perfectnesse for the eating in the first year. If the Gardener would bestow seeds to profit, he ought to make little furrows on the bed, well a foot distant one from the other, being in breadth and deepness of halfe a foot, which after fill with old dung finely broken, and black earth in like manner small, in which so handled, bestow the seeds to the depth of the middle joynts, and after cover them lightly with fine Earth, not pressing or treading it down. And as soon as the plants have yeilded forth leaves sufficient great, the owner ought to water them often, and to continue the like watering in a ground very dry, until the herbs yeild or send forth heads both tender and sufficient big, when the plants shall be well grown up, the Gardener must cleanse and purge daily the beds of weeds, and dung all about the roots of the plants (if he will credit *Columella*) store of ashes, for this kind of dung the said Author reporteth to be most apt and agreeable to that pot-herb, of which by the kind of the dung, this herb taketh the Latin name.

The owner or Gardener must have a speciall care, that he bestow not the seeds in the earth with the contrary ends downward, for these will bring forth Artechokes crooked, weak and very small, if we may credit the Neapolitane *Rutilius*. If the owner would have the herb yeild heads or Artechokes without prickles, he must (after the instructions of the Greek writers of Husbandry) either break the sharp ends of the seeds, or make blunt the prickes (before the bestowing in the earth) on some stone rubbed: which also many affirme to come to passe, if the Gardener paring off the rind of the Lettice root, and shreading or cutting the same into many small pieces, doth after the bestowing of the seeds into each piece, diligently set these a foot distance asunder, will after yeild heads the like.

The Gardener shall possesse Artechokes of pleasant savour, if he lay the seeds to steep for three daies before the sowing, in the juyce of the Rose, or Lilly, or oyle of Bayes, made with the sweet Almonds, or in any other pleasant juyce or liquor, which after the drying in the aire from the Sun beames, he committeth them to the earth, for on such wise handled, the fruits yield the same savour as the liquor in which the seeds were soked and received. For by a like example, the heads shall savour of the Bay, if the owner steep them with the leaves of the Baytree, or he otherwise making holes bestow the seeds within the

Bayberies, before the committing to the earth: and a like practise may he exercise in all seeds that be great.

The fruits of the herb named the Artechoke, wil become sweet and delectable in the eating, if the owner (before the committing of the seeds to the earth) do steep them two or three daies, either in new milke, hony, sugred water, or wine aromatized, and after the drying in the aire, doth then bestow them in beds a foot distance one from the other: the Artechokes be set in harvest, which is about the moneth of October, that these may yield plenty of fruits or heads, ought to be those bearing big leaves and stalks, which big stems grown or shot up in the middest: which big leaves after serve to none other purpose, but to be broken from the bodies, and the plants to be bestowed again in beds, which stems in like manner cut off and cast away, as serving to no use, wel turned in with dung: these set in such manner, that the tenderer leaves grow upright, and the stemmed in the middle being low broken off, to be diligently covered with light earth. And herein the Gardener must have a care to the watering of them, at times needfull, if the seasons sufficiently moisten not, either in winter, or in any other time of the year, to set forward or procure speedily the Artechokes to come: and set again the tender plants in well dunged beds, covering them wel about with Ashes and black earth, the better to beare and suffer the cold winter time, which in the year following will yield new fruits.

Many skilful Authors write, that if the leaves of the Artechoke be wel covered in the ground, about the beginning of winter, they wil after become not onely white, but pleasanter in the eating, whereby to serve among the winter meats.

Here I think it profitable to the owner to know, that the big leaves or branches ought yearly to be broken off, from the old stems or bodies, lest the elder in their yeeld might be hindred, and the younger plants in farther distances set, that these may prosper and send forth their fruits the better, for such is the fruitful and plentiful yield of this plant, that the brances or great leaves broken off from the tender stems, and set again in the earth, will after cleave and joyne together, as certain report, and oftentimes to yield in the same year, both the stem and outward roughnes with pricks on it. The skilful writers of the Greek husbandry wil, that the owner or Gardener in the opening and digging away of the earth, to cut them up with a sharp hook, leaving some part of the root in the earth, which so pulled up, and anointing the root with soft dung, set again in a wel laboured ground, turned in with old dung wel three foot asunder, and often water them when the drie season commeth, until the plants shall be sufficiently strengthened in the earth.

Those which the Gardener mindeth or let run or grow unto seed, such shal be separate from the young plants, as *Palladius* willeth, and cover the heads either with a thin Pot-shard, or Bark of a tree, in that the seeds are commonly wont to be corrupted through the Sun or showers of rain, and by that meanes these to perish and come to no use, which if the seeds be either burnt with the Sun, or putrified with the moisture of showers, will after yield to the Gardener no commodity in the bestowing in the earth.

The owner or Gardener may not gather the fruits of the Artechokes all at one time, for as much as the heads ripen not together, but one after the other, so that the owner ought then gather the fruits, when as these onely have flowers below in form of a Garland, not before that time; wherefore if the Gardener do stay until all the flowers be shed, the fruits wil be the worser, and lesser delectable in the eating.

The Gardener must carefully look unto, that the Mice haunt not to the roots of the Artechokes, for once allured through the pleasant tast of them, they after resort in great number from far places, to the marvellous spoile of the roots, as the Greek *Varro* in his worthy instructions of husbandry hath diligently noted, yet not leaving the same without a help and remedy: for he reporteth, that the sharp assault and enterprise of them is withstanded and driven away, if the Gardener either lap wool about the roots, or Swines dung, or bestow the Fig-tree ashes in the like manner about them.

The Moles in like manner do marvellously harme, and be injurious to the roots, insomuch that through their often casting, and hollowing of the ground, the hollow plants are procured to fall or leane through feebleness in the earth, for remedy of which annoyance, the Gardener may either bring up and learn a young Cat or tame a Weasil, to haunt daily in those places.

There be which set the plants of the Artechoke in a fast and dry ground, to the end the Moles should not so lightly in their working overthrow them.

The owner which would understand and know other helps, let him resort unto those experiments, which we have uttered in the first part.

CHAP. XIV

he Envive, otherwise named the Succorie, or sower Lettice, serveth rather for the use of Medicine, then for other purposes, so that by a travel caused to grow acceptable in the garden, forasmuch as this of it selfe by nature is evermore sower, although it be a kind of the Lettice, which ought often to be removed and changed into sundry places, that the nature of it may on such wise be altered, with lesser tarvel to the Gardner.

The Endive thus bestowed in beds, may wel abide the cold season of winter, wherefore in cold Countries, this better agreeth to be sown near the end of Harvest, and wel grown up, to be removed and laid again in the earth, that these in the lying, may on such wise become white, if so be (before the covering) the herbs be strewed over with river sand, and often watered (if not holpen by showers of rain) which then cover with light earth, letting these so rest until by a diligence in the watering, they become sufficiently white for Sallets, or other purposes: the young plants of the Endive are not to be removed, before that four leaves be sufficiently sprung up, and these cut at the ends of the roots, as wel as the tops of the leaves, with soft Cow-dung anointed about the roots, before the bestowing in the earth, which lightly covered, water so long, until the plants be sufficiently strong in the earth.

The succory is of the nature of the Endive, which in like manner

What skill and diligence is to be learned in sowing, and workmanly ordering, both of Endive and Succorie.

retaineth the proper bitternesse, being not like removed and ordered as the Endive: this desireth moist ground, and the earth to be wel laboured, when four leaves be come up: the plants after the removing, ought again to be set in a wel dunged earth, and that these may yield faire, large, and long leaves; let the owner after the leaves be somewhat more shot up, on the middle of them lay a piece of a Tilestone, for by the weight of the same will the leaves spread out, and enjoy more tufts, or grow thicker. By this workmanly ordering, wil the bitternesse of the leaves be removed, and they aptly serve in the winter time for the use of the Sallets, if so be the plants be set again in the end of August, or rather in the beginning of September, when the leaves are shot up big, and in pulling up, the earth not knocked off the roots, but with soft Cow-dung the roots gently anoint about, and bestowed after in beds wel turned in with dung.

The leaves laid along in wel dunged beds (to be white) cover so over with loose earth that the roots may lye upwards; and over them, lying a long in the earth, make some coverture in the form of a harbouring place, or rather strew upon them the chaffe of corne, for the better defence of the cold and bitter winds.

Certain report that the like may be purchased, if the owner after certain leaves of the Succory shot up, bindeth together with a brown thred, and covereth them after a pot of earth, to the end that those may daily draw by the roots a nourishment from the earth, which by the same meanes shall purchase both a whitenesse and tendernesse, and lose a great part of the proper sowernesse.

CHAP. XV

What care, skill, and secrets are to be learned in the sowing, and workmanly ordering of the Lettice.

he Garden Lettice desireth a well laboured ground, fat, moist and dunged, appearing for the more part by the fourth day above the earth, so that the seed in the earth be not burned of the sun, or the ground unfruitful: the seed may be committed to the earth, al the year through if the place for the growing shal be battle, dunged and moist. The Seeds may be sown in beds thick together and in the moneth of March or beginning of April, in that the tender plants cannot indure the nipping frosts nor cold aire. The seeds which the ower bestoweth in beds in the moneth of September, will be so hardened for the winter time, that the plants may well endure to be removed and set at any time, and watered for two or three dayes together, unlesse these be otherwise moistned with the daily and sweet showers of the aire. And in committing of the seeds to the earth, the owner ought to have a care for watering of the beds, least the heat consisting in the dung, breatheth or casteth the seeds forth of the earth.

The plants risen or sprung up well four or five leaves above the earth, ought then to be removed and set again into a fat ground, a good distance one from the other, and to water them wel at the roots, so that it freeze not, nor the season be very hot.

The owner or Gardener may not remove (to set againe) the small or common Lettices, but the greater which will become crisped and thick (named of divers, the Romane Lettice) that yieldeth white and far bigger seeds: these if the Gardiner bestoweth again in beds, will shoot up far fairer, and greater in Tuffe, and tast pleasanter, if he especially break away the first leaves before the setting of them in beds, forasmuch as the first outward stalks have much milk in them, which will lightly become bitter through the heat of the sun.

If the owner would possesse faire and white Lettices, he ought to bind the leaves up together with a thread, wel two dayes before the plucking up and setting again in other beds: which so done, he must straw thick over, with river or sea sand, which the worthy *Pliny* seemeth onely to ascribe to those which yield the white seeds, whose nature is such, that they best indure the cold winter. But if these through the default of the place, season or seeds wax hard, the Gardener may procure the plant to grow tender, by plucking them up, and setting them in wel wrought beds.

The Lettice spread into a breadth, if so be the owner either setteth it asunder, or when it is grown into big leaves, the tops gently cut off, it be pressed down with a turffe of earth, Tile, or Potshard, whereby it may the lesse shoot up into a stem. For thorough the waight thus laid upon, the plant kept under is forced to creep, and shed forth into a breadth, as the singular *Florentinus* in the Greek husbandary, and after him *Columella*, to these *Plinie* and the worthy Neapolitan *Rutilius* utter.

The Lettices are caused to grow broad, round, thick of leaves, crisped, and low by the earth, if the plants removed when they be shot up a hands breadth, be after the cutting away of the hairy roots anointed wel about with new Cow dung, and in heaping the earth wel about them, be often watered: and assoon as these are grown to a more strength, to clip the tops of the leaves off with a sharp pair of sheers, and to cover them with pots of earth new filled, in such manner that the tops eaten or pressed down, may grow tufted round up, and white, as the said *Florentinus* (in his Greek instructions of husbandry) reporteth that he did.

If the owner mindeth to injoy Lettices sweet in tast and smell, let him (two dayes before the pulling up) bind up the tops of the leaves hard together, for by that means in the father growing, wil the plants be the fairer, sweeter; and whiter. Herein remembring that at the tying (on such wise) of the plants, and they stronger grown, to be then pressed down, as afore taught, with either Tile or potshard or Turffe of the earth.

The skilful *Florentinus* (doth also affirm) that the plants may be caused to grow sweet and pleasant in smel, if the owner bestoweth of the Lettice seeds, into the citron seeds, before the committing to the earth, which likewise the Gardener may performe, by infusing the seeds in either damaske or musk water, for certain dayes.

Here I think it not impertinent to the matter, to recite in this place the marvellous devise of *Aristoxenus Cyreneus*: this man as *Plinie* writeth, leaving his proper Country, for the earnest desire he had to Philosophie, and setting a felicity in banqueting dishes, watred at evening divers Lettices (as they grew on the earth) with Wine and honey mixed together, and with the same liquor so long filled them, until the herbs had sufficiently drunk: which after he had left them unto the next day, boasted that he had purchased delicates from the earth; this no doubt a worthy invention for a proper banquet, but no Philosophy consisting in it, therefore leaving further to report of this, we will return to our former matter.

The Lettice obtaineth a tenderer leaf, or the leaves become the tenderer, if the root (as aforesaid) be diligently anointed about with the best Cow-dung, and watred at needful times with river or running water, or the tops of the leaves, as I afore writ, tied close together with a thread, well two dayes before the pulling up and setting again.

If the Gardiner desire to have a plant to grow of a marvellous form, and divers in tast, he shall with an easie cost and light travaile (as the skilful Greek *Didimus* reporteth) performe the same, if he will properly make a hole into a round pellet made of Goats dung, and into the same put of the Lettice, Cresses, Basill, Rocket, and Radish seeds (as the *Rutilius* writeth) and that ball wrapped in dung, be bestowed in a well laboured earth; the furrow not being deep, and soft dung laid over, with the light earth; and this often and gently (or by little and little) springled with water: for the radish shooting down performeth the root, but the other seeds into a height, the Lettice rising withall, and each yeelding the plant in their proper tast.

There be some which in two or three terdiles of the Goat or sheep bruised, and made up into a ball, bestow the foresaid seeds, and tying this in a linnen cloth, do set it into the earth, with the like care and diligence, as above is uttered.

Many of the Latin writers of husbandry taught the same in an other manner, by gathering whole leaves of the Lettice, growing next to the root, in the hollow pits and places of which leaves the owner so bestow, except the Radish (as *Rutilius* writeth) or the Parsley (as *Ruellius* instructeth) all the afore named seeds, which leaves anointed about with soft dung, to be set into a well dunged ground, and the seeds diligently covered over with earth.

If any would possesse Lettices for the Winter turn, he ought to conserve them as *Columella* instructeth) after this manner, in plucking first away the outward leaves round about, that the tender leaves left apparant and uncovered, might well be salted in an earthen pot or other vessell, and left covered for a day and a night, after such manner, until these with the help of the salt, yeeldeth forth a Brine.

The brine throughly purged away with fresh water, and the liquor pressed forth of the leaves, to let them lye abroad on a Lettice, until the leaves be sufficient dry, then to strew the dry Dill, and Fennel on them: after this to lay the heaps or handfulls of the Lettices into the vessell again, on which to powre the liquor made of two parts of Vinegar, and one of the Brine: after this, so to thrust down the whole substance with a dry thickening, that the liquor may flote and appear well above all, which on such wise ordered, must diligently be tended upon, that as often as the substance above seemeth lye bare and uncovered, to fill alwaies up with the said liquor, but with a Spunge keep clean the lips and outside of the pot, washed diligently about with fresh Conduit water, and this so often use, as need shall require.

CHAP. XVI

he Garden Purselane, how diligently the same is bestowed, so much the larger it spreadeth on the earth, and yeeldeth the thicker leafe. This desireth to be sown in February, March, April, May, and June, and in no other times, for this herb cannot well indure the cold season. This plentifully yeeldeth and spreadeth, being bestowed in beds well turned in with old dung, or in ground very fat of it self, or otherwise sown amongst Coleworts, Onions and Leeks. And after these have joyed a yeare in the Garden, they will yearly come up, without paines to the Gardener, of the one accord; yet the herbs desire every year to be often watered, to the end that these may yield the bigger Tuffe, and thicker leaf.

What care and skill is required in the sowing and ordering of the Purselane and Rocket.

The seeds ought to be sown under the shadow of trees, and in an harbour where trees grow not too thick, for these otherwise bestowed under a thick shadow, grow thin and small of leaf. The Purselane is one of the Garden herbs, served first in Sallets, with Oyle, Vinegar, and a little Salt, as well at the mean, as rich mens Tables, yea this for a dainty dish with many served first at Table in the winter time, preserved after this manner.

The greatest stems and leaves of the Purselane without roots were gathered in that the smaller steeped (lightly decayed and withered) and these with water clearly and throughly cleansed from the fine Sand, hanging on, and the filthy or corrupt leaves if any such were, clean purged away; and these so long they dryed in the shadow, until they were somewhat withered, for otherwise (through the plenty of moisture) they either moulded or rotted in the lying. After these were they infused in Verjuce made of sowre grapes, strewed thick over with green Fennel bestowed in an earthen pot glazed within, or for lack of it, in a sweet vessel of wood: after this, the whole sprinkled wel over with Salt, laying green Fennel again over the Salt, and sundry courses of Purselane, with Salt and Fennel bestowed to the filling up of the pot, and over the upper bed of Purselane again, a thick course of green Fennel strewed, which setled the whole mixture down into the pot.

These being done the liquor which was tempered or mixed with two parts of Vinegar, and one of Verjuyce made of Grapes was poured upon in such order and so full, that the same reached up to the brim or lip of the vessel. The same prickle or sauce at the end, close covered with a lid, was up in a place to be preserved far from the beams of the Sun coming, least the substance through the standing of the place, might gather a vinew or mouldines over the same: which also as they affirm may be avoided, if the Purselane be not suffered to lie floting above, but alwaies covered wel over with the liquor: when they used and served it at the table, they afore cleansed it with warm water or wine, the pouring sweet Oile on the Purselane, they set it as a first dish on the table, to procure an appetite to the guests set down to meat. The Rocket is added to the Lettice in Sallets, to the end it may temper the contrary vertue of the same, so that the Lettice is seldom eaten with meat without the Rocket, and the Sallet on such wise prepared is caused the delectabler, and yieldeth the more health to man. And the worthy *Galen* in his Book *de aliment. & facultat.* willeth no man to eat Lettice or Purselane without the Rocket, nor the Rocket contrary-wise in any Sallet, without Lettice or Purselane, that in as much as the one cooleth and harmeth the veneriall act, the other through the heating in the either matter profiteth man. The seeds may be committed to the earth, and the herb planted as wel in the winter time, as in summer, for it neither feareth the cold, nor any other distemperancy of the aire, nor this requireth great labour about the bestowing of the seeds in the earth, and after the coming up, it especially joyeth to be often weeded, but the seeds to be sown in a sandy or gravelly ground, ought afore to be well turned in with dung.

CHAP. XVII

What skill and diligence is required in the sowing and ordering of the Chervil, Smallage, Taragon, and Cresses.

he herb Chervil, joyeth to be sown in a wel dunged earth, in the months of February, March, and April: sometimes in August and September, to possesse the herb in the winter time, and this the better prospereth through the often watering, untill it be wel come up.

The smallage seeds ought to be sown in a well laboured earth, and near to a stone wall, or thick hedge, this herb well joyeth in shaddow, and commeth wel up in any ground. And after this herb be once stowed in the Garden, a man shall hardly weed it forth quite, and the Gardener may leave a stem or two, to shoot up into seed, from year to year; for this herb wil indure for ever, without any weeding at all. The owner may commit the seeds to the earth, after the middle or end of February, unto the beginning of September: this herb hath the like vertue and properties, which the Parsly possesseth.

The Taragon of the Garden, bearing seed like to the Flax, ought to be bestowed in a wel dunged earth, and after the plants shot up near a foot high, the Gardiner ought then to take up the whole bodies, and set them again in the selfe same earth, which often water, until they have taken strong root in the earth. The Taragon enjoyeth the like properties as the Rocket, and may not be eaten apart or alone, but rather with the Lettice, Purselane, and such like herbs.

The Garden Cresses is a sowre herb in tast like unto the Onion, which the Germaines (in many places) do often use in Sallets, but it seemeth that the herb is not eaten, without other cooling herbs matched with it, as the Littice, Sorrel, Purselane, and such like, which temper the fier or burning force of the herb, even as the worthy physitian *Galen* hath willed it, who forbad the Rocket to be eaten with the Lettice, that the contrary vertue might be tempered. This herb joyeth to be sown in moist places, as by smal Rivers or running courses of water, wells and springs: for no other labour (after the seeds bestowed) do they require, saving a daily watering, for the plants coming up, desire often times a day to be watered by little and little.

The seeds of the Cresses (after the mind of *Rutilius*) bestowed in beds with the Lettice, increaseth very well, for they joy in moisture, and hate the dung: and sown in a shadowie place, in February and March, the plants reasonably prosper and come forward.

CHAP. XVIII

he Bucks or Harts horn, whose leaves be sweet in tast, and somewhat faulty, is at this day sown in Gardens, and yearly used in Sallets, and requireth a small labour, before the bestowing in the earth, forasmuch as this herb so wel joyeth in the earth, not laboured and dressed, as afore prepared.

What care and skill is required in the sowing and ordering of the Bucks horne, Strawbery, and Mustard seed.

But if the owner mind to have the herb thick tuft, and faire to the eye, he must often clip the tops of the leaves, and press the head down by some waight, or properly tread with the foot on it: for on such wise handled will the herb be procured to grow downward, and into a breadth.

This especially in Sallets in summer time, although the same have no apt succour nor tast.

The Strawberies require smal labour and diligence in the bestowing in the earth, saving that these joy to be set in some shadowie place of the Garden, in that these rather desire to grow under the shadow of other herbs, then to be planted in beds alone: and planted under the shadow of high trees, these prosper without any trimming of the earth.

Here note a marvellous innocency in the strawberries, that although these creepe low by the earth, and that divers venemous, things creep over the herbs, yet are these in no manner infected with

Hellebore, iris, and a strawberry plant from a Tudor pattern book (early sixteenth century).

any venemous contagion, which is a note, that the herb (of property) hath no affinity with poyson. The herb by diligence of the Gardener, becommeth so great, that the same yieldeth fair, and big Berries, as the Berries of the Bramble in the hedge, and hereof it seemeth, that *Virgilianus Seruius* named the Strawberry, the Mulbery of the earth. Certain skilful men, by a diligence and care, procure the berries to alter from the proper red colour, into a fair white, delectable to the eye.

The Mustard seeds desire to be sown in a fat ground, and to be committed to the earth with fine powder dust, both before and after the winter, these after the coming up, require to be often weeded and watered. But the seeds may not be sown to thick, in that the plants multiply and spread into breadth. After the plants have enjoyed strong root in the earth, they are hardly plucked up by the roots, and the seeds may well be kept for five years, which the newer they be, so much the better to sow, and to be eaten. The goodnesse of the seed is known in the breaking or cracking of it between the teeth, whether the same be bound green or white within: for if this be white, the seed is old and nothing worth, neither to sow, nor to eat. The seeds which the owner would keep for to eat, those plants must he remove, after certain leaves sprung up, and set them a good distance asunder, whereby the tops may bush and spread the broader, but such plants, which the owner would have runne up to seed, those may he not change, nor remove out of the proper places.

CHAP. XIX

What skill and diligence is required in the sowing and workmanly ordering of the Leekes and Cives.

he Leek for that it is a root of the Garden to be eaten and often used in the Pot, therefore I will first treat of the same, which (as the most skilfull report desireth to be sown in a fruitfull and battle place, and lying especially open, whether the same be in a low place, as the worthy *Rutilius* writeth, and to these, that the beds be levelled, deep digged, diligently turned, and very well dunged. The Husbandmen in times past, noted two kinds of this herb, as the one which grew into a head, like the Onion, and the other into many divided blades, both long and straight, whose bush sprung up, is wont to be cut near to the ground, and this with us is named the unset Leek. The owner or Gardener which would possesse unset Leeks, ought to cut the green blades come up in the beds, after two moneths of the sowing. For these (after the mind of the learned *Columella*) will endure the longer, and encrease far bigger, if after this cutting they be removed and set again, and how often the green blades shall be cut, so often the herb is holpen with water and new Cow-dung. And use instructeth every carefull owner as the said Author reporteth, that in the removing, such skill must be used for the new setting, as when they be grown into a bignesse in the head, to be removed certain distances asunder, as four fingers breadth between either set, and when they shall be grown to a further strength, and bigness, to be again cut. The Leeks so often ought to be watered, dunged, and weeded, as need requireth the same, and the place is to be often raked over, whereby the plants may increase the better, through the help of the often killing and casting forth of the unprofitable herbs or weeds. As touching the Cives & unset Leeks, they may like be bestowed in the earth, as the Leek bearing the head: And the seeds of these may be committed to the earth at any time, if so be the owner enforceth not for the yield of the seeds, but they otherwise ought to be sown in the moneth of December, January and February, for the gathering and occupying after the moneth of March, unto the midst of of August. And the plants after the sowing, when the blades be well shot up, ought lightly to be troden down with the foot, and not to be watered for four days after. When the young and tender blades be shot out of the seeds, and that the owner mindeth to have the heads grow bigger, he ought not after the pulling up to set them again, before all the small roots be cut away, and the green blades nigh half cut off, which done the small potshards, or Oystershels, be laid (as it were) right under each head, and then diligently covered with earth, whereby the heads may so increase the bigger: in the which doing, the worthy Greek *Sotian* forbiddeth the the watering of them till four days after (if a drouth ensue) otherwise water them not at all. The skilful Neapolitane *Rutilius* instructeth, that when the Leeks be grown to a fingers bignes, by cutting the blades half way, and the hary roots quite (least these feed and draw away of the substance) then in the setting in earth mixed with sand and anointed fresh with Cow-dung, let the plants be distant in beds well four or five fingers one from the other, and when these have sent forth roots sufficient long, let the owner (gently putting under his dibble) raise softly the heads, that these remaining (as hanging on the earth) may on such wise fil the rooms or empty spaces by the greatnes of the heads growing. And that in fewer words I utter this instruction, if so be the owner would enjoy unset Leeks, he may bestow the seeds in beds the thicker together. If these do grow into a head, then the thiner in the earth, which shall cause them to prosper the better through a daily weeding, and feeding with fresh cow-dung.

The seeds ought to be committed to the earth, in the months of April, May, and June throughout, to possesse the herbs in the summer time, in the harvest, September, and October, for to enjoy the plants in the Winter time; but these especially require to be often weeded and dunged, which grow into heads: the Leek shal yield a far bigger head and stem, as after *Columella, Rutilius* wrote: yea before them both the worthy Greek *Sotion*, if in thin linnen clouts, or clohes much worn, the owner shall bestow and tye up many Seeds together, which so hardled, to cover diligently with soft dung and earth, and immediately to water them so lying in the earth, for these thus knit up (through the running of the seeds into one) will send forth Leeks of a wonderfull bignesse, which practise also may the husbandly Gardener try in the other seeds of plants.

A like experience will come to passe, if the owner bestow a Rape seed into the head of a Leek, without making a hole, with any Iron instrument, which so handled, set into the earth, for on such will it grow very big, as both *Rutilius* and divers Greek instructers of husbandry report. There be some, which making holes in the head with a wooden pricke, or piece of elder Cane, or else a Reed sharpned, bestow (in place of the Rape) the Gourd seeds. Others there are, which taking up so many seeds as they can handsomely retain with three of the fingers, and powred into a thin reed, do commit those to the earth, with soft dung covered and laid about, which practise doth even like agree to the former uttered.

The said Greek *Sotion* commendeth and affirmeth, that immediately after the seeds shall be sown, the soft earth of the Beds be troden with the seed into small and shallow furrows, and the Beds for three daies (as if they were neglected) not watered at all but in the fourth day, to be holpen through the sprinckling of water on the beds, for such wise handled, the blades comming up, will grow (as he reporteth) the more bushie and fairer to the eie, yet if the owner between sowing and planting, shall mixe sand with the earth, the blades will shoot up the fuller and bigger.

The said worthy Greek *Sotion* addeth and affirmeth, that if the owner shall eat a little Cummine seed before before, he shall breath forth no stinking savour at all of the Leek, although he shall eat a great handful at a time of the Leeks, for by eating of the Cummine seeds is the strong savour extinguished or put away.

Here out of *Petrus Crescentius* I have added, as a matter worthy of the noting, that the Leek seed thrown into a vessell of Wine, causeth that the wine sowreth not, but rather that Vinegar returneth into wine, that is, putteth away all egernesse.

This to conclude, conceive that the Leeke in the eighteen day after the sowing, do shoot and appear (for the more part) above earth, and do endure for ten years, after which time to yield seeds, and die.

CHAP. XX

hat the Onyons have a body compassed and compact with many cartilages, there is none (I beleeve) which knoweth not.

The ancient Husbandmen (as witnesseth *Columella*) named these Onyons, because they grew in one round head together, yet not joyned together with so many heads round about, as the Garlike, which unto this day is familiarly named the Onyon of the Husbandmen with us.

The Onyons for the more part ought to be sow in the moneths of January, February, and March, in a fat earth, well dunged, moist, and diligently trimmed, which shot up to some height, ought to be removed in the moneth of Aprill, a good distance the one from the other, and these further grown, ought carefully to be weeded about, and often laboured to cause them grow the bigger, and to defend them (in time of a blustering wind) by helps set against. The worthy Neapolitan *Rutilius* writeth that the seeds desire to be bestowed in a fat earth, often turned and raked, moist and dunged, and red also, as the Greek *Sotion* in his Husbandry willeth: which afore ought to be cast up, that it may putrifie through the cold and frosts in the Winter time, (as the skilfull *Columella* uttereth, after these the earth to be dunged, and within two dayes after, the ground levelled worth, and cast or troden into beds, all the roots and unprofitable herbs afore cleansed out. These workmanly handled in the moneth of March, being a pleasant and a calme day, the South or East-wind (at that time blowing) the seeds shall workmanly be committed to the earth, with Savery intermedled between them (as *Pliny* willeth) for so the plants

What skill and diligence is required in the workmanly sowing and ordering of the Onyon.

prosper the better. The worthy Greek *Sotion* admonisheth the Gardener which would set Onyons, to cut away all the hairy roots and tops of the green blades (before the bestowing) whereby they may grow to big heads. Others there are, which onely pluck away the blades nigh to the root, for on such wise they send the juyce to the nether parts, to cause the head grow big: But these (after the mind of *Rutilius*) ought in this manner to be placed or set thin in beds, and both raked and weeded (if these not often) yet four times at at least, as *Pliny* willeth: who also taught that the ground be digged, and cast up three times before the bestowing of the seeds in the earth.

If the Gardener commit seeds to the earth in the wane or decrease of the Moon, he shall possesse small and sowrer ones, if the seeds in the increase of the Moon, then strong and big, and of a moister tast, with the sowrness maistred. But the same not to be unremembered or overpassed, that in all the kinds of Onyons, the same somewhat long and sharp, is wont to be sowrer then the round, and the red one more then the green, and the raw more then the boiled, the fresh also, more then that seasoned or powdered with salt, or the sodden one.

The Gardener or owner shall possesse far greater Onyons, if when there is a place or room for the setting again, they be layed in earth well laboured for twenty dayes space, and so long left drying against the sun, untill all the moisture be gone or drawn forth by the heat of the sun, after the instruction of the worthy Greek *Sotion*, which *Ruellius* (out of *Palladius*) seemeth greatly to mistake, in that he ascribeth the same to be done to the Dill, and not the Onyons, whose heads may also be bared, by plucking off the upper skin, before the setting again in the earth, do prosper the better, and yield the bigger seeds, if they be set in the earth well a hands breath asunder.

The heads to be eaten before the full ripeness, that these may be the sweeter, ought rather to be sown in a moist ground, among the young plants of the Cucumberr, Gourds and Melones.

If the owner will rightly possesse, and gather the seeds in due season, when the green stems are shot up high, and yield big heads, they are then to be guided with two small forks of wood, fixed on either side (as *Columella* willeth) that the stems, through the staies shoaring them upright, may not in any big winde knock the heads together, to the spilling and losse of the seeds on the earth, which are not afore to be gathered, that they enjoy a black colour, as after the Greeks, *Columella* and *Rutilius* likewise uttered.

The stems and knops, in which the seeds are contained, ought to be gatered in the increase or the wane of the Moon, in a fair and warm time, when the leaves or blades begin of themselves to wither, and dry, and that the seeds begin to appear black of themselves, for then ought the stems to be plucked up by the roots, which knit together in forme of Garlands, or otherwise bound up, to be laid in the sun to dry and ripen. The Onyons will continue long uncorrupted (as the said *Sotion* hath noted) if so the Onyons be put into water, or (as *Pliny* willeth)into a salty and warm water, and after laid in the hot sun, until

BELOW *and* OPPOSITE *Onions from John Gerard's* Herball.

Cepa alba.
White Onions.

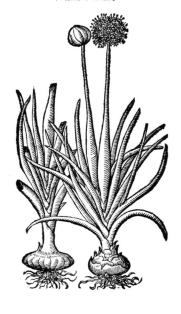

they be through drie, which let be hidden or covered with Barly
straw, and in such manner bestowed, that neither touch other by any
part. In many places, the Onyons being hanged in the smoke, and in
chimnies near to the heat of fire, and in such wise preserve them a
long time.

The ancient and skilfull writers of Husbandry utter, that if the
Gardener would possesse Onyons of a wonderful bigness in the head,
the seeds of the Onyons must be put within the seeds of Gourds,
which so handled, bestow in moist beds, well turned in dung, into a
like bigness will the heads of the Onyons increase, if the earth digged
round about, the small heads of the Onyons, in the heavingor lifting
of the earth, shall be lifted up, yet in such manner done, that the
heads not quite raised, out of the earth or plucked up by the roots, as I
afore uttered to be wrought with the Leek. The like also shall the
owner obtain, if boaring the head of an Onyon with a wooden pricke
in sundry places, and putting into the holes Gourd seeds, he bestow
them together in a well laboured earth.

But in this place I thought not to omit, that if the Gardener shal
commit the seeds of the Onyons in due time to the earth, they will
after grow into a head, but they shall yield less store of seeds. But if
the Gardener shall bestow little heads on the ground, the heads wil
after wither and wax dry, and be shot up into a round stem.

To these I add, that the Onyons plucked out of the ground and
lying upon the earth, or hanged up in ropes, do continue longer sound
in the Aire: but if we may credit *Aristotle*, in the summer Solstice,
these, as the Penny-royal, and many other herbs, do at the same time
flourish, which may be as if they were of a doubtful life, that one while
taking nourishment out of the earth, and another while from the
Aire. But the Onyons lightly bud and shoot out, not being in the
earth, and send forth faire green blades by occasion of the moisture in
the heads, but after the stem shall be full shot out, the heads wither.

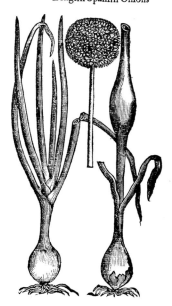

Cepa Hispanica oblonga.
Longish Spanish Onions

To which *Pliny* wrote, that the Nuts be contrary, in that these do
abate the strong savour of the Onyon. I read that many skilful
Gardeners used to sow the Onyons and Garlike near to Garland
flowers (but especally the Rose) to procure them to yield a sweeter
savour; and the same done by counsell of the ancient and the worthy
Pliny, which in my opinion, deserveth to be followed.

Truely, this one thing is greatly to be marvelled at, that the Onyon
alone of all herbs as *Plutarch* writeth, receiveth no damage of the
Moon, and hath contrary vertues of encreasing and diminishing to
her, for the Onyon becometh green, and buddeth forth in the wane or
last quarter of the Moon: contrary-wise she encreasing of light, the
Onyon then withereth and rotteth.

For which cause, the Egyptian Priests in time past, refused the
Onyon in their Religious meats, where otherwise, Fruits, Herbs,
Trees, and Beasts, receive a damage or diminishing and increasing
through the occasion of this Starre, so that the Onyon onely obeyeth
unto the contrary turnes of the Moon, whose preserving unto the

Winter time, *Columella* prepared after this manner: he chose the Onyons or Scalyons (that are all alike) which be not budded forth, or that green blades appeared, and these dryed afore in the hot sun, after which cooled again in the shadow, by strewing upon Time or Savory, he then laid them by courses, with either of these strewed between in an earthen pot, and by powring the liquor upon, which was three parts of Vineger, and one of brine: he strewed then a good handfull of Savery (in such manner) that the Onyons were couched or pressed under the liquor, which when they had drunk up the liquor, and seemed to lye dry, he poured upon and filled the vessel with the like mixture, and in an apt place set the pot to preserve them to use.

This one thing I will not omit, although the same may seeme childish, in that it is noted by the learned man *Cato*, who writeth, that the letters drawn and written with the juyce of the onyon are invisible, which then shew and appear evidently, when the paper shall be heated at the fire: to conclude, the Onyons set in the midle of August in red earth, do yield the year following their high stems and seed, but the worser will those be, which are bestowed in the earth, to serve green in the Lent time.

CHAP. XXI

What care, skill, and secrets to be learned in the sowing and ordering both of lesser, and greater Garlike.

 he Garlike much desired, and often of the Husbandman with fat beefe, and other sodden meates, joyeth in an earth especially white, diligently digged and laboured without any dung bestowed in it, whose cloves broken off from the head, ought to be bestowed on the borders of beds round about, well a hands breadth asunder, about the same time when the onyons are: and these with the beds or little ridges made (in form to such in the field) to be high raised, whereby the plants coming may the lesser be harmed with the showres falling, and the naturall moisture consisting in the earth. The cloves set in the ridges and borders of the beds may not be deep, nor the earth raised on them like to hillocks (as many do) but in an even manner, and unto the middle joynts bestowed, which when they shall have yeelded or sent up three blades, then these to be diligently weeded about, for through the often doing they increase the better, and yeeld a bigger head.

The Neapolitane *Rutilius* (writing of the garlike in his Instructions of Husbandry) willeth that the seeds to be committed to the earth in the moneths of November, December, January and February, in a ground well digged and laboured, and the same white, without any dung bestowed in it, besides the earth the same time indifferent drie, and in a warme day: for the seeds on such wise handled, are caused to prosper and yeeld the better. Although the learned *Plinie* seemeth to write that the seeds bestowed in the earth do slowly come up, whereby these in the first yeare onely yeeld a head no greater than a Leeke, but in the second yeare they grow divided, and in the third yeare come to their full growth and perfection, and such some suppose to be the fairer and seemlier.

The seeds of the garlike with us, better agree to be bestowed in the moneths of September, October, Februarie and March, in a earth white, indifferent dry, and well laboured without dunging. If any happen to remane in beds (as *Rutilius* reporteth) after the seeds fully ripe an gone, those then renew in the yeare following of the owne accord, both in the roote and blade, yeeld seedes the same yeare, which may after be sowne in well laboured beds, to send forth green Garlike; if the owner would possesse Garlike both great and big in the head, then before the same be shot up into them he must workman-like, tie all the tops of the green blades to an other growing next to it, which after tread softly down with the feet.

The worthy *Rutilius* willeth, that when the stemme beginneth to appeare, to cover the same with earth after the treading downe, which in such manner to foresee, that it increase not into a bush, or many blades, this so handled in the hard treading down, to be daily applied that the juice may run to the root, and cause the head to wax bigger. The like of which *Plinie* in his first time experienced. The worthy *Sotion* in his Greek observations of Husbandry, and also *Rutilius* with certaine others report, that if the cloves of Garlike heads be committed to the earth, and the like pulled out of the ground, when the Moon shall be descending and under the Horizon (as hid to us) that the stinking savour will (in a manner) be distinguished, so that the breath of the eaters, shall very little be felt; which *Plinie* seemeth somewhat otherwise to utter, instructing that the heads (unto the same purpose) ought to be bestowed when the Moon shall be under the earth, and to be gathered when the Moon shall be in conjunction with the Sun.

The said Greek *Sotion* seemeth to affirme, that the Garlike heads may be caused to grow sweet of savor, if in the setting the kernels of Olives (after the joyning with them) be bestowed together in the earth, or the sharper ends blunted on some stone, and then committed to the earth, or else in the setting, that lies of the Olives be bestowed with the cloves. The singular *Didimus* (*Ruellius* noting the same) uttereth, or rather *Sotion* (as the Greek Copy sheweth) that the loathsomenesse or stinking savour by the eating of Garlike-heads is abolished, or put away, if the green and raw bean be soon after eaten: Others there are, which will the root of the Beet to be eaten, after the rosting under hot embers, affirming the same to be sufficient to remove the strong savor: Also with the like remedy *Menander* one of the Greeke writers witnesseth, as *Plinie* writeth of him, the savor to be dissembled and shid. Our later writers of Husbandry and Physick report, that the ranke savour of Garlike may be extinguished, with the onely eating of greene Parsly-blades.

The commodiouser and apter time for the gathering of the Garlike-

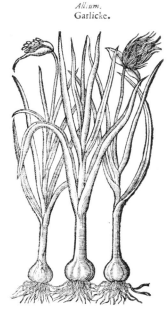

Allium.
Garlicke.

BELOW *and* OVERLEAF
Garlicke from John Gerard's
Herball, *1597.*

heads, is in the decrease or wane of the Moon, the day being drie and faire, when the blades be withered, that they leane or hang downe.

Many of the ancient Writers of Husbandry utter, that the Garlike heads will endure a long time, and be to better purpose afterwards, if they be either hid in chaffe, or after the tying together hanged up in the smoke. There be others which after the infusion of the heads awhile in warm salt water, and letting them dry, do likewise hide them in chaffe.

Allium sylvestre rubentibus nucleis.
Wilde Garlicke with red cloues.

But the heads handled after either manner, do for the more part remaine barren, or prosper not after the bestowing in the earth: To others it was sufficient to have dried them over the heat of the fire, that they might after grow. The learned *Plinie* uttereth, that those heads of Garlike be of a sowre tast, which possesse the more cloves round about, and he addeth that no more lothsomenesse or strongnesse of savour doth consist in them after the seething, then in the onion like ordered: Nor he omitteth not, that the Garlike heads afore eaten to be instead of the white Neeswort for the Pioners, if they mind to avoid and escape the hazard of death. There is another wild Garlike which the Greeks name, *Ophioscoridon*, in English, *Ramsies* growing of the owne accord in the fallow fields, through which the Kines milke by feeding on the greene blades, is caused to savour of the Garlike, yea, the cheese made of the same milke, doth render in the eating the like ranknesse of savour. The Husbandmen name this both the wild and Serpentine Garlike.

This Garlike on such wise boiled, that it may not grow againe, and bestowed in beds, doth greatly avail against the harm of birds to seeds, as afore is uttered in my first part, there writing, that the same of *Plinie* is named *Alum*. But here cometh to mind a marvellous matter, not to be over-passed, which is, that neither the Weasel, or Squirrel, will after the tasting Garlike, presume to bite any fowles, by which practice, Pullets and other fowles in the night being sprinkled over with the liquor of the Garlike, may be defended from harm of either of these.

There is yet a matter more worthy the remembrance, and the same far marvellouser, which *Volateranus* uttereth, that in his time hapned a husbandman to sleep open-mouthed in the field by a haycock, cast up in the harvest time, which when he had unwittingly suffered an Adder to creep into his body, with the eating incontinent of Garlike heads, was (as by a certain preparation against poison) delivered, yet the venome and death of the Adder consisting or remaining within the body distilled and shed forth in co-eating, a matter to be marvelled at of the wise.

But this also is marvellous in the Garlike, that if it be boyled with a salt liquor, the same doth effectuously destroy the mites or little wormes in either peasons or beanes, so that the walls or floores of the barnes be wet with this mixture. Here also I thought not to overpasse the marvellous discord of the Adamant-stone and Garlike, which the Greeks name to be an *Antipathia*, or naturall contrarity between them, for such is the hatred or contrarity between these two bodies, (lacking both hearing and feeling) that the Adamant rather putteth away, then draweth to it Iron, if the same afore be rubbed with Garlike, as *Plutarchus* hath noted, and after him *Claudius Ptolomeus*; which matter examined by divers learned, and found the contrarie, caused them to judge that those skilfull men (especially *Ptolomie*) meant the same to be done with the Egyptian Garlike; which *Dioscorides* wrote to be small Garlike, and the same sweet in tast, possessing a beautiful head, tending unto a purple colour. There be which attribute the same to *Ophioscorido*, which *Antonius Microphonius Biturix,* singular learned man, and well practised in sundry skills, uttered this approved secret to a friend whom he loved: And the same as last shall here be placed, that divers Garlike heads hanged on the branches or trees, doe drive farre off birds from the spoiling of fruits as the like *Democritus* noted in the Greek Instructions of husbandry.

That the big Garlike named of certain skilfull Authors, the Africa Garlike, is of a far bigger increase then the Garden garlike with us, which the worthy Greek *Sotion, Columella,* and *Rutilius* instruct, that the cloves to be broken from the head, and bestowed in a white ground, well laboured and dressed without any dung, and set in high ridges of beds, to the end the naturall moisture of the earth, nor showres falling may offend.

The time commended for setting of the cloves is in the moneths of January, February, and March, but some will to bestow them in the earth, from the beginning of October, unto the end of November, well a hand bredth a sunder, and unto the middle joynts, or rather a finger deep in the earth, which growne up to some height, to be often weeded about, and the earth diligently raked, whereby the plants may the better prosper.

These further growne up, the skilfull teach, to tie the tops of the blades by two and two together, which done, to tread the blades down with the foot, that the juyce by the same means may run to the root to increase the heads bigger.

The other instructions needfully to be learned, may the owner conceive by the former taught of the garden Garlike, which for the Physick benefits deserveth a place in every ground, especially in the Husbandmans garden.

CHAP. XXII

he Scalions better prosper and come up, being set then sown, for when they are committed to the earth in the seeds, the owner may not hope for a seemly growth of them, before the second yeare. The owner may bestow the Scalions in well dressed beds, from the beginning of

What care and skill is required in the sowing and ordering both of the Scalion and Squile Onyon.

November, untill the end of February, for to enjoy the proper yield the next Spring following: and they require to be likewise set in the ground (as afore taught) to the Garlike. But they are to be plucked up to use, before that the March violets be in their full pride and flourish: for if these be longer suffered, as unto the time of the perfit flourishing of the violets, they are then found feeble and withered. And for to know when the Scalions are ripe, it behoveth the Gardener to marke whether the blades beneath be withered; for on such wise seen, denoteth the full ripenesse of them. And to possesse Scalions with big heads, it behoveth the Gardiner to bestow round about the roots soft Cow dung, and to water them often, which grown to a reasonable heigth, he must also tread down and order as afore uttered in the using of the Leek.

The Squill onyon better commeth forward in the Garden being set with the head, then sown in the seed, for when the seeds are committed to the Earth, they yield slowly their seemely bush and heads.

The owner may bestow the heads of Squil onyons in well laboured and dressed beds, so that the ground be of a drie nature, and tending unto a saltness, whether gravelly or sandy, for they desire a like diligence to be bestowed on them, as is afore uttered of the Onyon and Garlike.

The ancient and latter writers report, that there are two kindes of the Squill onyon, as the Male and Femall, the Male yeilding white leaves, and the Femall black. This strong by nature, will continue in the hanging up, (in a shadowie place) a long time green, and it lightly groweth (as *Theophrastus* writeth) bestoweth in drie earth, and speedily shooteth up to a heigth, it keepeth fruits to be preserved, especially Pomegranets, the stalks afore broken off: and this is said to beare flowre thrice in a yeare, fore shewing by it, the three seasons of committing seeds to the earth, as the first time of bearing flowers, to signifie the first time of plowing, the second time of flower bearing, the second time; the third, the last time: for how many times these appear, even so often is the earth accustomed to be laboured.

The flower also of the Squill onyon (as *Beritius* writeth) shooting up in a straight stem, if so be it doth not hastily wither, signifieth the large or plentifull yield of fruits.

CHAP. XXIII

What care and skill is required in the preparing and ordering of the Garden Saffron.

As touching the Garden Saffron, it joyeth to be bestowed in a mean and chalkie ground, and evermore well laboured, and it may very well be set in the beds, where the onions have been newly plucked up. The Saffron refuseth watering and moisture, for which cause the heads ought to be set in beds, between which furrowes be made, that these may receive the moisture falling, which they greatly feare.

Besides these the heads are greatly indamaged through the resort of mice, and moles, which greatly covet to feed on the roots or onions of the Saffron.

The remedies against these two noyous beasts, are fully taught in my first part, which the reader may resort unto.

The heads are rather to be bestowed in the earth, than the seeds, in that the seeds (after the committing to the earth) prosper not.

The heads are to be set on ridges, in the month of April or May, and the heads laid on a heap, to lie and wither in the shadow from the Sun beames, for the space of eight dayes before, which done, to set them with the hairy roots in the earth welled laboured and dressed and at length one by another well halfe a hand bredth asunder, and three fingers deep. Certaine there are which will them to be set for the better yeeld, after the midst of August unto the middle of September, letting these to remaine for two or three years, and that every year in the month of Aprill and May, the leaves or blades then dry to break off orderly, the other prospering to weed about, and to raise the earth after two fingers deep, but in such manner, that the heads be not touched.

After that the herbs be sufficiently cleansed, whenas the flowres be withered and dead, especially in August, and towards Harvest, which flourish not above a moneth, then these are to be gathered in the morning after Sun-rising, and after the drying by a gentle fire to be kept together in bagges of leather, in a close and dry place.

And this one thing as marvellous, is worthy to be noted, that the root or onion standing quite out of the earth, yeeldeth notwithstanding the proper flowre of continuance but a day or two after the full opening, at the season of the yeare; but the head afterwards (as deprived of nourishment) withereth and rotteth.

The blades be fresh and green all the winter through, in that the heads be ful of juice, and sufficient strong to indure the cold season: When the Saffron is set, and in the third year digged up, there are round about each head five or six heads growing, and joyned together within the earth.

The best Saffron is the same, which is fresh and new, and excelleth in the goodnesse of colour, in such manner, that the tops in which the seeds be contained be white, and mixed with a rednesse, the chine also is not lightly broken, and rubbed in the hand coloureth the skin, and is in savour comfortable, with a great sharpness, And this is named the Orientall Saffron.

CHAP. XXIV

What skill, and care, and diligence is required in the workmanlike sowing and ordering of the Nauewe.

The Nauewe and Turnups are sowne after one manner in the earth, well turned up, and orderly dressed, or if the owner wil in earable ground, and will indure in a manner any aire; yet these desire a drie ground, rather lean and gravelly, and diligently turned up.

The seeds well prosper, bestowed in a fine powdered earth, well laboured afore, and to possesse faire Nauewes, let not the seeds be above three years old, for being elder the seeds run into Coleworts: If the plants in the coming up appear too thick together, the owner may pluck them up, and set them thinner in other well dressed place: These also in the growing up ought diligently to be weeded, and the earth to be digged about, and let the greater and fairer still grow, to possesse their seeds, which in the moneth of August diligently bestow in a well laboured earth.

To commit seeds to the earth, the owner ought to stay untill the ground be well moistened with flowres, for bestowed soon after they prosper and come the speedier up: But the owner or Gardener ought in any case to take heed that he bestow not the seeds in any shadowie place, for the shadowie places are disagreeable and hurtfull to the plants, although the ground be good, fertile and well laboured.

The property many times of the ground doth alter the Nauewe into a Turnup, and Turnup into a Nauewe.

The owner ought to gather the Nauewes in the moneth of November, and to possesse them all the winter time, he must burie the roots in sand lying in a seller, that he might not onely eat of them in the Winter time, but all the Lent through.

The worthy Nauewes be those which are rather long, and as they were crisped, and not big, and posessing few roots, at the most but one seemly root, and the same strait and sharp downward.

There be which make a singular composition of the Nauews with Radish roots, a little salt, honey, mustard, delectable spices, and Vinegar; yea, the same may be made without spices, both wholesome and profitable.

CHAP. XXV

he Rapes be not much differing from the Navews and Turnups, saving that these be bigger, and sweet in the eating. For the Rapes or Turnups be much greater, and in the eating pleasanter then the Navews; The Rapes require a like ordering and dressing of the earth, as afore uttered of the Navew, which for truth ought to be rather sowne in the moneth of September, then in any other time. In a moist earth well dunged, diligently turned in and dressed; for by that meanes they prosper and come the better forward, and are caused to be fairer, tenderer, bigger, and sweeter of taste through the cold season following, like as the hoary frosts, snow, and cold mists, then in the dry and warm season of the year.

What care and skill is required in the sowing and rightly ordering of the Rape and Turnup.

After these be come up, and ready to be removed, the owner must carefully see unto, that the leaves be not gnawne neither of spiders, nor by any other vermine or worms, and for the avoiding of like anoyance, it shall be profitable for the Gardener (wel a day before the committing of the seeds to the earth) to mix the seeds with the powder or dust of plank boards, or rather with the soot of a Chimney, which after wet with water, to the end that the seeds may receive some moisture, and being thus ordered, bestow the whole together in the earth the next day following.

The skilfull Neopolitane *Rutilius* reporteth, that the Rape or Turnup (as the Navew) prospereth under every aire, and desireth to be bestowed in a fat and loose earth, and the same so loose, that it in a manner falleth to powder, whereby the seeds may prosper, and come the speedier forward.

The seeds also are to be bestowed with fine powdred earth, to the end the Plants may not come up too thick together, about the end of July, unto the midst of September; and if rain happen not the day before, then the day following, moisten the ground with water gently

Turnips from John Gerard's
Herball.

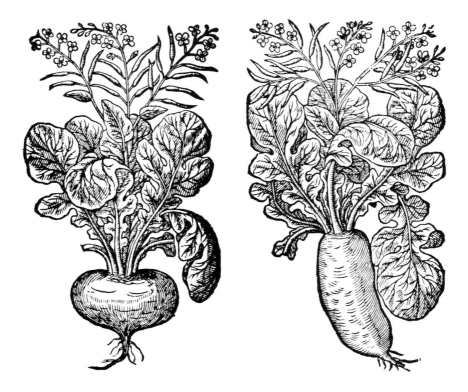

sprinkled upon.

If the seeds committed to the earth be bestowed thin, the plants in the coming up (by diligence of the Gardener) will increase the bigger; for which cause, where the plants grow thick together, and these come to good strength, the owner may pluck up sundry, and bestow those a good distance asunder, whereby they grow the bigger in root.

And for the better furtherance of their growth, the owner shall sundry times water and weed about the plants: The seeds may be sowne in the open field, and where corn grew, if so be the ground be diligently ploughed, and the weeds weeded forth, these after the bestowing in the earth may the owner onely cover with the Harrow or Rake, because the seeds lie shallow on the ground.

The seeds joy in an open field, far from the shadow of trees, in that these lying under shadow be much harmed; if the owner mind to commit seeds to the earth in a dry season, he may then bestow them in some wel dressed place being moist and shadowie, thick together after the manner of the Colewort.

After this, when the plants be well grown up, and the earth sufficiently moistened with showres, the owner may remove and set the plants in larger places well dressed, from the end of August unto the entring of the Sun into *Libra*, or middle of September.

The Rapes to serve the winter time, ought to be gathered in the moneth of October, and those which are the fairer, by plucking away the outward leaves, may be set again in well dunged and dressed earth, to yeeld seeds the Summer following.

And to preserve the Rape or Turnup roots to serve the winter and Lent time, the owner may work after this manner, by washing first the roots, and these raw, bestow in ranks one upon another, and in each rank strew salt, fennell seeds and sauerie, or onely cover them with salt, close couched, and on such wise letting these remain for eight dayes, powre so much faire water upon as will cover them, which done, let the vessel stand in some vault, or seller, to serve for the above said times, or longer if the owner will, if so be he fill up the vessell, when these lie bare and drie. These hitherto *Rutilius* in his Instructions of Husbandry.

Detail of an old woman peeling turnips. From a painting by David Teniers the Younger (1610-90).

This one thing is marvellous, and worthy the noting, so small a seed to increase in root to such a bignesse as we many times see them, of which the like hath been seen to have weighed thirty, yea, forty pound weight, to the admiration of many.

The owner ought especially to take heed that the seeds to be committed to the earth, be not above three years old; for the ground otherwise of the Rapes will change and bring forth Coleworts.

For to injoy fair and big roots, let the owner new set those roots which are grown into a finger-bignesse, well a span distance one from the other; which done, and these somewhat more grown, the owner ought to tread down with the foot, and diligently cover the heads thick with earth, whereby the juice of the leaves and stalks may run to the increasing of the roots.

The roots after the gathering in the moneth of November, may likewise be preserved to serve the Winter and Lent time, as afore is uttered of the Navew.

CHAP. XXVI

What skill and diligence is required with the secrets to be learned in the sowing and ordering of the Radish.

The Garden Radish with us, is better knowne, then I with pen can utter the discription of the same, for in a manner every person as well, as well the rich as the poore, the Citizens as Countrimen, when their stomack is slack or irketh at meat: they then to procure an appetite to feeding, by the same root, by cutting the roots either into a length on each side, or into round slyces, doe workmanlike season them with salt, heating them for the more delight in the mouth, between two dishes, supposing a more tendernesse caused to the roots, through the like doing: whose care and diligence in the bestowing of it in the earth, ought, (after the mind of *Columella*) to be after this manner; that the beds, before the bestowing of the seeds, be well laboured, and workmanlike turned in with dung; and when the roots be grown to some bignesse, then the earth to be raised and diligently heaped about them, for the roots shall be naked or lie bare of earth, that both the Sun and ayre beat upon them, then will they become in their further growth, both hard and hollow like to the Mushrome, as *Plinie* reporteth, which prescribeth to these both a loose and moist earth.

The worthy *Rutilius* (in his instructions of husbandrie) uttereth, that the Radishes refuse a hard, sandy, and gravelly ground, and do joy in the moisture of the aire: besides, these ought to be sown in beds a good distance asunder, and the earth deepe digged after a late or new rain fallen, except the place by hap shall be moist, and soon watered.

The seeds committed to the earth, ought immediately and with diligence, to be covered light with a Rake, and neither dung bestowed within, nor strewed upon the beds (although *Columella* otherwise willeth) but onely chaffe of Corne, as after shall further be uttered.

The skilfull practised in Garden matters report, that these better prosper being orderly set, then curiously sowne, and that these to be bestowed in the earth, as both sown and set, at two times of the yeare, as in the moneth of February, and beginning of March, if the owner shall enjoy the roots timely, and in August unto the middest of September, if the owner would enjoy them much sooner: and these then bestowed in the earth, are without doubt far better, forasmuch as the Radish in the cold season, groweth and encreaseth especially in the root, and is the same time tenderer, whereas the plants otherwise in the faire and warm season, runne up into a leafe or stem. Yet this manner of tryall, to possesse them in sharp Winter, is little use with us, because the Radish can ill abide the bitter ayre, which once bitten and tainted with the frosts either therewith, or soon after dyeth: yet the learned *Plinie* writing of the Radish, uttereth the same to joy so much in the cold ayre, that in Germany hath sometimes been seen a Radish, which grew in compasse so big as an infants middle.

The skilful *Aristomachus* in his learned instructions of husbandry, willeth that the leaves of the Radish in the winter time be broken off, and thrown away, and to heape the earth high about them, least puddles of water do stand in the beds, for the roots on such wise increase and be big in summer time.

Howsoever the roots shal be handled, certain it is, that the cold ayre and frosts do increase and sweeten the roots (as afore uttered of the Rape) if so be they may continue in winter time: for the cold ayre converteth the increasment into the roots, and not into the leaves, although that those (as *Theophrastus* uttereth) doe wax then hard in many places.

The roots are caused to grow the sweeter in eating, and more delectable in taste, if the leaves be broken off (as *Pliny* hath noted) before the Radishes shoot up into a stem.

And the leaf of the Radish, how much the smaller the same shall be, even so much the tenderer and delectable root will it yield, which by watering with a salt liquor, or pickle, causeth to breath forth the bitternesse quite, if any such rest or be in the root.

As the like *Pliny* wrote, that the Radish is to be fed, yea and willed the roots for the tendernesse, to be often watered with pickle, or salt water.

The Egyptians watered with Nitre, to the end the roots might be commendable in sweetnesse and delight to the mouth, which possesse a Cartilage and thick, rinde: to these, in many roots, sharp in taste, yet delectable in the eating, which are part left bare above the ground becometh tough and hard, through the occasion afore uttered, and hollow (like to the Mushroom) unlesse they be wel covered about with light earth.

There are Radishes supposed to be of a feminine kind, which be so sharp, and these possesse smaller leaves, and to the eye be a fairer

Raphanus orbiculatus.
Round Radiſh.

ABOVE *and* OVERLEAF
Radishes from John Gerard's
Herball, *1597.*

green, as *Rutilius* writeth.

If the owner covet to enjoy sweet roots in tast, then after the counsell and mind of the singular *Florentine*, let him steep the seeds for two dayes before, in either water or hony, or Cuite, or else sugred water, and these dried in the shadow, to commit them orderly to the earth.

If the Gardener desire to possesse faire and great roots, let him (after the mind of the aforesaid *Rutilius*) when the roots be grown to some bigness, pluck away all the leaves, saving two within to grow still, which done, cover the earth often over the heads to grow the sweeter and pleasanter.

A like experience in causing the root to become marvellous big, doth *Plinie* skilfully utter and teach, after this manner, by taking a great dibble, with the which making a hole in the earth wel six fingers deep, fill it up with fresh chaffe, after bestow a seed of the Radish with dung and light earth over the mouth, covering the same in like manner even with the earth; these performed, the root will grow and encrease unto the bignesse of the hole.

The skilful practitioners report, that the goodnesse of the Radish is known by the leaves, which the sweeter they be (after the manner) so much the tenderer and more pleasant are the roots in the eating: the like teacheth or sheweth the rinde, which the thinner the same is, so much the delectabler is the root in the tast of the mouth.

The thin bestowing of the seeds in well dressed beds, from the end of August unto the midst of September, and after the coming up diligently weeded about, with leaves broken off, the light earth covered about, and after watered with salt water, doe procure the roots not onely to wax, or grow the bigger, but tenderer and sweeter in the eating, forasmuch as the salt pickle very much abateth the bitternesse consisting in them, as by a like we customably see, that these be eaten with vinegar and salt.

And the plants better prosper, coming up in an open ayre, then bestowed in a shadowy place, where in the increase, the roots be much hindered.

If the owner happen to commit seeds to the earth in a drie season, let them be sown the thicker in beds, and if the same may be in a moist ground lightly watered.

The plants grown to a reasonable height above the earth, and that showres have moistened the ground a day before, the plants may then be removed, and set into beds wel laboured and workman-like dressed, which by diligence bestowed, grow the better and pleasanter in the eating.

That the Radish may not be harmed with the garden fleas, *Theophrastus* willeth to sow in the beds among them, the pulse named *Erum*.

Other singular helps for the most herbs, may be learned in my first part, which I have gathered for the most part out of ancient writers: Here is not to be overpassed, that in the Radishes a bitterness

Radicula sativa minor.
Small garden Radish.

consisteth according to the thickness of the rinde, as the worthy *Pliny* uttereth, which writeth that these also do offend the teeth, by blunting or setting them on edge.

But in this place commeth to mind, a secret very pofitable, and to be esteemed with Vinteners, which the Author freely uttereth to them.

If the Vintener cutteth a Radish into slices, and bestoweth those pieces into a vessel of corrupt Wine, doth in short time draw all the evil savour and lothsomnesse (if any consisteth in the wine) and to these the tartness of it like reviveth, which if the root be not able to rid and draw quite forth this default, let the same immediately be taken forth, and (if need shall require) put a fresh root like ordered. For this no doubt hath been proved, and profiteth many by understanding of this secret.

Raphanus fativus.
Garden Radifh.

This no doubt is a secret very marvellous, that the Radish in no wise agreeth to be placed or grow nigh to the Vine, for the deadly hatred between them, insomuch that the Vine neer growing, turneth or windeth back with the branches, as mightily disdaining and hating the Radish growing fast by: if we may credit the learned *Plinie, Galen*, and the Neapolitane *Rutilius*, which seeme to have diligently noted the same.

And the reason they report to be like (as afore uttered of the agreement of the Colewort with wine) which is through the hid discord of natures consisting in them, so that if the places were changed, yet for all the removing, will they in no manner joy together.

Of which *Androcides* affirmeth the Radish and Colewort, to be a singular remedy against drunkenness, so that the ancient in Greece commonly joyned and matched the drinking of wine, with the Radish, as I afore uttered in the Chapter of the Colewort, so that no marvel it is if that these be used so common.

The Radish in time past hath been in much account, and so worthily esteemed, that *Moschion* the Greek wrote a large pamphlet of the worthy praises of the same yea the Radish before other meats, was so preferred in Greece, that at *Delphos* in the temple of *Apollo*, the Radish was esteemed as Gold, the Beet as Silver and the Rape or Turnup as Lead.

The Radish also is said to polish very fair the Ivory, and buried in a heap of Salt, doth alter & reduce the same into a watry pickle.

The Radish to conclude, in the removing and setting again, looseth the sharpnesse resting in it, and this hath a singular delight in the rind, so that the same be new gathered and not too old of growth, therefore by the example of many seldome eaten, do unadvisedly refuse and omit the using of it.

And drawing to an end, I thinke it right profitable to utter the making of Vinegar with the Radish, as the learned *Petrus Cresoentius* (in his work of Husbandry) hath noted the same, the roots of the Radish (saith he) being dried and brought to fine pouder, and bestowed into a vessel which hath wine in it, let stand to settle (after the well labouring and mixing together) for certain daies: which done, the owner shall enjoy a Radish Vinegar, very laudable and much commended for the disolving and wasting of the stone in the Kidneyes, and many other painfull griefs.

CHAP. XXVII

What care and skill is required in the sowing and workmanlike ordering both of the Parsnip and Carot.

 he seeds of the Parsnep and Carot, require one manner of diligence in the sowing, and to be bestowed in a ground painfully digged, well turned in with Dung, and workmanlike dressed before: but the seed to be committed to the earth, may not be bestowed in beds very thick together, to the end these in the encreasing may grow the fairer and bigger.

The plants are in like manner to be set, and at those times sown as afore uttered of the Radish, as sown in December, January, and February, to serve in Lent and spring time, but these better commended, to be sown in harvest time, to enjoy them all the Lent.

The Gardiner which would possesse faire and big roots, ought to pluck away the leaves often times, and to cover light earth on the heads, as afore uttered of the Radish: besides these grown to some bignesse, at the least so big as the finger, ought to be thinner set, and often weeded about, whereby the roots may grow bigger and sweeter in the eating.

Detail from Pieter Casteels (1684-1749), Peacock and Rabbits in a Landscape.

CHAP. XXVIII

he Garden Poppie (after the minde of the Neapolitane *Rutilius*) ought to be committed to the earth, in the moneth of September, if it be in a hot and dry place: but the seeds in colder and more temperate places, may be bestowed after the middle of February, unto the end of April, and sown in beds among the Coleworts.

The diligence and skill to be used both in the sowing and ordering of the Garden Poppie.

The Plants come the better forward, if so be Vine branches or other boughes of trees be burned in the places, where you after mind to bestow the seeds. To be briefe, the seeds of the Poppie and Dill, require the like order and diligence in the bestowing in the earth, as afore uttered of the herb Charvill and Arach.

CHAP. XXIX

he ancient in time past confounded, or rather contrary matched the Gourds with Cucumbers, as the like also *Plinie* did, and *Euthidemus* the Athenian in his book which he wrote of pot-hearbs, named the Gourd, the Indian Cucumber, and *Menedorus* a follower of *Erasistratus* defineth two kindes of the same: the one, to be Indian, which as he uttereth, is the Cucumber: and the other to be that, which is named the Gourd. The Cucumber besides (after the sentence of *Varro*) is so named for the crooking of it, and the Greek physitians named it both *Sicyon* and *Sicys*, for that it stayeth and represseth (as *Demetrius* writeth) the venerial act, through the coldness consisting in it.

What skill, diligence and secrets is to be learned in the sowing and ordering of the Cucumber.

But leaving further to utter of the kindes, let us come to the matter in teaching what diligence is required, about the well handling of the Cucumber.

The Seeds after the minde of the Neapolitane *Rutilius*, desire to be bestowed in furrows not thick together, and these raised well a foot and a halfe high, but in breadth three foot, and between the furrows must the owner leave spaces of eight foot broad, whereby the Cucumbers (in the growing) may freely wander and spread abroad.

These after the comming up need neither to be raked nor weeded about, for that in their first comming up, they joy and prosper the better by growing among other hearbs, of which these are greatly strengthned and aided.

The plants creep along on the earth, and spread into branches much like to the Vine, which for the weeknesse of the stalke are caused on such wise to spread abroad on the ground, except these be otherwise shored up in their growing, with props workmanly set in the earth, for the better staying up of the weak armes and branches,

that the fruits corrupt not by lying on the earth.

The seeds for the most part, appeare by the sixt or seventh day after the sowing: being sufficiently moistened with store of water for that space and time, by a pot or pots of water dropping continually downe with a list or wollen cloth hanging forth of the mouth of the pot, which manner of watering is named filtring.

This kinde of watering, is one of the chiefest matters required, in that the plants prosper and come speediest forward through the much moisture, in which they mightily joy: Yet these are much hindered, and greatly fear the frosts and cold ayre. For which cause the plants ought at such cold times to be workmanly fenced with mattresses of straw diligently spread over them. The skilfull *Rutilius* writing of the workmanly ordering of the Cowcumber, willeth the seeds to be committed to the earth in the moneths of March, and for danger of the cold frostes, to cover the beds with mattresses of straw, unto the middle of May, at which times the plants ought to be removed, and set againe into beds well dunged, and thick laid for to run forth, and creep abroad on the ground, but the plants yeeld the more; if they be bestowed in beds well filled with earth and dung, and these raised above a foot high.

In the bestowing of the Seeds in the earth, the owner ought to have a care, that he set the seeds in beds a length, and these well two foot asunder one from another, herein considering whether the seeds be broken by the eight or tenth day following, which found either hard or broken, doth denote a perfectness or goodnesse of the Seeds: But these in a contrary manner discerned soft, are unprofitable, and to be cast away, in whose places others require to be set, proving by the sixt or eight day, if the Seeds be broken or otherwise soft, which in a contrary manner seen, bestow others in the places as above taught.

The plants after the comming up, need not be weeded in any manner, for as much as the plants better prosper and grow the fairer, by comming up among other hearbs, of which these take a nourishment.

If the seeds before the sowing, be steeped for two dayes in sheeps milke (as *Rutilius* willeth) or in water and honny, as *Plinie* instructeth, or in Sugared water, which cause the plants, after their perfect growth, to yeeld cowcumbers, both sweet, tender, white, and most pleasant, as well in taste as in sight (as the singular *Columella* hath noted) and before him the Greek *Florentinus*, also after both, *Plinie* and *Palladius*, to all which experience confirmeth.

ABOVE LEFT *A watercolour illustration of the opium poppy, from c. 1568 by Jacques Le Moyne de Morques (1530-88).*

ABOVE RIGHT *Detail from Jan Van Kessel (1626-79)* Vertumnus and Pomona.

The Gardiner which would possesse Cucumbers timely and very soone, yea and all the yeare through, ought (after the minde of the Neopolitane) in the beginning of the spring, to fill up old worne baskets and earthen pans without bottomes, with fine sifted earth tempered afore with fat dung, and to moisten somewhat the earth with water, after the seeds bestowed in these, which done when warme and sunnie daies succeede, or a gentle raine falling, the baskets or pans with the plants, are then to be set abroad, to be strengthened and cherished by the sun and small showres: but the evening approching, these in all the cold season ought to be set under some warme cover or house in the ground, to be defended from the frosts and cold aire, which thus standing under a cover, or in the warme house, moisten gently with water sundry times, and these on such wise handle, untill all the Frosts, Tempests, and cold aire be past, as commonly the same ceaseth not with us, till abut the middest of May.

After these, when opportunity or an apt day serveth the Gardener shall bestow the Baskets or Pannes unto the brimme, or deeper in the earth, well laboured or trimmed before, with the rest of the diligence to be exercised, as before uttered: which done, the Gardener shall enjoy very forward and timelier Cowcumbers then any others.

This matter may be compassed, both easier, in shorter time, and with lesser travell, if the owner, after the cutting of the waste branches, doth set them in well laboured beds, for these in far shorter time and speedier, doe yeeld faire Cucumbers.

This one thing I think necessary to be learned, for the avoiding of the daily labour and paines, in the setting abroad and carrying into the house, either halfe tubs, baskets, or earthen pannes, which on this wise by greater facility may be done, if so be the Gardener bestow the vessells with the plants in Wheel-barrowes, or such like with Wheeles: for these, to mens reason, causeth marvellous easinesse, doth in the bestowing abroad, and carrying againe into the warme house, as often as need shall require:

The young plants may be defended from cold and boisterous windes, yea, frosts, the cold aire, and hot Sunne, if Glasses made for the onely purpose, be set over them, which on such wise bestowed on the beds, yeelded in a manner to *Tiberius Cæsar*, Cucumbers all the year, in which he tooke a great delight, as after the worthy *Columella*, the learned *Plinie* hath committed the same to memory, which every day obtained the like, as he writeth.

But with a lesser care and labour, may the same be performed, as *Columella* writeth, if in a sunnie and well dunged place (saith he) be sundrie roddes set a row, aswell of the Osier or Bramble, and these so planted in the earth, after the Equinoctiall of Harvest, to cut a little within the earth, whose heads after the wiser enlarging with a stiffe woodden prick, to bestow soft dung either within the pithes of Osiers and Brambles consisting in the middes: these done, to fixe or put seeds of the Cucumber into the places, which after the growing to some bignesse, joyne with Osiers, and brambles.

For the plants on such wise growing, are after not fed with their owne, but as it were by another mother roote feeding, which by the same meanes yeeld Cucumbers, that will indure the cold season and frosts.

The learned *Plinie* uttereth the same matter, admonishing here the reader of the wrong instructions of *Columella*, although he seemeth to alledge an Authour, for which cause it shall be to great purpose to heare the sentence of *Plinie* in this, who removing the error of *Columella* uttered, that Cucumbers may be enjoyed all the yeare green, instructeth and willeth, that the greatest roddes of the bramble be set againe into a sunnie place, where these be cut, well two fingers long, about the equinoctiall spring or middle March, and into the heads of these after large holes made, the seeds to be bestowed lying especially within the pitches of the Brambles, and filled with soft dung, which done, that fat dung and fine Earth, after the well mixing together, ought to be thicke laid, and diligently heaped about the roots, which may the better resist the cold.

But howsoever these ought to be handled, it well appeareth, that *Plinie* doth disagree with *Columella*, in this instruction.

For *Plinie* willeth these to be set about the Equinoctiall spring, but *Columella* about the Equinoctiall Harvest, as the Neapolitan *Rutilius* interpreted and noted the same, to whom, as it should seeme, he bare a favour.

The plants much feare the thunder and lightning, for which cause the Gardener may not set nor remove them at those times: besides, if the tender fruits be not covered over with sheets or thin Coverlets, when such tempests or stormes happen, they commonly after perish and wither.

The Gardener minding to possesse long and tender Cucumbers, ought to set under the young fruits growing, an earthen panne, Bole, or halfe tub, filled with faire water, well five or six fingers, yea, halfe a foot distance from them, for these by the next day, will be stretched unto the water, so that setting the Pannes lower into the earth, or raising the fruits higher, ye shall daily see them stretched forth towards the water, unto the admiration of the owner, for the length of them: which deprived of their vessels of water, shall in a contrary manner see them winded and crooking, so much these joy in the moisture, and hate the drouth: the fruits likewise will grow of a marvellous length, if the flowres be put to grow within hollow Canes or Pipes of the Elder: but the same is otherwise to be learned of the Oyle, for as the Cucumbers so deadly hate (as *Plinie* writeth) that setting vessels of the oile, in steed of the water under them, they after bend and winde away, as disdaining the licour, which the owner shall well trie and see that these to have bended so crooked or winding as an hooke in one nights space.

But there must be a speciall care, as *Columella* (after the Greek *Florentinus* (admonisheth, that no woman, at that instant, having the reds or monethly course, approacheth nigh to the fruits, especially handle them, for through the handling at the same time they feeble and wither.

If she in the place be like affected, she shall after kill the young fruits, with her onely look fixed on them, or cause them to grow after unsaverie or else corrupted.

The Cowcumber will yeeld fruits without seeds, if three dayes before the sowing, the seeds be steeped in Oyle *Sesasininium* or Savin Oyle (as the Neopolitan *Rutilius* hath noted) or that the seeds afore be steeped in the juice of the hearb named of *Plinie, Culix*, or as the same in Greek may be conjectured to *Coniza*, in English Flebane.

The like shall be wrought, if the first armes or branches (after the condition of the veins) be on such wise digged about, that only the heads of them appear naked, which a third time to be like barred, if need shall so require, yet such a diligence to be exercised in the same, that what branches grow out, and spread on the earth to be workemanly cut away, preserving onely the stemme and branches that last shoot forth: which on such wise handled, yeeld fruits with the onely Pulpes, having no seeds in them.

If the Gardener desireth to enjoy Cowcumbers, having Romane

BELOW LEFT *A watercolour illustration of a marigold by Jacques Le Moyne de Morgues (1530-88).*

BELOW RIGHT *A watercolour illustration of camomile, from c. 1568, by Jacques Le Moyne de Morgues (1530-88).*

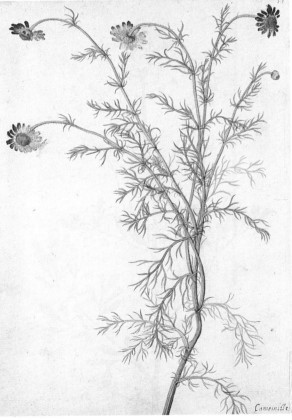

letters, strange figures, and scutchins or armes imbossed on the greene rinde without, he may after the lively countersetting of formes on the Moulds of wood, bestow of the potters clay, or plaister of Paris unto the thicknesse of a finger, which like handled, and cut into two parts, let drie in a faire and hot place, that these may the sooner serve to use, after bestow into the hollow moulds, framed to a like bignesse and length as the fruite of the young cowcumbers, which fast bound about, and so close together, that no aire breath in, let these on such wise hang untill the fruits have filled the moulds within, which they joy to doe, and be ready to be gathered.

For the young fruits of property, by the report of the skilfull, do so much desire or be so wonderfull desirous of a new forme, that into what workemanly vessel or mould the young fruits be bestowed, they by an earnest will and desire represent the figures counterfeited within, as the same is found noted in a singular work of Husbandrie which, why *Rutilius* may ascribe to *Gargilius Martialis*, I see no reason.

To be brief, as the cunning of the mould shall be, such will the beautie of the fruites be: for many fruits have been seen (as *Plinie* reporteth) which presented the image of a winding Dragon on them.

BELOW LEFT *A watercolour illustration of a gherkin cucumber, from* c. *1568, by Jacques Le Moyne de Morgues (1530-88).*

BELOW RIGHT *A watercolour illustration of mallow and 'Flag fly' by Jacques Le Moyne de Morgues (1530-88).*

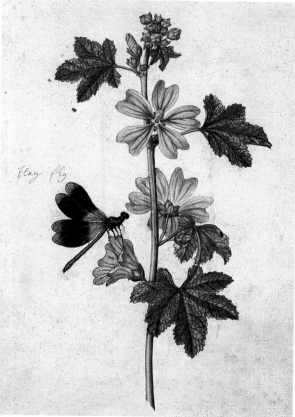

The owner minding to injoy Cucumbers, a long time fresh and faire, ought to bestow them in white wine lies uncorrupted or not turned, the vessel after the well pitching without, covered with a heap of sand in some low seller or vault in the ground.

The Cucumbers do like continue a long time, if they be bestowed in a proper Pickle, made of water and salt.

But the freshnesse and delight of them, will a longer time be preserved, if after the husbandly instructions, the owner hang them so high in Barrells or Firkins, being a quarter filled or somewhat lesse, that these in the hanging doe in no manner touch the vineger.

And the vessels shall be diligently pitched about, which the owner prepareth to serve to this purpose, that the force of the vineger, in no manner breatheth forth, for this by nature is otherwise penetrable, and pierceth through the thinnesse of parts. And by this practise, may the owner at due times, all the winter through, make delectable Sallets of them.

The Cucumbers (by report of the skilful) are the longest time preserved fresh and green, if so be these are bestowed in a Glasse vessel, filled with the purest distilled vinegar, which if the owner will, he may also preserve a long time, if that he cut them off, whiles they yet be young and small, and these bestow in a vessel of hot water to be scalded, which done, lay the Cucumbers abroad all the night time, to be throughly cooled, after lay Cucumbers into a vessel filled with a sharp Pickle, made of water and salt: for this will preserve them, by the former meanes, untill new doe come or may be had.

The ancient report, that a Pickle may be made, to preserve the Cucumbers and Gourds a long time, with salt, vinegar, Fennell, and Marjoram, if so be the Cucumbers in some vessel, be laid by courses, and these above named, strewed between.

There be others, which affirme, that these may a long time be preserved fresh and green, if they be bestowed into the Pickle made of Vinegar and Mustard seed wrough together.

The learned *Pliny* willeth the Cucumbers to be laid in a furrow made in a shadowie place, strewed after the form of a bed with sifted sand, which on such wise handled, to be covered over with earth and dry Hey.

Atheneus reporteth, that the Cucumbers be biggest and fairest to the eye, at the full of the Moon, so that these receive an increase according to the Moons light, through the watry moisture consisting in them.

For which cause, if the Gardiner mindeth to enjoy fair and big Cucumbers, let those be gathered at the full of the moon, wherein the decrease or wane of the Moon, they be then slenderer and not so sightly to sale.

To these, this *Atheneus* (favored of *Plinie*) addeth, that how often it thundereth and lightneth, the Cucumbers (as striken with fear) turn and bend.

This one thing is marvellous, that Moiles and Asses are exceedingly delighted with Cucumbers, in so much that they receiving the savour far off, are by a marvellous delight allued to runne and breake into a place, where these many fruits grow. For which cause, the hedges and banks about must be strong made, whereby they in no manner, break in to tread down and wast the Cucumbers.

But the same is more marvellous which in the Greek instructions of Husbandry is noted, and of many hath been proved, that if an Infant being sick of the Ague, and sucking still of the breast be laid on the bed made of the Cucumbers to sleep, being framed of like length to the Child, and that he sleepeth on the bed but a little time or a nap, he shall immediately be delivered of the same, for while he sleepeth, all the feverous heat passeth in the Cucumbers.

If the owner would enjoy Cucumbers, having but little water in them, he must dig a furrow, of a reasonble depth, and the same filled half up with chaffe, or the wast branches of Vines or trees, finely broken, cover over with earth, into which then bestow the seeds of a reasonable distance asunder, and in the comming up, water not the plants, or these moisten very little, but in the rest order the plants as afore taught.

To the loosing and purging of the body it also belongeth: if the owner shall steepe the seeds in the roots of the wild Cucumber bruised, either Ruberb, Turbith, Agarick, Ellebore, or any such like made into a Potable water, for three dayes together, or for five dayes together, after the Plants shoot up, doth often moisten them with this liquor, he shall after enjoy fruits, which will gently purge the belly.

And they may be caused to work the stronger, if the roots, while they send forth the branches, be digged about, and the smaler roots upward cut away, in the places of which, a quantity of the Ellebore, and some other purging simple laid, and the earth diligently covered about.

CHAP. XXX

ll the kinds of Gourds, require the same travell and diligence in the bestowing in the earth, as afore uttered of the Cucumbers, which after the larger setting asunder and often watering, appear (for the most part) above the earth, by the sixt or seventh day after the bestowing in beds.

What skill and secrets are to be learned in the sowing, and workmanlike ordering of the Gourd.

The weak and tender branches, shot up to some height, and coveting by a certain property in nature upward, require to be diversly added with poles to run up in sundry manners, as either over a round and vaulted Harbor, to give more delight, through the shadow caused by it, and the seemly fruits hanging down, or else by poles directed quite upright, in which the Gourd (of all other fruits) most earnestly desireth, rather then to run branching and creeping on

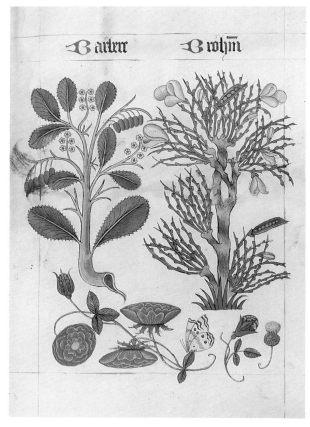

ABOVE LEFT *Barberry and broom with butterfly, thistle, and roses. From a Tudor pattern book of the early sixteenth century in the style of the Low Countries.*

ABOVE RIGHT *Strawberry and birch with two sprays of birdseye. In common with many Tudor plant illustrators, the artist was not working from live specimens, but copying or possibly drawing from memory: this illustration was incorrectly labelled 'Blackberry'.*

the ground like to the Cucumbers.

The plants love a fat, moist, and dunged loose ground, as the Neapolitan *Rutilius* in his instructions of Husbandry hath noted, if a diligence be bestowed in the often watering of them, the plants require a lesser care and travell, in that they are very much furthered, by the store of moisture, although there may be found of those, which reasonably prosper with small store of moisture, or being seldom watered, and that they of the same yield fruit of a delectable tast.

If the owner or Gardener happen to commit seeds to the earth in a dry ground, and that the tender plants appear above the earth his care shall then be to water them plentiful for the speedier shooting up, after this manner: by taking certain pots filled with water, into which tongue of cloth afore laid to the bottoms of the pots, that these may the workmanlier distill and drop often on the plants, through the stooping forward of them: which no doubt profiteth greatly the plants in drough and hot seasons.

The longer and smaller have few seeds in them, and for the same more delectable in the eating; yea, these are better accounted of, and sold in the Market.

The Gardiner, minding to commit of the seeds to the earth, ought afore to steepe them in a Bole or Panne of water for a night, whereby the seeds apt to be sown, may the surer be known, which he shall well perceive by those resting in the bottome, of the cunninger sort preferred and used, but the others swimming above, as unprofitable, and serving to no use, are willed to be throwne away.

The chosen seeds are to be set in beds together with three fingers unto the middle Joynts, and sharper ends fixed upward, but the beds afore ought to be digged two foot deep, and so many broad, and the seeds bestowed wel three or four foot asunder, one from the other (in these filled up with old dung,) well turned in with the earth: or rather to procure them speedier to grow and yield the fruit the sooner, let the beds be filled with hot Horse dung, new taken out of the stable.

If the Gardiner would possesse Gourds of divers formes, as long, round, and short, it behooveth him to choose and set the seeds accordingly. For those seeds taken out of the neck of the Gourd, shall the owner after the counsell of the singular *Columella*, learned *Plinie*, and *Rutilius*, set in well dunged ground, with the sharp ends upward. Which after the well watering (as above taught) yield fruits long in form, tenderer, and better esteemed. The seeds taken out of the midst of the belly, and set into the earth with the big ends upward, do

BELOW LEFT *Daffodil and carnation with besom, wooden fork, saltbox, and broken eggcup. From an early sixteenth-century Tudor pattern book.*

BELOW RIGHT *Violet and woodruff with two sprays of flowers. From an early sixteenth-century Tudor pattern book.*

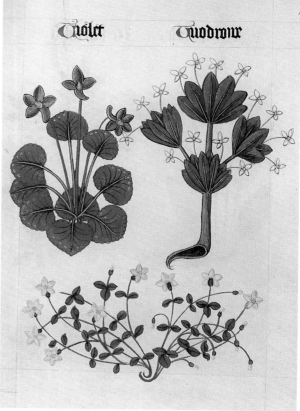

yield (after the husbandly handling and watering) great fruits, round and large, of which after the thorow drying, and meat taken out, be Bottles and other Vessels made, to serve for divers uses, in that these grow far larger in the belly, then any of the other kinds.

The seeds taken out of the bottome of the Gourd, and set with the grosse or big ends upward, do also yield after the workmanlike ordering, fruits both great and large, yet these far lesser and shorter. And the seeds in generall, in what place they be set, ought to be bestowed in earth wel dunged, and the rather with hot horse dung, new taken out of the stable, if these be set in the moneth of March. But the seeds in no manner, may be bestowed in low places, least showers of raine falling, hinder and corrupt the fruits, through the overmuch water cloying and standing in the Alley or other low place: the plants shot up to some height, ought to be diligently weeded about, and the earth heaped high up, and when need requireth in the hot seasons, to water them often.

If the seeds happen to be set in a earth smally laboured, and hollow, when the plants be somewhat grown above the ground, the owner ought to dig away of a good depth (from the young plants) the earth round about, that the roots may the freelier runne and spread abroad: the plants further growne and shot up, may the owner erect to run and spread like to a Vine well a mans height.

If the plants happen to be anoyed with the Leke or Garden fleas, the owner shall remove and drive them away, by the onely setting of the herb Organie, in sundry places among them, on which (if they happen to light) they either are incontinent killed, or caused to encrease but few after, as the Greek writers of husbandry, in their skilfull practises witnesse: out of which with diligence we have also gathered these, that to the owner or Gardener may happily appear profitable; as the Gourd (a matter somewhat strange) to yield fruits without seeds, if the seeds before the setting be steeped for three dayes at the least, in *Sesaminum*, or Savin oile, as the Neapolitan *Rutilius* uttereth, or in the juyce of that herb infused, named *Conyza*, in English, Fleabane.

The like may be wrought, if after the condition of the Vine, the principallest and first stem shot up, be on such wise digged about, that all onely the head of the same be left bare; which as it shall encrease, must the owner repeat: yea, a third time if need shall require the same.

And in this doing, must the owner have a care, that as the branches spread for (whether upright or on the ground) to be cut away, herein preserving onely that stem, which shot forth last.

The Gourds on such wise handled (as the Cucumber afore noted) wil yield fruits without seeds, possessing onely Cartilages, and a soft pulpe within. If the owner would possesse fruits timely and very soon, then (after the instruction of the Greek writers of husbandry) bestow in earthen pans or old baskets without bottoms, fine sifted earth intermedled with dung, about the beginning of the spring, in which

Pumpkin gourd from Fuchsius Fuchs, De Historia stirpium, *1542.*

the seeds set, sprinckle and moisten sundry time with water: after this, in faire and sunny dayes, or when a gentle shower falleth, set them abroad, but when the Sun goeth downe, bestow the baskets with the plants within the house again, and these like order so often (and water when need requireth) until all the frosts, tempests, and cold seasons be gone and past. After this assoon as oppertunity and time will serve, and that a faire day be present, bestow all the baskets and pans of earth unto the brim, in well laboured and dressed beds, and applie that other diligence required, through which the Gardner shall possesse, timely fruit, as well of the Gourds as Cucumber.

The same matter shall the owner bring to passe, and cause with lesser cost, travail, and time, if he cut away the wast branches of the Gourds, or tender shoots of the Cucumbers, for on such wise handled, they speedier yield and send forth their fruits.

If the Gardener coveteth to enjoy divers formes on Gourds, or sundry caracters on Cucumbers, let him bestow the flower or tender young fruit of either, as the same shall yet be hanging on the branch, into a mould of like bignesse, as the fruit: which so handled, will after cause the Gourd or Cucumber, to possesse on the upper face, the like figures or caracters, as were afore imprinted within the mould.

For the fruit of either, after the mind of *Gargilio*, so much desireth a new form, that it like representeth the image or figure imprinted within the mould. Insomuch that of what form the mould of the Gourd shal be fashioned, on such manner shal the fruit grow within the mould: And *Plinie* for confirmation of the same reporteth, that he sow many Gourds fashioned in their full growth after the form of a winding Dragon. If the owner endeavoureth to possesse long and slender Gourds, he must bestow the young fruits new grown, and hanging still on the Vine branches, either into a trunck of wood, or a long Cane bored through all the joynts, which in time growing, wil stretch & shoot forth into a marvellous length. For the substance which should encrease into a bredth, is caused through the hollow pipe to stretch and grow slender, whereby the narrownesse of the hole so hindering the bignesse of growths, procureth the fruit to run into a length, as the like Gourd by the same occasion, *Plinie* saw to extend well nine foot of length. The like fruits altogether shall the Gardener purchase, if under the Vines, he set of some deepnesse in the ground earthen pans filled with water, and they distant well five or six fingers from the Gourds hanging downe. For by the morrow or next day shall he see the fruits stretched even down to the water, by which feeding and handling of the pans with water, they may be caused to grow of a wonderfull length.

But the pannes for a time removed or taken away, will cause the fruits to crooke and winde upwards, so much of property they joy in moisture, and refuse or hate the drowth: yet of the oyle is otherwise to be learned, forsomuch as they deadly hate the same as *Plinie* writeth, which if in the stead of water it be set under the fruits causeth them by the next day to winde another way.

Gourd plant from The Grete Herball, *1526.*

RIGHT *Wild clary and rosemary with two birds and two sprays of cornflowers. From an early sixteenth-century Tudor pattern book.*

FAR RIGHT *Foxglove and Fennel with ladle, spit, pestle, and metal tool. From an early sixteenth-century Tudor pattern book.*

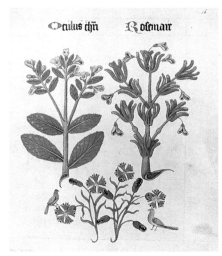

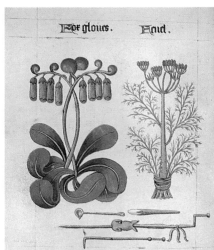

Sperage and sage with a castellated stone building, trees, and peacock. From an early sixteenth-century Tudor pattern book. 'Sperage' was an early word for asparagus, and this may be the artist's impression of what it looked like.

If this likewise they cannot doe, yet doe the writhe, and as it were disdaining of the same, crooke upward after the manner of a hooke, as a like forme of the fruit may be tried in one night space.

This one matter ought especially to be cared for, as *Columella* after the Greek *Florentinus* warneth, that no woman come or very seldome approach nigh to the fruits of the Gourdes or Cucumbers, for by her onely handling of them, they feeble and wither, which matter if it shall happen in the time of the Termes, doth either then slay the young tender fruits with her looke, or causeth them to be unsaverie, and spotted or corrupted within. The Gourds determined to be kept for seed, ought after the minde of *Rutilius* the Neapolitane, to hang still on their vine, unto the winter time, and cut or broken from the same, to be dried either in the Sun, or in the smoke: for the seeds otherwise are prone to putrifie, and not after profitable to any use.

The Gourds and Cucumbers will indure, and be kept along time fresh and faire to the eye, if they be hid and covered with white wine lees, not over eger or sowre, in the hanging downe in pipes or hogsheads. They be in like manner defended and preserved by bestowing them in a pickle or brine. But they will a long time continue fresh and faire (as the worthy instructers of husbandrie report) if so be they hang so high within the vessels, that they be nothing neere to the vineger. And the vessels appointed for the onely purpose, shall diligently be pitched over and round about, least the spirits of the vineger in the meane time breath forth, and by nature otherwise is penetrable, through the thinnesse of parts. The Cucumbers may in like manner be kept for a long time, if they shall be bestowed in a vessel of distilled vineger: for on such wise they putrifie not, as hath been tried of the skilfull searchers of secrets.

Thus by these practises, may the owner injoy faire Cucumbers and Gourds all the winter to use, which if the Gardener will, shall he also preserve a long time, if while the fruits be tender, he cut them off, and

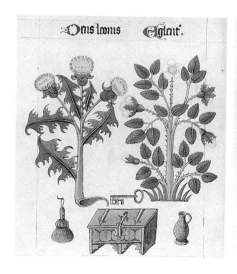

FAR LEFT *Dandelion and eglantine with tassel, chest, and pewter jug. From an early sixteenth-century Tudor pattern book.*

LEFT *Thistles and teazle with a moated castle and a stork in the nest. From an early sixteenth-century Tudor pattern book.*

scalde them in hot water, and after lay them abroad all the night to coole, and bestow them on the morrow into a sharpe pickle or brine, made for the onely purpose, which on such wise handled, will marvellous well indure, untill the new be come.

In this place cometh to minde, and that very aptly, the same which *Atheneus* boasted, as touching his strange feast that he prepared for his friends, especially in that he served them with greene Gourds for a daintie dish, in the moneth of January, which so pleasantly savoured and eate, as if they had been new gathered, in a manner. Which like, by studie and diligence of the Gardeners that exercised this art, they supposed them to be preserved.

As the like *Nicander* long before *Athaneus*, and many others report, who will the Gourds to be first dried in the aire, and stitched through the heads with a strong packthread, to be after hanged up in the smoke, that the pots filled with them may leasurely soak all the winter, and drinke in of the Brine.

At this day in France, through all the winter moneths, are the Gourds hanged up in the roofes of their houses, to be preserved for daintie dishes green, when occasion offereth to use them, especially those which are named the Citrones, that far longer indure, and be not so lightly subject to putrifying.

The fruits of the Gourds, Mellons, Pompons, and Cucumbers, may be caused to loose and purge, like to many others, if the seeds be steeped for a night and a day in the licour made with *Ruberbe, Agaricke, Turbith, Senæ, Colocynthis, Scamonie*, or other simple purging medecines and those after the bestowing in the earth, watered for five dayes together, and five times every day. When the Gourd is felt unpleasant, the fruits by the steeping, may after receive what savour and taste the owner will, if the seeds before they be committed to the earth, be infused for a time in any pleasant licour, whether the same be damask or musk water, for the plants shooting

Pea and Rose with a naked youth with bagpipes, and a naked child with pipes and tabor. From an early sixteenth-century Tudor pattern book.

up of, these will yeeld fruit of like savour, as well being sodden as raw, after the condition of the Cucumber.

The like altogether may be wrought or caused without any art, if whiles the fruit is a seething, you bestow in the licour what taste, colour, or savour you desire to have. For the Gourd and Cucumber are of sucha kinde, that they be void of any qualitie.

The rinde of the fruit of the Gourd grown to full ripenesse, becommeth so hard as wood.

The Gourd planted in the ashes of mens bones, and watered with oile, yeeldeth fruit by the ninth day, as the ancient *Hermes* affirmeth. Which man, for that he teacheth vaine matters, for the same cause he giveth me occasion to credit him weakly. Yet experience doth many times cause the uncertaine to prove certaine.

CHAP. XXXI

Of the rare helps and secrets of the Pompons, Mellons, and Musk Mellions.

he ancient, both of the Greek and Latine writers of Husbandrie, attributed the Pompons and Mellons, to a kinde of Cucumbers which they confessed, very neer to agree with them, in that the Cucumbers, in their growth have been seene, to be changed into Pompons, and Mellon Pompons, which two kindes of fruite, doe differ in themselves, especially in the forme and quantity: for when these appeare to exceed in bignesse, they are then named Pompons, but they growing round, and in forme of an Apple fashioned, are by a

Jacques Linard, Still Life with Peaches, Plums and Melon, *1642.*

bie-name of the Pompon and Apple, named Mellon Pompons. For which cause *Palladius* nameth all this kind of forme Apples, Mellons; or as if a man should say he named them apple-wise, or Quince-like, which are not wont to hang, as *Plinie* writeth, but to grow round on the ground, and they are then grown to ripenesse, when the stalk is parted from the body, and a sweet savour from the belly striketh to the Nose. Further, those growing after the formes of the Quince, which properly are named Mellons, have a harder and tougher meat then Pompons, and they not onely enjoy lesser wrinckles in the rind, but be drier, grosser, whiter of flesh, and have more seeds then the Pompons.

The other kind, named Cytrons, be in form and colour like to the Citron, and the leaves of the branches divided into many smal parts after the form, feathers, or wings of Birds.

The other kind named the Winter Pompons, are nothing so big of growth, as be the common Pompons of the Garden.

But the best kind of all, are the Mellons, next the Turkish pompons, and those made sweet by art, when the Seeds before the bestowing in the earth, are for a night laid in water well mixed with Sugar, or honey.

The Mellons and Pompons hardly come up in any Country, at due time of the yeare, without labour, cost and diligence of the Gardener in hastening them forward, nor these caused well to spread and yield before the great heat of the year be come, which season, some yeare, hapneth divers, and intermedled with cold, and either over dry, or over moist; which much hinder the ripening of them in the harvest time, and toward the vintage. For which cause the Gardener ought to hasten the fruits forward by dung, and heat of the beds, which alwaies procure a more health to persons. The seeds of Mellons to be committed to the earth, ought to be such which have been kept within the fruit, unto the full ripenesse of the same: for these then taken forth of the Mellon be more worth, and reserve in them the proper substance within the bodies. If the owner would possesse the fruits of the Mellon timely, he ought afore to infuse the seeds in luke warm water, for six or ten hours, and those after to bestow in beds, prepared, about the tenth day of March, well three or four foot distant one from the other, and the beds to be cast well two foot high, and so many broad, and to fill them with old dung finely broken, and with black earth sufficiently loose wrought together, for on such wise handled they yeeld a bigger, fuller, and pleasanter fruit. Certaine skilfull Gardeners bestow horse dung in beds, so hot as the same cometh forth of the stable, to cause the plants far sooner to shoot up, and they turn upward six or ten of the seeds of the Pompons with the sharp ends downward, as certain do four or five of them to come up, and those they lightly cover over, with much beating or treading the earth downe on them. *Rutilius* in his husbandry, willeth the seeds both of the Mellon and Pompon, to be thin set in beds, in such manner, that the seeds be placed well two foot asunder, and the

A Spanish melon from John Gerard's Herball, *1597.*

places well digged and diligently turned in with fine dung, for the plants joy in a libertie, that they may spread at will hither and thither, and are greatly holpen by other herbs, growing among them, as the Cucumbers are, so that they shall need but little raking and pulling away of other herbs.

After these, for danger of the cold and frosts, the owner may cover the plants and beds with light mattresses made of straw, or with mats spread on rods, shored up with the forkes set at each corner of the beds, or he may for a seemlier sight, laie abroad bords or tables on pillers or other fraimes of stone, set at each corner of the beds in such manner, that the bords may be lifted off, when the sun shineth hot, and cover again, at the going down of the sun, or when the cold aire is felt.

And assoone as the Mellon hath yeelded leaves sufficient great, the Gardener ought to water the same gently and softlie, with a sift sharpened at the end hanging forth, and broad at the other end, resting within the Pot or Dish full of water, which on such wise continually moistneth (by the drops falling) the Earth verie drie.

The Mellons further growne, the owner ought to remove, and set the plants againe, when the fruits are yeelded so bigge as Orenges, and this especially must be done after the middest of May, when as the cold of the yeare is wel spent, that otherwise might hinder the growth of them, and set well six foot distant one from the other, in beds diligently dunged and laboured.

The Pompons purchase a far greater sweetnesse, and pleasanter in taste, if the seeds afore be steeped for three dayes in water well mixed with Sugar, or in water and honey named Mulse; and in like manner the fruits are found sweet in the eating, if the seeds steeped in new Cow milk, be then set wel in dressed beds.

The Pompons in like manner will obtain a savour of Roses, if the seeds afore be laied among dry Rose leaves for twenty or thirty dayes together, and those after with the leaves, set in wel dressed beds, or the seeds steeped in Rose-water, or other odoriferous liquor, which after the drying in the shadow, then as afore uttered, committed to the earth, as the worthy Author *Florentinus* in his Greek instructions of Husbandry writeth, and after him the like that worthy *Rutilius*.

Here I think it a matter not to be omitted, that Cats by an earnest desire cover the Pompons, for which cause the owners must have a care to looke diligently thereunto.

To procure Pompons to continue a long time without decaying or corrupting, let the owner water the plants for a time, with the juyce of Houseleek.

The other matters to be learned, are fully taught in the secrets of the Cucumbers and Gourds, where many devises are uttered, that may be used common. As if the owner would enjoy timely fruits, and having strange forms on them, big, laxative, and without seeds, let him diligently read and consider the former Chapters, both of the Cucumber and Gourd.

The Mellons and Pompons ought then be gathered, when the stalks begin to feeble, and the fruits to yeeld a pleasant savour in the eating, at which time the owner must diligently take heed of Cats, that have an earnest love and desire to them, as afore is uttered.

Also the Gardener ought to conceive, that those named the winter Pompons, doe never grow to a full ripenesse on their beds, and for that cause to procure them speedily to ripen, he must (after the gathering) hang them up in the roof of the house, and eat of those, when they appear yellow within.

CHAP. XXXII

 here afore we have sufficiently written of the apt placing and workmanly ordering of the most hearbs and fruits, both for the pot and sallets, and for their benefits for the use of physick: in this part following (for a further increase and comfort of the simple) we purpose to intreat not onely of the artly placing of sundrie physick hearbs, but to what uses these serve for the aid and benefit of health.

Worthie instructions about the sowing and setting of sundrie physick hearbs, to these of the greatest number of fragrant hearbs, and pleasant flowers: and first of the blessed Thistle.

And of these we intend to begin with that worthie hearb named the blessed Thistle (for his singular vertues) aswel against poysons, as the pestilent ague, and other perillous diseases of the heart: which to many at this day is very well known, although great controversies have been amongst the ancient Phisitians, about the true description of the hearb: for both the name and forme of the hearb, doe declare the same to be a kinde of thistle: yet the learned *Rutilius* writing of the blessed thistle, came neerer to a troth, and faithfuller described the forme of the hearb, in that he affirmed the same to have a big stalk, and leaves crisped with prickles (after the condition of the Endive) the flower yellowish, and seeds small, contained within the soft downe, (as in the other thistles) and that they doe late wax ripe.

This hearb named the blessed thistle, requireth to be sowne in a well laboured ground, and the seeds ought to be committed to the earth in the first quarter of the moone, but those not to be bestowed in beds above three fingers deep.

The hearb also joyeth and well prospereth comming up among Wheat.

CHAP. XXXIII

What care and secrets are to be learned in the sowing and setting of the hearb Angelica.

he hearb *Smyrnium*, which at this day of all the Physitians and Poticaries throughout Europe is named *Angelica*: this when in the first year it shall come up of the seed, yeeldeth stalks of a foot and a halfe high, a finger big, round, tender, smooth, and bending back to the earth: these also divided and spread forth into two, or three, and many times four smaller stalks or armes, in whose top are leaves in forme like to the leaves of the Smallach, but far greater, and those, divided into three parts, sharp fashioned at the end, and growing unto twelve fingers in height and breadth, and green all the Winter.

In the second or third year, the stemme shooteth up, out of the middle of the leaves, and in height two or sometimes three cubits, increasing within a thumb bigness for the most part, round jointed, whitish and smooth, and as the same were sprinckled with dusty spots and hollow within, beset also with leaves in joynt forme, much lesser then the abovesaid. This also hath little branches and certain stemmes shooting forth, in whose top are great tuffes, well five or six inches broad, and those in forme imbossed round, and full of whitish flowers, in which doe after succeed two seeds, conjoyned together, long, cornered, and of ashie white colour: those also contained within the huske, be long, plain, black without, white within, and the tough kernel covered with a rinde or pilling sharp edged. This increaseth in root many times so big as the hand can clapse about, and sometimes bigger, yea, it sendeth forth the root before the stemme be come up, which root increaseth in years well a foot of length, or into many parts divided, being black without, and white within, big, soft, and full of Juice, which being cut, sendeth forth a yellow Juice, or licour from the inner side of the rinde, and a like licour is contained in the veins of the leaves, but the same more watery.

The root, seeds, and leaves possess an eager taste, fretting the jawes, somewhat bitter, thin, and aromatick or sweet smelling.

The most effectuous of all the parts, is the proper licour, next the seeds, then the root, last the flowers and leaves.

The hearb Angelica joyeth to be sowne in a well laboured earth, and the same rather drie than moist, for the harming by wormes, after the comming up, this requireth to be diligently weeded about and seldome watered. This Angelica flourisheth and beareth flowers in the moneth of July and August.

CHAP. XXXIV

he Valerian groweth up with a long and high stem, jointed and hollow, bearing on the top a tuffe, and flowers purple mixed with a whitenesse, or white mixed with a rednesse, after the form of Organy, the root as big as the little finger, and white, with many other small roots branching in the earth, and these yellowish of colour, sweet in savour. And this doth *Hieronimus* book report to be true Valerian, and that rare to be found, which for the rarenesse, is at this day sowen in many Gardens. The Valerian cometh very well up, being bestowed in a moist and well dunged ground, and the herbe after the coming up, requireth to be often watered, untill it has yeelded a high stem.

What care and diligence is required in the artly sowing of the herbe Valerian.

CHAP. XXXV

he Bytonie is an herbe, having a slender stem, and foure square growing in many places a foot and a half high, and leaves long and soft and indented round about, like the Oken leaves, and sweet smelling, among the which, greater leaves are those growing nigh to the root: in the top of the stems is the seed, cared after the manner of Saverie, the roots spreading small, and beareth purple flowers.

The herbe Bytonie joyeth to be sown in a moist and cold ground, and by a brick or stone wall, to enjoy the shadow of the same, for the herbe much delighteth to stand in the Sunne beams.

The diligence required in the bestowing of the herbe Bytonie.

CHAP. XXXVI

he Lovage joyeth to grow by waies, and under the Eeves of an house, it also prospereth in shadowy places, but especially delighteth to grow near to a running water.

This in the growing sendeth up a long and slender stemme, like to Dyl, jointed with leaves round about like to the Melyote, sweet savouring, tenderer and softer, towards the top smaller and much more divided. In the top of the stemme groweth a tuffe, in which consisteth the seed black, hard, and long, like to the

The skill and diligence required in the artly bestowing of the Hearb Lovage.

Fennell seed, being sharp in taste, and sweet in smelling, it also beareth flower, and hath a pale root within, but black without, sharp, sweet savoring, tender, full of juice, and byting the jawes.

The hearb for his sweet savor is used in bath, but the seed is of greater effect in medicine.

CHAP. XXXVII

What care and skill is required in the bestowing of the Herb Elecampane.

 he herb Elecampane groweth up with a long stem, big and mossie, and the leaves with mossy hairs on the one side, on the top of the stem, being many times a mans height, is a big yealow flowre growing, in which the weeds are contained, and those by feeling procure itch.

The root within the earth, reddish without, and white within, big, sharp in tast, and sweet smelling. The root is digged up at the beginning of summer, and sliced, dried in the sun.

This especially flourisheth in the moneth of July.

The Elecampane may not be sown, in that the seeds bestowed in beds prosper not, but rather set the young buds broken tenderly from the root, in earth wel dunged and laboured afore. And those begin to set in the month of February, well three foot asunder one from the other, in that those send forth big leaves, and long roots spreading in the earth.

CHAP. XXXVIII

The care in the bestowing of the herb Pepperwort.

 he Pepper-wort is a seemely herb, yielding leaves greater and broader then the Peach or Bay-tree, and those thicker, greener, and softer, the herb also growing a foot and a half and sometimes two foot high, with a stiffe and round stem, bearing on the top white and very small flowres; after these, a small seed and long root.

The leaves are sowre, and bite in tast like Pepper on the tongue, for which cause this is rightly named Pepper-wort; this groweth every where in Gardens, and well ordered in the ground, endureth for two yeares, in certaine places also (as witnesseth *Ruellius*;) it continueth green ten years. It flourisheth or beareth flowres in the month of June or July, and next yeeldeth the seed.

The Herb Pepper-wort, ought to be set before the beginning of March, after the growing up, to be clipped and cut like the Sives, but this not often, for after the first day of November, the herb ought not to be cut, least it perisheth or drieth through the cold season ensuing. The herb prospereth and continueth two years, if the same be well dunged about, and diligently weeded.

CHAP. XXXIX

he Herb Celondine shooteth up a foot and a halfe high, and sometimes is more slender of stem, bearing many leaves and those like to the Crowfoot, but softer and to a yellowish colour tending, yeelding also a yellow flowre like to the Violet.

The juyce in the herb of yellow colour like Saffron, biting the tongue, sowre, somewhat bitter and strong savoring. The root above all one, but within the earth shed into many yellow hayrie roots: it commonly growth in shadowie places, by walls, and in stony heaps: this flourisheth at the coming of the swallows, and all the Summer, but it withereth at the departure of them.

The Celondine commeth up in any earth, yet doth the same more joy bestowed in a shadowie place, and the seeds ought to be committed to the earth in the moneth of February, which after the coming up, will endure for two years, if after the shedding of the seeds, the stems be cut away, well four fingers above the roots.

The care in the bestowing of the Celondine.

CHAP. XL

he hearb Filipendula groweth in stonie and rough places, as on hils, bearing a leaf like to the wilde Parsenip, or Parsly, the stem big, and a foot or somewhat more in height, yeelding on the top a white flower in the month of July, after that the seed like to the Orache, and a big root, out of which many round heads or kernels grow.

The root ought to be digged up in the end of harvest, which indureth for ten years.

The Filipendula commeth well up in any earth, yet doth the hearb more joy, being sowne or set in a stonie or gravelly ground: the Seeds require to be committed to the earth in the moneth of April, and to be like ordered, after the shooting up in the weeding and watering as afore taught of the other hearbs.

The care in bestowing of the hearb of Filipendula.

A Necessarie Table to the Second Part of this Book, briefly shewing the Physical operations of every hearb and plant therein contained, with the vertues of their distilled waters

[The table below, intended by Hill as an index to his medicinal notes, has been retained to give an idea of the kinds of ailments for which the various plants were prescribed. Ed.]

A fully equipped laboratory for preparing distillations.

A

Angelica cureth poisons, cleareth a bloud, and preserveth the body against the plague.

Angelica availeth against the pesilent aire, it recovereth all inward griefs, it helpeth ruptures, it amendeth the dimness of the sight, the bite of a dog, the heat of the fever, deep wounds, reneweth flesh, &c.

Angelica aswageth the ache of the hibs and the Goute, it cureth new and old ulcers.

Artochoke reformeth the savour of the mouth.

Artochoke causeth urine and veneriall act.

Artochoke amendeth the hardnesse of making water and the ranke savour of the Arme pits.

Artochoke strengthneth the stomack, and helpeth the privie places, that men children may be conceived.

Arage or Orage helpeth the stopping of the liver, it ceaseth the shedding of the gall or yellow Jaundise, it casteth up choller, softneth the belly, healeth impostumes, swellings, swimmings, drawing of the winde short, expelleth worms, provoketh vomiting, helpeth a hot liver, it looseth the belly, and delivereth the pain of the bladder, helpeth the ague, profiteth against spitting of bloud: it helpeth the matrice, draweth a thorne or naile out of the skinne: it looseth rough nailes from the fingers, it helpeth the hot goute in the feet, it softneth the belly being hardened by heat, and removeth swellings.

B

Beete looseth the bellie, provoketh urine, purgeth the body of evil humors: it helpeth the smelling, the paine of the eares, and of the gums, it procureth haire to grow and killeth lice, nittes, and dandrie: it healeth whelkes, blisters of scalding and burning, gripings of the belly, stayeth a loose bellie, driveth away the wormes of the bellie, helpeth the obstructions or stoppings of the Liver, the corrupted spleene and the shingles.

The discommities of the Bette; it gripeth and biteth the stomack, and increaseth evill humors.

Beete softneth the bellie, cureth the biting of a Scorpion, the beating paine of the temples: it profiteth the Oile on the milt, it profiteth the Oile on the milt, it restraineth the tearms.

Borage procureth gladsomnesse, it helpeth the giddinesse and swimming of the head, the trembling and beating of the heart, it increaseth memorie, and removeth melan-

cholie, and the kings evill it doth only comfort.

Buglosse prevaileth for the roughnesse of the throat and cough, it procureth gladsomness, it purgeth red choller, it expelleth the noisome humours of the lungs, it removeth the swelling of the feet: it preserveth a good memory, it comforteth the heart, and engendreth good bloud.

Bucks horne helpeth the griefs of the joints, it bindeth, it putteth away the fever.

Betony stayeth belching and rawness of the stomacke.

Bitonie profiteth the diseases of the matrice, and all inward grief.

Bitonie purgeth all poison, it profiteth frensie persons, falling sicknesse, palsie, ach of the hips: it helpeth digestion, stayeth vomiting: it expelleth the ague, &c.

Bitonie fastneth broken bones, dissolveth clotted bloud.

Bitonie stayeth the spitting of bloud: it helpeth the eies bruised, and the paine of them: it helpeth the pain of he eares: it causeth cleernesse of sight, removeth tooth ach, the quotidian, tertian, quartain ague, the grief of the bladder, &c.

Bitonie asswageth the paine of the gout, &c.

Blessed thistle causeth urine, helpeth the megrim, restoreth memorie and hearing, helpeth the diseases of the lungs, purgeth fleume of the stomack and bloud, helpeth consumption of the lungs, gripings, provoketh sweat, breaketh the stone, and helpeth the monthly Termes. It comforteth the braine and sight, purgeth the bloud in the eyes, stoppeth the bleeding at the nose, purgeth the Uvula and ceaseth the spitting of fleume.

Blessed Thistle helpeth a weake stomack, procureth appetite, abateth heat, consumeth evill bloud, provoketh sweat, strengthneth the palsie members, recovereth the lungs exulcerated: it profiteth against the dropsie, helpeth the plague, impostumes, cankers and falling sicknesse, it is a present remedie against the plague, the fever of the stomacke, and the quartaine, it cureth greene wounds, pushes, swellings of the plague, any burning, the chollick, scabs, a stinking breath: it helpeth womens privities: it helpeth stitches, pleurisies, and infants incombred with the falling sicknesse.

Blessed Thistle expelleth poison with two examples.

C

Coleworte helpeth the hardnesse of making water, the canker fores, the ulcers in the pappes of women, aches in the joints, hardnesse of hearing.

Coleworts procureth the monethly course of women, it cureth the sorenesse of eies: it profiteth against the eating of venemous mushromes: it maketh children to goe speedilier alone, cutteth the disease of the Spleene and Jaundise: it cleanseth the scurse and leaprie: it amendeth the voice and grief of arteries: it cureth the bite of a dogge, it helpeth the Reume and falling of the uvula: it helpeth the bite of a Serpent or Adder: it cureth the gout, joint sicknesse, old ulcers, purgeth the head, draweth the termes or reddes downe, and qualifieth inflammations.

Coleworts asswageth great swellings: it breaketh botches, staieth the shedding of haire, the disease of the spleen: it cureth eating ulcers, canker sores, griefes of the flanks or sides, head ache, a drie cough: it

drieth a moist belly.

Coleworts bringeth these discommodities: it hardneth the belly, it harmeth the fleumatick, and women having the redde course on them.

Chervill provoketh urine, and sendeth downe the terms in women: it looseth fleume: it putteth away gripings of the belly, it ingendreth winde: it killeth wormes in the belly: it healeth a canker: it ceaseth ach in the hips: it recovereth the dandry of the head: it healeth running sores, it healeth the bit of a mad dog, it breaketh the stone of the bladder, and provoketh urine, it dissolveth the bloud gathered into knobs.

Chervil healeth impostumes behinde the eares.

Cresses dryeth superfluous humours, it expelleth the dead youngling: it easeth the cough and looseth the brest: it availeth against the palsie of the tongue.

Cresses restraine the distillations of the head, cleanse the braine and paine of the head,

Turnips, a cabbage, and some asparagus painted in the 1690s by Claude Aubriet.

help against the palsey, provoke neesing, and amend the lethargie and sleeping out of measure: dryeth the uvula, helpeth infections of the head, as knobs and dandrie: stayeth the going out of the fundament, expelleth the round and flat wormes in the body, these help the griefes of the breast, the ach of the hips, and griefe of the loins, purchase a readier understanding, and wit, remove the chollick proceeding of a cold cause, help the strangurie, removeth the paine of the teeth, and doth asswage the swelling of the milt.

Carots amend a cold reume, the paine of the stomack, stopping of urine, and chollick, a dry cough, the hard fetching of breath, the fluxe of the head, remove winde, heat the stomack, help the stopping of the liver, the vexing of the belly.

Ciccorie cureth scabbed places, causeth a faire skin, recovering the stopping of the liver, it purgeth the matrice: it helpeth the liver, the vexing paine of urine, the kings evill, the plague, burning agues, pestilent pushes, the gout proceeding of heat, and cureth the shingles.

Celondine the juice of the hearb cleareth the eyes, removeth the Pinne and webbe, being mixed with salt Armoniack. The hearb removeth the dimnesse of sight, the juice cleanseth the Leaprie, the root draweth away the Jaundise, and helpeth the tooth-ach, and healeth Tettors or shingles: the hearb removeth the chollick passion, the pouder of the root cleanseth and healeth ulcers, healeth the Canker of the mouth, bones or sinews being annointed with the same boiled in vinegar with the pouder of Roses.

Celondine boiled in Rose water, and a quantitie of Triackle added to the same, is a most effectuous remedie against the plague.

Filipendula is of quality hot and dry in the third degree.

The leaves and stemme of the Filipendula drunke in wine and hony mingled together, help the after burthen, and furthereth the birth of the childe: the root brought to pouder, helpeth the kings evill and strangurie, the stone, paine of the kidnies, and ach of the hips. Taken in wine, it removeth the swelling and coldnesse of the stomack, a hardnesse of fetching breath, and all sicknesses, proceeding of cold causes.

The water of Filipendula beeing drunke Morning and Evening, unto the quantitie of three ounces at a time, recovereth the plague. The same also being drunke four omnces at a time, is good against poison, and also dissolveth and cureth the stone of the kidnies and bladder.

E

Endive prevaileth against the stopping of the liver and milt, against the simple and double tertian, against the heat of the liver, against burning impostumes, it draweth hot pushes, it cureth the Cardiacke passion, it stayeth the flix, it helpeth the kings evil the shingles, hot impostumes and swellings, asswageth headach, the spitting of bloud, the excesse of sperme.

Elecampane amendeth the cough, the ache of the hippes, expeleth grosse humours, ceaseth the hard fetching of breath, it procureth urine, &c.

Elecampane is profitable against poyson, against the pestilent aire and plague, &c.

Elecampane recovereth strength and helpeth the strangurie.

G

Garlike heateth the body, extentuateth grosse humours, it expelleth wormes, cureth the bite of a Snake, taketh away black and blew spots.

Garlike harmeth the cholerick person.

Garlike putteth away inward swellings, openeth impostumes, killeth lice and nits of the head, moveth urine, helpeth toothach proceeding of a cold cause, stayeth the shedding of haire, cureth ulcers, removeth lepry, procureth a clear voice, and removeth an old cough, correcteth the stomack, cooled drieth up the moisture of the stomack, it is a preparation against the bite of a serpent, relieveth the dulness of sight, healeth tetters and whelks, it resisteth poison, removeth urine, procureth Terms, draweth down the after burden, cureth the bite of a mad dog, helpeth the digestion of the stomack, the kings evil, frensie persons, dropsie, it staieth the fluxe, an old cough proceeding of a cold cause, it helpeth wormes in children, expelleth the broode wormes in bodies, it cureth the bite of venemous things the swellings of the bladder, healeth ulcers of the lungs, dropsie being of a cold cause: it helpeth the griefs of the lungs and difficultie of urine, headach, toothach proceeding of a cold cause, itch, the paine of going often to the stoole, expelleth a quartaine, cureth the pippes of hennes, it helpeth the stone.

Garlike profiteth against contagious aires.

Gourd comforteth the stomack, looseth the bellie, helpeth the heat of the eares, profiteth leane men, purgeth gently, helpeth the cornes of the toes, fastneth loose teeth, and helpeth the toothach, the inflammations of the liver and bladder, impostumes, provoketh urine, helpeth all agues, asswageth the heat of the liver, the inflammations of Infants heads, the burning gout, the inflammatons of the eies, asswageth rumors, ulcers on the privie places, looseth the bellie, cooleth burning fevers, helpeth the shingles.

LEFT *'Tongue plants'. From Giambattista Porta's* Phytognominica, *1588. There was a theory current at the time that many medicinal plants bore a likeness which would reveal their potential curative use – in this case, for ailments of the tongue (Doctrine of the Signatures).*

L

Leek cureth the bite of a venemous beast, helpeth the difficulties of making water, stayeth the spitting of bloud, dulleth the sight of the eies, offendeth the stomach.

Leeke juice sodden draweth downe the Termes, procureth urine, obtaineth a superfluous heat, stayeth the bleeding of the nose, causeth vomiting, and putteth away drunkenness being eaten raw.

Leeke amendeth an old cough and the ulcers of the lungs, healeth pushes, the grief of the eares and the toothach: it purgeth ulcers, removeth the bloud clotted in brused members, stayeth the fluxe of bloud after birth, ceaseth the bleeding of the nose, profiteth against paines of the hippes, stomacke, ceaseth an old cough, helpeth the dropsie, staieth the flixe of the belly, and helpeth a hoarse voice.

Nero accustomed to eat an unset leeke with oile for his sounding voice.

Leeke helpeth the paine of the head, it prevaileth against the exulcerations of womens privie places, looseth the difficultnesse of making of water, aydeth the deliverie of the childe, for the spitting of bloud and staying the bleeding of the nose is very profitable, cleanseth the wounds, helpeth the ach of the hips, recovereth the wasting of the lungs.

Lettuce procureth sleep, causeth good bloud, helpeth digestion, looseth the belly causeth plentifulnesse of milke in the breasts, sharpneth the sight, cooleth impostumes, helpeth the dropsie, cureth the shedding of sperme, procureth sleep being laid under the coverlet, and profiteth cholericke persons.

Lettuce is noisome unto married men: it dulleth thd sight of the eies, it abateth the venereall act, it harmeth the fleumatick: the overmuch eating of Lettuce is as perillous as Hemlock.

Lettuce helpeth the Tertian ague, it looseth the belly, it represseth drunkennesse.

Lettuce procureth sleep.

Lovage helpeth digestion, expelleth superfluous humours, it ceaseth inward griefs, it expelleth poison, causeth urine, &c.

Lovage expelleth the stone of the kidnies and bladder, &c.

M

Marigold helpeth the after burden of a woman, stayeth the fluxe of pissing of bloud, it killeth the worms, it healeth pushes, and stoppings, and griefs of the liver, comforteth the stomack, and procureth appetite to meat, heateth a cold breast, asswageth the paine of the teeth, it recovereth the palsie, and fit of the plague: is a preparative against the plague, it helpeth the quartaine, it helpeth the milt or cold stomack.

Mintes uncurdeth milke.

Mintes stayeth the belching of the stomack and vomiting, it profiteth against the long wormes in the body, it helpeth the swolne privities, asswageth the fluxe of the bellie, and scouring with bloud, it stayeth the reddes in women, it healeth ulcers on the infants heads, quickneth the spirits, bringeth appetite, amendeth the default of the nostrills, retaineth the fluxes of bloud, softneth the pappes, and defendeth them from mattering, it looseth the belly, procureth a seemely colour, profiteth the spitting out of bloud, asswageth the head ach, and the noise in the

An apothecary's shop of the seventeenth century with customers presenting their prescriptions and assistants preparing, selecting, and weighing out the herbal remedies. Professional apothecaries would in time lessen the need for home-made remedies such as those that Hill describes.

eares, it removeth the dimnesse of sight, it amendeth the strong savour of the mouth, it helpeth the teeth, and purgeth the gums, and healeth the blistering of the tongue, it comforteth in cold sicknesses, it stayeth the will to vomit, and helpeth the shingles, it dissolveth and cureth impostumes, and helpeth the spottes in the eies.

Mallowes or Holihock remove a hot cough, recovereth the lunges blistered, and is a singular remedie against the consumption of the lungs, healeth the putrified sores of the throat and mouth, looseth the belly, and helpeth the hoarsenesse of the voice, it ripeneth any impostume and softeneth it.

Mustard seed heateth and ripeneth, it breaketh impostumes without paine, it cureth the biting of a venemous beast, it helpeth the palsie of the tongue, and availeth against all palsies, it helpeth the dropsie, the blistering of the mouth, the swelling of the throat, it procureth a good memorie, it helpeth a cold gout, sciatick, and feeblenesse of sinewes, it removeth the dimnesse of sight, and putteth away the spots and webbe in the eies, it causeth thirst, and provoketh the veneriall act.

Mustard seed preventeth the falling sicknesse, it purgeth the braine, it cleanseth the braine from humours, it amendeth the fall of the Uvula, and ulcers of the throat, it draweth downe fleume from the head, it removeth the swelling of the Jawes, it helpeth the suffocation of the matrice, it ceaseth the ach of the teeth comming of cold, it breaketh the stone in the bladder, and procureth the Termes, it causeth a cleer voice.

N

Navewes nourish much, profit the stomacke, increase sperme in man, prevaile against poison.

O

Onions maintaine health, cure ulcers, remove spottes in the bodie, profit the eares running, help swellings in the throate, and the cough, remove the griefe of the stomacke, open pilles, cleare the eies, remove the pin and web, amend the bloodshotten eies, recover the haires shed away, the biting of a mad dog, &c.

Onions eaten rawe harme the members.

Onions harme the chollerick, and profiteth the fleumatick person.

Onions stay the dropping of the eyes, help ulcers of the privities, paine and noise of the eares, Disenteria, griefe of the loines, the water between the flesh and the skinne, cure slumbering, and impostumes, paine of the breast, spitting of grosse humours, purgeth the stomack, cureth warts.

Onions often used, ingender evill humours, procure thirst, swellings, windinesse, head ach, cause to become foolish, they nourish nothing.

Onions twice sodden nourish.

Onions eaten rawe cutte grosse humours asunder, open the veines, provoketh Termes and urine, increaseth appetite, purge the head, remove the white spots on the face, heale kibes, remove the redde and wan spots of the face, healeth scabs, asswageth fluxes and gripings in childbed, heale impostumes speedily.

A sixteenth-century English apothecary preparing medicinal oils.

P

Pimpernell is especially applyed for poyson, it driveth venemous blood from the heart, it ceaseth the headach, it healeth a green wound, ulcers and other wounds, by experiment tried upon a cock: moveth sweat, expelleth poyson, removeth the disease of the hippes, the cough, and purgeth the breast, and stone of the kidnies and bladder, and removeth the strangurie: the gripings of the bowels, the stopping of the liver and milte, it putteth away any fever: an experiment against the physick of the Lunges.

Parsely doth incarnate Ulcers and Carbuncles, it doth dissolve the impostumes of the pappes, it amendeth the stopping of the Liver: it provoketh urine, it stayeth loosenesse of the belly, strengthneth loose parts and helpeth the stone, it healeth the shingles, the hardly making of water, and softneth the hardnesse of the Pappes: it healeth the Kidneyes, removeth Ulcers out of the mouth, and Jaundise, and helpeth womens monthly course: it is delectable to the stomack, it expelleth winde in the bodie, removeth scabbes, and maketh a faire skinne: It helpeth the swelling of the stomack, and Dropsie, it cleanseth the Liver and Leapry, and removeth the paine of the Loines and Bladder, it prevaileth against a Fever, it procureth a sound braine and perfect memorie, and purgeth the blood, asswageth the Strangury, and helpeth the biting of a madde Dogge.

Parsely seeds are the principall causes, the Roots the next, the leaves as third in working.

Purselaine asswageth hotte and Cholericke fluxes, and helpeth the burning Fever, helpeth the Teeth being on edge, helpeth the Shingles, hindereth venereall act, and abateth sleepe, it expelleth the wormes in the belly, it stayeth the flux Disenteria, ceaseth the Tooth ache, it helpeth the stomacke swollen, it cooleth inward heat,

A woodcut of 1531 shows the various stages in the use of medicinal herbs: their cultivation, the learned discussion over their properties, their preparation and preservation, and finally the treatment of the sick.

amendeth the Ulcers on the privities, it healeth an hot impostume, it removeth the Ulcers of the head.

Purselaine helpeth swolne eyes, and spitting of blood, it removeth the burning Fever, it quallifieth the heat of the stomacke, it stayeth Womens monethly course, it stayeth the bleeding at the Nose, and the head ache, it extinguisheth the heat of the eyes, it stayeth Disenteria, it strengthneth both the Kidneyes and Bladder, it helpeth burning Fevers, it killeth the wormes in the belly, and stayeth the spitting of blood; it helpeth excoriation in womens bowels, and the rawnesse of privy places; it helpeth the head ache, it mitigateth a furious heat, it helpeth the Navels of Infants, it stayeth the loose Teeth in the head, it asswageth the kernels and Ulcers in the mouth, it mitigateth the desire of often drinking, it removeth warts; it asswageth the gout, and inflamation of the Paps, the fall of the Uvula &c.

Parsenep and Carots removeth the venereall act, procureth Urine, and asswageth the Chollerick, sendeth downe the Termes in Women; it profiteth the Melanchollicke, encreaseth good blood, helpeth the straightnesse of making water, amendeth stitches of the sides or plurisies, the bite of venemous beast, it amendeth the eating of Ulcers, the wearing of this root is profitable.

Poppy procureth sleepe, helpeth the Rheume, Cough, and lacke of sleepe.

Poppy recovereth a dry Cough, Consumption of the Lungs, Rheume, and debility in sleeping, it draweth heat out of an Ulcer, helpeth a hot Liver, strengthneth the joynts, removeth the rage of the goute, profiteth against the Ague.

Pompons or Mellons, are easie of digestion, comfort the heart, asswageth unnatural heats in the stomack, they take away sunne burning and foule spots.

Pompons profit the flegmatick and cholerick person.

Pompons which are round, loose the belly, and cause Urine.

Pompons asswage the running of the eyes.

Pompions mitigate the venereall act, clenseth the skinne, causeth Urine, purgeth the loynes, Kidneyes, and bladder, heale ulcers, and cease speedy boyling.

R

Rocket encreaseth the Sperm, causeth the venereall act, causeth a giddinesse and paine in the head, encreaseth a strong heat, is hurtfull to the head, encreaseth milke in women and nurses, causeth urine, softneth the belly, comforteth the stomack, helpeth digestion, recovereth blacke scares unto whitenesse, amendeth pimples or pushes in the face, killeth nits and wormes in the head, helpeth bruised bones, and bitings of venemous beasts, the Jaundise, and hard swelling of the Milt, &c.

Rapes or Turnup sharpneth the sight, yeeldeth nourishment, extinguisheth heat and dry blood, it stirreth the venereall act, cureth scabbes, helpeth digestion, hot gouts and kibed heeles.

Radish eaten before or after meat, causeth wind, dulleth the braine, eyes, and reason.

Radish profiteth the flegmatick, helpeth the Stone, stopping of the Urine by gravell, procureth vomiting, stayeth belchings, the Kings evill, the cough, profiteth against poyson, and to the handling of Serpents, it helpeth the noise of the eares, the stopping of the Liver, it availeth against all sortes of poysons and diseases, it cureth strokes of whippes or bruses, it cleareth scares and pimples in the face, it delivereth the quartaine Ague.

Radish profiteth against the stopping of the Milte, it delivereth the water betweene the skinne, and swolne milt, it eateth out the Canker of Ulcers, amendeth the cold cough and fleume, it procureth vomitings, it causeth mushromes to digest, it helpeth gripings in women, procureth Milke, sendeth downe the Termes and wormes in the belly, asswageth the swelling in the Throate.

S

Saffron amendeth the hard fetching of the breath, procureth a faire colour, comforteth the heart, causeth healfull blood, removeth poysons from the heart, causeth long breath, expelleth Infections, helpeth impostumes in the breast, moveth the venereall act, and causeth Urine, helpeth head-ache, procureth the Termes, removeth the yellow Jaundise, it profiteth an ulcered breast, stomack, liver, lungs, kidneyes and bladder, it helpeth the gout, impostumes, swellinges, the griefes of any sore, feeblenesse of the heart, palsie, the griefe of the eyes, the distilling of eyes, removeth drunkennesse, and diseases of the eares.

Sperage helpeth the Palsie, Kings Evill, Strangurie, a hard Milt, and stopping of the Liver, it recovereth the shedding of the

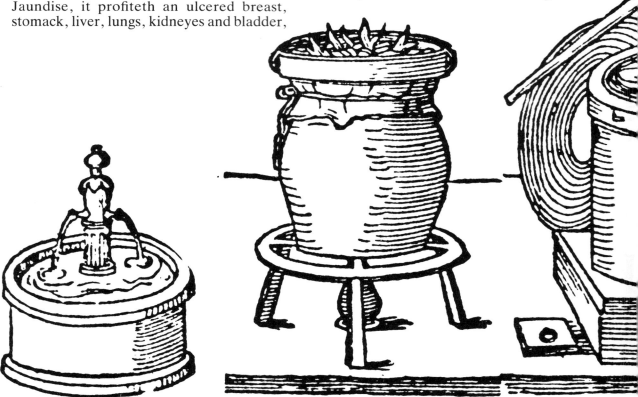

gaule, it removeth the swelling of the belly and cholick, it procureth Urine, and dissolveth the small stones in the bladder, it helpeth the griefes of the womens privy place, it profiteth against the stinging of Bees, it helpeth the hardly making of water, the paine of the gummes, teeth, mouth, breast, and chine of the back, it removeth the venereall act, and looseth the belly: the dropping paine of the Urine, the difficultnesse of the same, the flix Disenteria: it cleareth the kidneyes, and stopping of the Liver.

Spinach softneth the belly, moysteneth the body, removeth the griefes of the breast and lungs, it profiteth in hot causes, it nourisheth more then Araga, it asswageth the Choller, it helpeth the sorenesse of the throat, hoarse voice, the hardnesse of breath, the cough &c.

Sorrell procureth appetite to meat, preserveth against the plague, it ripeneth sores, it asswageth the flix Disenteria, the paine of the belly, and abortment of the stomack, it helpeth the leapry, and Ringwormes, and rough nailes, the itch of the body, the paine of the eares and teeth, the kings evill, the head-ache, any sickness comming of heat, Jaundise, the reds of women, all fluxes of the belly, the swelling of the milt, the burning of the Fever.

Strawberry leaves helpeth hot impostumes.

The strawberry amendeth the hardness of the splene, the stone, healeth wounds and Ulcers, procureth the termes, staieth the bloody flixe Disenteria, and causeth urine, it helpeth inflamations of the Liver, and clenseth both the kidneyes and bladder, it helpeth aches, and provoketh urine, it fasteneth the Teeth, and stayeth the rhume:

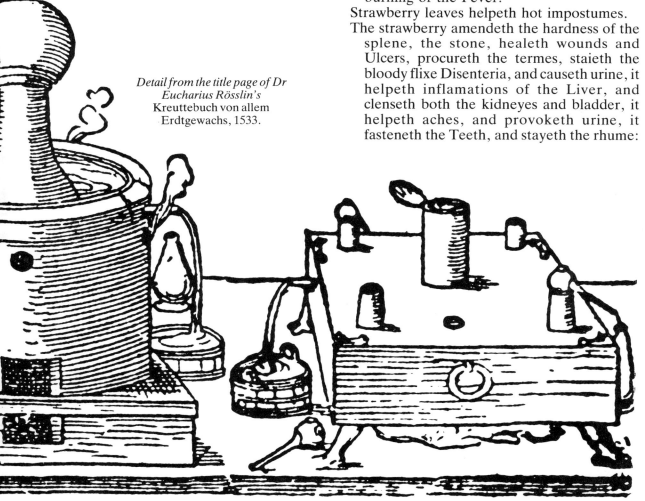

Detail from the title page of Dr Eucharius Rösslin's Kreuttebuch von allem Erdtgewachs, 1533.

it is good for cholerick stomackes, it putteth away the impostumes of the throat, it removeth the rednesse and pimples which happen on the face through the heat of the liver, it asswageth the rednesse of the eyes, the Jaundise, fetching the wind short, & cooleth thirst.

Scalions or squill Onions move venereall act, cut the tough matter in the stomack.

Squill Onion amendeth the dropsie, the fetching of wind hardly, the defaults of the Liver, the Ague, exulcerations, purgeth fleumes, and the belly, causeth vomiting.

Squill Onions amendeth the hard fetching of breath, an old cough, griefes both of Liver and Lungs, expelleth wormes, Melancholly, Apoplexie, falling sicknesse, the stone, purgeth the matrice, causeth the ache of the hips, fasteneth the teeth, amendeth the savour of the breath, helpeth the hearing, driveth away warts, chappes of the feet, running scabs, the dandry of the head, the bite of Serpents, procureth haire to grow, amendeth the foule gummes, the sight of the eyes, griefes of the sides, expelleth all diseases of the bodie: also it killeth mice &c.

T

Time removeth joynt sickenesse, purgeth Choller and Humour, it helpeth the passions of the bladder, the swelling of the belly, it removeth the griefe of the hippes, loines, and sides: it amendeth the breast, and the inflammations of Hypochondria, or the flanckes, it amendeth melancholly, blearnesse of the eyes, and the paine of them: it asswageth the griefe of the cold gout, the stifnesse of limmes it asswageth the swelling of the Testicles, it purgeth the bowels: it hepeth the hard fetching of breath, and falling sickness, it breaketh the stone of the kidnies and bladder, it helpeth the stinging of a Bee.

Black Time is not to be used.

Time which hath a purple flowre, is commended: all Time is mightily hot.

Time healeth the bite of an Adder, or Snake, it helpeth the spitting of blood, it stayeth the Rhume comming of a cold cause, it easeth the cough, and a cold stomacke, the headache, frensinesse, Letharge, and often slumbering, it openeth the stoppings of the Liver and Milt, and moveth urine, it recovereth the bites of venemous beasts, it helpeth the swelling in the throat, it stayeth bloody vomitings, it heateth the stomake, it removeth wind in the bowels, it ceaseth the strangury, it moveth urine, and expelleth the stone.

V

Valerian provoketh sweat, and urine amendeth stitches, killeth mice, moveth the termes, prevaileth against the plague,

helpeth the straightnesse of breath, the headach, fluxes, and Shingles, procureth clearnesse of sight and healeth the piles.

W

Valerian from John Gerard's
Herball, *1597.*

Water of the herb Valerian distilled amendeth ulcers; old sores, swellings, piles, broken Ruptures: it cleareth the eyes, expelleth wormes: it profiteth against a pestilent aire, impostumes and ache of the hips, it provoketh sweat &c.

Water of the roots of Valerian distilled removeth poyson; the Quotidian Ague and stitches.

Water of white Poppie distilled, cureth the red spots of the face, procureth white hands: it helpeth the head ache proceeding of heat: it extinguisheth any heat.

Water distilled out of Gourds, looseth the belly, ceaseth thirst, the cough; helpeth the stone, purgeth the kidnies and bladder; quallifieth burning Fevers.

Water of mellons distilled, helpeth the stone, procureth Urine, cleanseth the kidneyes, cooleth the Liver, ceaseth thirst, breaketh the cough, expelleth heat and swellings.

Water of the blessed Thistle distilled, putteth away headache; comforteth memory, helpeth giddinesse and all griefes of the eyes; Consumption of the body, breaketh the stone, cureth burnings.

Water of the leaves of Elecampane expelleth the grief of the stone, helpeth the person broken, comforteth head, strengthneth the stomacke, amendeth the hard fetching of breath; the cough, plurisie, poyson, the stone and terms of women; causeth urine &c.

Water distilled out of the root of Elecampane healeth an inner Rupture; asswageth the griefe of the stone, provoketh Urine: it sendeth the dead youngling out of the belly; it asswageth the swelling of the Testicles, it ceaseth the cough &c.

Water of Strawberrie leaves distilled removeth the Kings evill, it looseth the breast, purgeth the lungs, helpeth the cough, cleanseth the leaprey; it mitigateth the heat in the eyes, it ceaseth overmuch sweating; it is healthfull for the stopping of the Liver.

Water of mustard seeds distilled amendeth Ulcers of the Gummes; it helpeth the consumption of members; it heateth the marrow in the bones: this water profiteth against a cold diseases in the joynts.

Water distilled out of Leeks remedieth the spitting of cold blood; it profiteth a barren woman, it stayeth the bleeding of the nose, it helpeth a costive belly and ache of the hips; purgeth the kidnies and bladder, procureth Urine, expelleth the stone, healeth wounds; it profiteth exulcerations and fracture of womens places.

Water distilled out of Onions recovereth swellings, caused by the bite of a mad dog; asswageth head-ache and tooth-ache, causeth haires to grow, expelleth wormes.

Water distilled out of Garlike helpeth the swellings in the throat: also the greene sicknesse and swelling of the splene.

Water distilled out of Rapes, helpeth gallings, burnings, scaldings, swellings of the face.

Water distilled out of Radish, helpeth digestion, the Kings evill, worms of the belly, clenseth the stomack: it openeth all manner of stoppings, extenuateth the humours in the lunges, clenseth the breast, causeth a cleare voice.

Water of Radish recovereth poysoning taken in meate or drinke, helpeth the Quartaine, draweth downe the Termes, and helpeth the stone, asswageth the stinging of the Bee, profiteth against the venome of a spider, helpeth the pricking of the side, cleareth the eyes and the face: it removeth yellow or blackish spots by heating: also the swelling of the throat and cleareth the Kidneyes, breaketh the stone, and causeth Urine, and expelleth the water betweene the skin.

Water distilled out of Parsneps, helpeth the palsie, moveth the venereall act, and encreaseth the sperme, helpeth the painfulnesse in making of water.

Water distilled out of the root of Lovage, helpeth an inner Rupture, helpeth the stone, provoketh the terms in women, removeth the swellings of womens places, and ceaseth the cough &c.

Water of Colewortes stayeth womens reds, it profiteth the birth of a child, the dropping of the Urine: it stayeth a loose belly.

Water of the red Coleworts softneth the belly, putteth away the giddines of the head, helpeth the Apoplexie, the Cramp, Palsie, Inflammations, Swellings, Ulcers within the bodie and without.

Water of the white Beete, prevaileth against the stone, it ceaseth the vexing pain of joyntaches.

Water of Sorrell prevaileth against the plague: it removeth all inward heats, ceaseth thirst, and helpeth the liver and milt: also removeth the shingles, scaldings, or burning, the kings evill: it cooleth the burning heat of Agues.

Water of Pimpernell helpeth the stone of the kidneyes and bladder, and purgeth the reyns: it helpeth the plague, profiteth women whose matrice is cold, and fendeth downe the reds, it helpeth the shaking of the members: it expelleth griefe from the heart, and evill humours, and provoketh Urine, it profiteth against poyson, and causeth a white skine.

Water distilled out of Borage, asswageth the griping, and swellings of the belly: it cureth

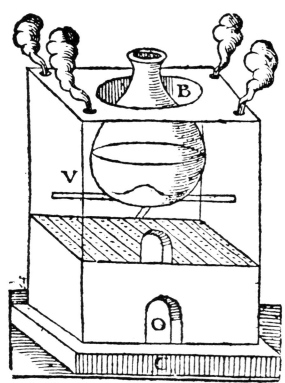

An illustration from Thomas Hill showing his favoured equipment for distilling.

Disenteria, and hardnesse of fetching breath: it comforteth the heart and braine, and rendereth a helpe to memory and wit: it purgeth all blood and frensinesse: it ceaseth the stinging of a Bee or Spider: it procureth clearnesse of sight; it removeth the ringing and paine in the ears: it comforteth the heart, it helpeth the Rhume, burning Fevers and Jaundise, it cooleth the Liver: it helpeth the flix Disenteria, the painfull fetching of breath, and decay of minde, the weake braine: it purgeth the blood, and pricking about the heart and breast: it clenseth the leaprie and scabs, and stayeth the stilling of the head, the head-ache, the burning of the eyes, the ringing of the eares.

Water of Marigolds distilled, recovereth all defaults of the eyes, and procureth cleare eyes, and also putteth away the griefes of the head.

Water of Parsely distilled, profiteth against the stone of the Kidneyes and Loines: it purgeth the kidneyes, and bladder, and greatly provoketh urine.

Water distilled of running Time, strengthneth the head, braine, and stomack: it also procureth appetite to meat, it removeth the noise and rumbling of the belly, it softneth the hardnesse of the stomack, and moveth Urine, it comforteth the sight, and consumeth distillations of the head, it helpeth a quotidian ague, it amendeth a cooled Liver and Milt, and healeth the bowels exulcerated, it openeth the stopping of nostrils, and eares, it restoreth hearing, helpeth giddinesse, stayeth desire to vomit, & expelleth the gripings of the belly, it breaketh the stone, and moveth urine, it cureth brused members.

Water of Marigolds or Holihock distilled, cureth the breaking out of the mouth, as also the outward and inward heat, the Shingles, Ulcers and all swellings, it cureth all inward heats of Fevers, it cooleth all impostumes of the Lungs and sides, it mitigateth the flux Disenteria, the hot dwellings of womens places, the kidnies & bladder, it expelleth the stone, it procureth sleepe in a hot Fever, and ceaseth thirst.

Water of Mints distilled strengthneth the stomack, and digesteth the meat received, it helpeth the stopping of the Liver and Milt, it openeth the waye of the Urine, it procureth an appetite to meat, it stayeth belching and vomiting, it recovereth a stinking breath, and putrified Gummes, it stayeth founding and giddinesse, it purgeth the matrice, it dissolveth the milke curded in hard pappes, it healeth Ruptures within, it restoreth the Uvula fallen, it healeth the scabs of Children, it helpeth wormes, and heateth a cold stomack.

Water of Cichory cooleth the heat of the stomack, it preserveth from the plague, it cureth curbuncles, it stayeth the rising of the lungs, and stoppeth the flix Disenteria: it openeth the stopping of the Liver, it helpeth the swelling of the Uvula and throat, helpeth wasted members, and the bite of venemous beasts, helpeth the Ulcers in the eyes, and the dimnesse of sight, the pin and web &c.

Water of Lettuce distilled, Profiteth the Liver, it cooleth the blood inflamed, if stayeth the flix Disenteria, it amendeth trembling of members, and helpeth sleepe, it helpeth women lacking milke, it ceaseth a drie cough, it molifieth the throat, cleanseth the breast and lungs, ceaseth thirst, tempereth heat of the stomacke, Liver & kidnies, it looseth the belly.

Water of Chervill distilled, helpeth men bursten and hurt by grievous fals, and resolveth the blood clotted in lumps, it profiteth against the stone of the Kidnies, it looseth the belly; it procureth a good stomack, comforteth the heart, putteth away shaking of the Fever, is healthfull for the head, and comforteth the senses, it removeth the paines of the lungs.

Water distilled of Strawberrie, amendeth an unnatural heat, ceaseth thirst proceeding of the Liver, or of choller, it cooleth the liver, looseth the brest, refresheth the heart, purgeth the blood helpeth the Kings evill, prevaileth against the stone, loines and kidnies, it cureth blisters in the mouth, it procureth womens Termes, helpeth a broken legge, healeth all foule legs, it cureth filthy wounds, and asswageth swellings of the face, helpeth the leprie, purgeth blood, removeth spots out of the eyes, and comforteth nature expelleth poisons, asswageth burning humours, and comforteth conception, staieth watering in the eies, & cooleth heat in them, restoreth a dim sight, it cureth pimples in the face.

Water of Berony distilled, putteth away dropsie, jaundise and ague, cureth diseases of the kidnies & milt.

FINIS TABULÆ.

INDEX

Numbers in *italics* refer to illustrations

ACKNOWLEDGEMENTS

The Warden and Fellows of All Souls College, Oxford: p55 Warden Hovenden's map of All Souls, c. 1585.

Barnard Castle, Bowes Museum: p192 Jacques Linard *Still Life of Peaches, Plums and Melon*, 1642.

The Bodleian Library, Oxford: p30 *(bottom)* Romance of the Rose, French, late fifteenth century, Ms Douce 195 fol 26; p113 *(top)* Tradescant's Orchard, first half of the seventeenth century, Ms Ashmole 1461 fol 141; p117 Tudor pattern book, early sixteenth century, Ms Ashmole 1504 fol 10v; p125 *(top right)* ibid fol 13v; p125 ibid *(below right)* fol 4v; p128 *(top left)* Tradescant's Orchard, first half of the seventeenth century, Ms Ashmole 1461 fol 15; p128 ibid *(bottom left)* fol 145; p156 Tudor pattern book, early sixteenth century, Ms Ashmole 1504 fol 15r; p167 ibid fol 17r; p186 *(left)* ibid fol 5; p186 *(right)* ibid fol 21; p187 *(left)* fol 9v; p187 *(right)* ibid fol 19; p190 *(bottom left)* ibid fol 17v; p 190 *(centre top)* ibid fol 16; p190 *(top right)* ibid fol 15v; p191 *(top left)* ibid vol 8v; p191 *(top centre)* ibid fol 18v; p191 ibid *(bottom right)* fol 24v.

BPCC/Aldus Archive: p21; p28; p38; p60; p103; p192.

The Bridgeman Art Library: p18 Jacob Grimmer (c. 1626-89), *The Spring* Musée des Beaux Arts, Lille; p30 *(top)* Lucas van Valkenborgh (c. 1530-97), *Vegetable Market* Kunsthistorisches Museum, Vienna; p31 *(top)* The Bradford Table Carpet, English sixteenth century, Victoria and Albert Museum; p31 *(bottom)* Thomas Robins (1716-70) *Panoramic View of Charlton Park*, Cheltenham Art Gallery and Museums; p113 *(right)* from The Hours of Anne of Brittany c. 1510, The British Library; p116 David Teniers II (1610-90) *A cat tended by an old woman teased by rats in a farmyard*, Christie's, London; p128 *(right)* watercolour by Jacques Le Moyne de Morgues, c. 1568, Victoria and Albert Museum; p176 *detail* from Pieter Casteels (1684-1749) *Peacock and Rabbits in a Landscape*; p178 *(left)* & p179 *(right)* details from Jan van Kessel (1626-79) *Vertumnus and Pomona*; p178 *(right)*, p179 *(left)*, pp182-83 watercolours by Jacques Le Moyne de Morgues c. 1568, Victoria and Albert Museum.

The British Library, London: p26 Add Ms 20698 f17; p42 Add Ms 18852 f3v; p65 Add Ms 19720 fol 117v; p86 Add Ms 19720 fol 10; p95 Add Ms 19720 fol 165; p121 Add Ms 19720 fol 80.

The British Museum: p105; p107; p108; p123 engravings by Wenceslaus Hollar from *Diversae insectorum figurae*. Photographs courtesy of The Paul Mellon Centre for Studies in British Art.

Christie's Ltd, London: p89 Lucas van Valkenborgh, *Spring*, 1595; p171 David Teniers II (1610-90) *detail An old woman peeling turnips in a kitchen*.

Devonshire Collection, Chatsworth: p53 Pieter Andries Rysbrack, *View of the Orange-tree garden and Rotunda*, Chiswick c. 1729-31. Reproduced by permission of the Chatsworth Settlement Trustees. Photo courtesy of the Courtauld Institute of Art.

Fotomas Index: p71; p83; p102; p189; p200; p204; p210.

Sonia Halliday: p19 *April* from Kloster Frauenthal Zug, Switzerland, now in the Darmstadt Museum; p120 *March* one of the labours of the months, French late sixteenth century, Rouen Museum; p125 *(left)* stained glass window showing Jonah before Ninevah by Abraham van Linge, 1631, Christ Church, Oxford.

The Mansell Collection: p34; p37; p49; p50; p57; p59; p61; p63; p66; p67; p68; p70; p84; p96; p98; p106.

Reproduced by courtesy of the Trustees, The National Gallery, London: p27 *detail* from A follower of Joos de Momper II, *A Music Party before a Village*, 1633; p91 Jacob van Walscapelle (1644-1727) *Flowers in a Glass Vase*.

Reproduced from *Medicine and the Artist (Ars Medica)* by permission of the Philadelphia Museum of Art: p207; p209.

Rijksmuseum, Amsterdam: p119.

Sotheby's, London: p22 *detail* from a follower of Paul Brill, *March and April, A Fantasy View of the Villa Medici, Rome*; p127 Northern French School *A Woman seated at a fruit and vegetable stall*, 1607.

Victoria and Albert Museum, London: p24 Embroidery of Abraham and the Angels, English, mid-seventeenth century; p73 Embroidery, English third quarter of the seventeenth century; p203 Watercolours by Claude Aubriet c. 1690-95.

Gemäldegalerie, Vienna: p78 David Teniers II (1610-90) *Vertumnus and Pomona*.

Illustrations from Printed Books

N. de Bonnefons *Le Jardinier Francois*, Paris, 1658: p87.

D. H. Cause *De Koninglycke Hovenier – Nederlantze Hesperides*, Amsterdam, 1676: p54.

Crispin de Passe *Hortus Floridus*, Utrecht, 1614: p23; p82; p92; p93.

Charles Estienne *L'Agriculture et Maison Rustique* . . . Paris 1569-70, trans. London 1616: p46-7; p56; p81 *(bottom)*.

Fuchsius Fuchs *De Historium Stirpium*, Basle, 1542: p130; p135; p188.

John Gerard *Herbal* London, 1597: p138; p143; p145; p147; p155; p160; p161; p163; p164; p170; p173; p174; p175; p194; p215.

The Grete Herbal, London, 1526; p100; p189.

Thomas Hill *The Gardener's Labyrinth*, London, 1652: p9; p17; p44; p48; p55; p64; p80 *(top)*; p81 *(top)*; p85; p216.

Hortus Sanitatis, 1536: p29; pp 110-11; p136.

Das Kreüterbuch oder Herbarius, Augsburg, 1534: p99.

Gervaise Markham *A Way to get Wealthe*, London, 1638: p33; p36; p79.

Leonard Mascall *A Booke of the Arte and Maner howe to plante and grafte all trees*, London, 1562: p72.

Giambattista Porta *Phytognominica*, Naples 1588: p204.

Dr Eucharius Rösslin *Kreuttebuch von allem Erdtegwachs*, Frankfurt, 1533: pp 212-13.

Leonhart Thurneisser *Historio sive descriptio Plantarum*, Berlin, 1587: p101.